POOR DISCIPLINE

Studies in Crime and Justice
James B. Jacobs, Series Editor

POOR DISCIPLINE

Parole and the Social Control
of the Underclass, 1890–1990

JONATHAN SIMON

THE UNIVERSITY OF CHICAGO PRESS / CHICAGO AND LONDON

Jonathan Simon is associate professor of law at the University of Miami.

The University of Chicago Press, Chicago 60637
The University of Chicago Press, Ltd., London
© 1993 by The University of Chicago
All rights reserved. Published 1993
Printed in the United States of America
02 01 00 99 98 97 96 95 94 93   5 4 3 2 1

ISBN (cloth): 0-226-75856-7
ISBN (paper): 0-226-75857-5

Library of Congress Cataloging-in-Publication Data

Simon, Jonathan.
    Poor discipline : parole and the social control of the underclass,
  1890–1990 / Jonathan Simon.
        p.   cm. — (Studies in crime and justice)
    Includes bibliographical references and index.
    ISBN 0-226-75856-7. — ISBN 0-226-75857-5 (pbk.)
    1. Parole—United States—History—20th century.   2. Socially
  handicapped—United States.   3. Criminal justice, Administration of—
  Social aspects—United States—History.   I. Title.   II. Series.
  HV9304.S54   1993
  364.6′2′0973—dc20   93-15876
                                                              CIP

⊚ The paper used in this publication meets the
minimum requirements of the American National Standard
for Information Sciences—Permanence of Paper for
Printed Library Materials, ANSI Z39.48-1984.

To my parents
MARLENE B. SIMON
and
WILLIAM SIMON

and to the memory of
DAVID RUDY SKLARE
1942–1990

CONTENTS

ACKNOWLEDGMENTS

This book began as a dissertation in the Jurisprudence and Social Policy Program at the University of California, Berkeley in 1987. Like all dissertations it was an experience of personal transformation as much as a work of scholarship. Like all personal transformations it was a product of many special people and circumstances.

I owe a special debt to my committee, Sheldon L. Messinger (Chair), Franklin E. Zimring, and Troy Duster for giving me the freedom to pursue my intuitions and the help to bring them home as empirical insights. I was also fortunate to have an informal committee of advisors on the project including John E. Berecochea, Robert Dickover, Malcolm M. Feeley, and Marlene B. Simon. Their uncompensated advice pulled me out of a number of blind alleys.

I am especially grateful to Sheldon L. Messinger who for the better part of a decade lent my intellectual efforts continuing support and confidence. His willingness to believe in the enterprise, even when it could not be articulated to the rigorous standards of his own work, has been an irreplacable gift.

The dissertation would not have been possible without the cooperation of the California Department of Corrections, and its Parole and Community Services Division. These agencies have a long history of pursuing critical evaluation of their operations and I am proud to be a small part of that.

No researcher of a complicated institutional setting can hope to succeed without tapping the embedded knowledge of those who work with it day by day. I would particularly like to thank Robert Anderson, Ronald Chun, Elmer Cox, Robert Dickover, Jerry Dimaggio, Robert Pomerenke, Robert Roenicke, and Glyn Smith. Their collective decades of reflection were invaluable. I would also like to acknowledge (if only abstractly) the scores of agents and their administrators, parolees and their families, lawyers and social workers, who allowed me to probe around in their work and lives.

My dissertation was the culmination of thirteen years spent as a student, activist, and café loafer in Berkeley California. Through three degrees, and what seems like many life times, the University and town have inspired, infuriated, and shaped me. These things I cannot repay or fully acknowledge.

I would, however, particularly like to thank those among my teachers and mentors whose intellects and ideals have most shaped this author and through him this book. My parents were my first and greatest teachers and to them I have dedicated this book. Hubert L. Dreyfus awakened my undergraduate mind to the task of thinking, and together with Paul Rabinow introduced me to the work of Michel Foucault. Jerome H. Skolnick taught me how to do field work in my first years of graduate school. David L. Kirp taught me how to see the individual stories which embody history. Robert C. Post challenged me to go beyond critique and ask questions about how to construct more just institutions. Judge William C. Canby, Jr., of the Ninth Circuit court of Appeals, taught me about the relationship between law, writing and integrity.

I would also like to acknowledge the special atmosphere of the Center for the Study of Law and Society, where these ideas were incubated. I am deeply grateful to all the faculty, staff, and students who made it feel like an intellectual home town. I am especially grateful to its "asylum keepers" Margo Rodriguez and Rod Watanabe.

I would like to express my gratitude for the financial support my work received from the Daniel and Florence Guggenheim Program in Criminal Justice Research, the Center for the Study of Law and Society, and the Earl Warren Legal Institute.

During the three years in which the dissertation became a book I moved to the University of Michigan and learned so much from my colleagues that they had to restrain me from starting all over again. While my time there was short, the influences and friendships are enduring.

A number of friends and colleagues provided readings of all or parts of the manuscript, including Anthony Amsterdam, Marianne Constable, David Garland, James B. Jacobs, John Kindon, Martha Minow, Austin Sarat, and Kim Scheppele.

The production aspects of this book have been far more pleasant than I imagined possible. I would especially like to thank my editor at Chicago, John Tryneski for making this as good a book as it could be. I am also appreciative for editorial work done by David E. Anderson in Chicago and my research assistants, Karen Coombs and Gregg Casalino at the University of Miami.

Finally, although she will undoubtedly consider this an archaic sexist ritual, I would like to thank my partner and now spouse, Christina Spaulding, for making me so very happy during these last five years.

The Crisis of Penological Modernism

In a period of "normal" science in penology a localized study such as this one of parole supervision would hardly need an introduction.[1] It would address itself in monographic proportions to the successes and failures of the institution studied. It would point to organizational impediments to the more complete realization of correctional goals and offer suggestions on how the system might be rationalized.

But it is impossible to treat penology today as a normal science or to assume that studies will pursue regional problems in a field of social endeavor whose basic aims and strategies are noncontroversial. In fact, the most basic assumptions about the penal system are in question, not simply by academics looking for a new angle, but by the people who administer the penal system itself. As David Garland puts it:

> The question that arises today is not one of institutional adjustment and reform. It is a more basic question which asks whether the social processes and ramifications of punishment can be contained within specialist institutions of any kind. This is, in a sense, a crisis of penological modernism. (1990, 8)

It is impossible for a study of a penal institution today to ignore this basic turmoil in the theory, practice, and aspirations of penality. Indeed, it was a situation brought up to me constantly by actors at all levels in the parole supervision agency I studied. As a researcher I could not very well attempt to measure the success or failure of the institution's technical operations when the very criteria of success and failure at work in the institution were contested.

---

1. For the way "normal science" works and its relationship to the form of scientific production see Kuhn (1962).

Instead, I tried to follow the institution itself, by looking at its efforts to define and present itself, to itself, to its clients, and to the public.

In lieu of the summary of technical problems with which such a study might have once begun it seems more relevant to identify the themes that most motivate reflection on penal institutions today: increasing public fear of crime and demand for punitive solutions to it, widespread uncertainty as to the viability of the basic concepts of modern punishment, and a vacuum of political will to reshape the exercise of the power to punish.

Punishment and Fear of Crime

In 1988 3.7 million adult Americans, one out of every forty-nine adults, were under some form of correctional custody.[2] For certain groups the numbers are even more sobering. One out of twenty-seven American men was under some form of correctional control (Bureau of Justice Statistics 1989b). For African-American men between the ages of 20 and 29 the proportion in 1989 was a staggering one out of four (Mauer 1990).[3]

The massive growth in custody over the 1980s is much discussed today among academic experts and government planners. Corrections has become the Pentagon of the state budgets, pushing other service priorities to the side and sending ostensibly conservative governments into a massive buildup of debt. Yet the politics of this development has seemed almost miraculous in its power and coherence.

Citizens in virtually every part of the social and political spectrum have felt insecure about crime and have strongly supported proposals to spend money on public safety by building a larger capacity to punish and control criminals. After nearly two decades of steady increases in the rate of incarceration, and despite a moderate decrease in the level of victimization during that period, overwhelming numbers of people tell survey researchers that courts need to be tougher with criminals in their communities (Bureau of Justice Statistics 1989a). Scholars of penality from the right and the left concur in the conclusion that public fear of crime is a genuine and massive feature of our present political landscape (Currie 1987; J. Q. Wilson 1986).

Crime is far from the only matter about which Americans are concerned. We live in a time of deep social anxiety, when questions of what to eat, where to live, and with whom to have sex are all answered with reference to the ques-

2. Up 38.3 percent from 1984.

3. Yet even this number is too aggregated to be fully useful because it hides the tremendous gulf that has developed within the African-American community between a substantial middle class and a large population existing in poverty (W. J. Wilson 1980). If class could be taken into account it is not hard to imagine that the real number might be much larger.

tion of risk. It does not take long, in a society where the largest supermarket chain is named "Safeway," to recognize that security is something which people demand, not just in general, but in each and every thing we do, experience, or consume.[4]

Insecurity is not in itself surprising. AIDS, revelations that our government knowingly exposed millions to radiation during the cold war, and the savings and loan crisis are just a few recent reasons why people in our society might feel that they cannot assume their security is being taken care of.[5] More surprising is the apparent paradox that during a period of general unwillingness to increase public spending to control pollution, diseases, and environmental disasters, the public has been highly supportive of spending on crime.[6]

What is fascinating about our political behavior in the market for public safety is how little it follows the objective distribution of risk. Across every crime category higher-income Americans are much less likely to be victimized than lower-income Americans (Bastian 1992, 6). Indeed, middle- and upper-class Americans living in the suburbs, those whose voices are most loudly heard in the political system, experience substantially lower risks of crime today than they did two decades ago (Bureau of Justice Statistics 1992, 7). Moreover, they can and do achieve the greatest reductions in personal risk by privately investing in suburban homes, better locks, private police, and the like (Newman 1972; Shearing and Stenning 1983), all the while paying through their taxes for a prison building boom with only a dubious connection to their personal safety.

If we try to treat preference for spending on crime as a problem of rational choice we miss the important symbolic role of crime control efforts. The choices we make of what to fear most are loaded with opportunities for scorning, stigmatizing, and punishing certain classes and institutions (Douglas 1966; Douglas and Wildavsky 1982). Likewise, the means selected for managing specific risks often represent symbolic levers with which to combat broader fears of social disorder which are powerfully concentrated in the imagery of crime, diseases, and war (Tesh 1988).

From the Jacksonians in the 1830s to the presidential campaign of 1988, crime has recurrently been a privileged site in the American conscience for expressing deep anxieties about class, race, and social order. The large litera-

4. As of 1990, Safeway Corporation was the largest food retailer in the United States (Hoover et al. 1990, 479).

5. If there is an irony, it is only in the fact that for the last two (in a haphazard list), it was a desire for security that led to these crises.

6. It may be that the public is dubious about the effectiveness of government programs in general, but if so, they could hardly be more confident in the long-term success of penal programs, which have regularly been condemned as failures for the last two centuries and currently have few admirers in opinion-making circles.

ture on the history of modern penality reveals that its development has always been closely linked to the ebbs and flows of such anxiety.

The transition to modernity in punishment, which began with the birth of the prison, was triggered, in large part, by anxiety about the populations of uprooted rural inhabitants that moved across Europe and North America in the early nineteenth century (Chevalier 1973; Rothman 1971; Foucault 1977). The wave of penal reform in Europe and North America at the beginning of the twentieth century (associated with the Progressive Era in the United States and the Edwardian Era in Great Britain) was designed to address the problems and new political strength of the increasingly organized and assertive industrial working class (Garland 1985; Rothman 1980).

As the Chicago-school sociologists of the early twentieth century well understood, social control is reproduced for the most part through the normal processes of social life itself, family, neighborhood, and occupational structure (Janowitz 1978, 27). Punishment plays a part in such an order, but it is largely derivative of the basic pattern of social control in social life. Punishment seems to emerge as an especially compelling symbolic lever on social order precisely at those times in history when economic and political changes undermine the ability of the prevailing social hierarchies to distribute risk effectively.

But this produces a paradoxical result. Punishment becomes important to social control at precisely those moments when it is most difficult to articulate a persuasive account of how it provides social control. When a class undergoes a rapid transformation in its social and economic base it can come to be seen as a "dangerous class" (Chevalier 1973). The social problems generated by geographic and social dislocation are, under such circumstances, viewed as evidence of moral or even biological degeneracy, which call for exclusionary and punitive social policies. At the same time the basic practices of punishment in society become problematized because of their uncertain relationship to the shifting grounds of social order. Historically this has generated powerful incentives to re-imagine the basic strategies of punishment (Cavender 1982, 21).

The rise of the prison appears to be closely tied to precisely such apprehensions among elite groups in European and North American societies experiencing the stirring of capitalist economic relations in the late eighteenth and early twentieth centuries. The geographic mobility, generated by the elimination of traditional economic opportunities for rural laborers (often decried as vagabondage by elites), created tremendous fears of crime and disorder while simultaneously undermining the effectiveness of traditional modes of punishment (Rothman 1971, 57–59). The accumulation of many of these uprooted into cities led to fears of biological contagion and political upheaval (Chevalier 1973). The prison, with its emphasis on confinement, separation, and discipline offered an appealing lever to use against the social evils associated with that period of profound economic change.

At the end of the nineteenth century, the class order in the United States and other industrial democracies was again shaken by the growth in the size and militancy of the industrial working classes and by the arrival of millions of new immigrants (in the case of the United States). Fears of social, biological, and political disaster were widely shared among elite classes (Painter 1987; Lears 1981). Once again innovation in the punishment of criminals stood out as a leading avenue for reestablishing social order.[7] Within a short period new programs designed to intensify the disciplinary capacity of penal regimes, and to bring discipline and order to bear directly on the "dangerous" in the midst of their communities, were implemented. Although lacking the associated influx of immigration, very similar strains and developments took place in Great Britain (Garland 1985).

This historical pattern leads to one of the most fundamental assumptions of this book: crises in penality do not arise primarily from the internal problems of punishing offenders but from transformations in social and political structures. The massive expansion of criminal custody over the last decade in the United States must be seen in relationship to changes in political economy including the restructuring of the labor force away from industrial employment (Bell 1973; Bluestone and Harrison 1982; Harrison and Bluestone 1988; Magaziner and Reich 1982), the emergence of an urban underclass living in zones of hardened poverty and made up primarily of minorities, and the heightened accountability of political power, what we legally call due process, that has emerged since the Second World War.

The most important of these for penality is the emergence of the underclass. However general the formal commands of the criminal law, the power to punish has always been primarily directed at the poor. Significant changes in the position of the poor vis-à-vis sources of social control inevitably bode ill for the existing strategies of punishment.

Young African-American men, so many of whom live under correctional jurisdiction, are a case in point (Duster 1987). Their employment situation has gone from bad (Kerner Commission [1968] 1988) to catastrophic, with over a quarter of those age 20 to 24, and 16 percent of those 24 to 54, reporting no income at all in 1984 (Jaynes and Williams 1988). Looking just at youth age 16 to 20 living in enclaves of poverty, the National Bureau of Economic Research survey found that of those not in school, only half were employed (Freeman and Holzer 1985). At the same time these youth have become the

---

7. While crime is probably the most significant point of concern in both the Jacksonian and Progressive Eras, the same assembly of social fears found outlets in innovations in the management of other problem groups including the mentally ill and school children (Rothman 1971, xiii–xx).

target of criminal custody to an unprecedented extent, so much so that criminal custody may now be the normal experience of life for many of them.

As participation in the criminal justice system becomes a more crucial element in the life of underclass communities it may add its own independent effects, such as furthering their economic marginalization (Bound and Freeman 1991) and further marking them as an irredeemable population (Gordon 1991, 197).

The relationship between the ordinary mechanisms of social control that function in and through social life and extraordinary ones like punishment is an extremely complicated problem. It is tempting, but surely too simplifying, to view the current explosive expansion of criminal custody as a direct response to the diminution of the ability of the labor market to create adequate relations of security for the urban poor. This study aims to provide a less sweeping, but more empirically rooted, analysis of this problem.

Instead of exploring the links between employment and crime (a worthwhile but distinct endeavor), this study examines the links between employment and the exercise of the power to punish. Modern punishment, which emerged with the prison and later expanded to include techniques like parole, probation, and juvenile justice, relied for its coherence on its fit with the disciplinary forms of social life being generated by the industrial labor market. The crisis of that labor market has generated a crisis of public security. The immediate public response has been to intensify the use of punishment, but because it has become decoupled from its anchors in the social discipline of industrial work, the result is greater levels of insecurity.

The Crisis of the Penological Idea

Penal practices, of course, aim to diminish the actual amount of crime and thus improve public safety directly. Yet, until recent times, we have rarely had a very precise picture of whether or not they accomplish this. Even today, when our statistical methodologies are far more capable, the question of what to measure continues to obscure the relationship between penal systems and public safety (Maltz 1984). Yet regardless of their objective effects on crime, penal methods affect public safety by creating more or less plausible accounts of control, which tie the object of fear into the predominant vehicles of social control and order in society.[8]

The meta-narrative of penality which has predominated for over two centuries is in crisis today, a crisis manifest in the inability of any current account of

8. It is not simply a question of success or failure in fighting crime. Western medicine has for the most part failed to diminish the lethality of most cancers, a class of diseases which the public clearly fears. Yet there is a widespread sense that regardless of failures, medicine possesses the proper epistemological and institutional strategies to eventually succeed. People continue to fear cancer, but they are not beset by the doubt that some other effective method is being overlooked by a deeply flawed system, a belief that seems to animate much disgust with the penal system.

penality to provide a plausible model of security. David Garland suggests that we are faced with

> a skepticism about a penal project that is as old as the Enlightenment with its vision of punishment as one more means of engineering the good society, or organizing institutions to perfect mankind. After more than two centuries of rationalization, even our "experts" have begun to recognize the limits of social engineering and the dark side of social order. (1990, 8)

This skepticism seems belied by the huge boom in the size of the population under custody of the penal system over the last two decades. During most periods of transition in modern penality, the expansion of sanctions has corresponded with the rise of a new vision about how penality should work. Today, for the first time, growth is linked to widespread doubt about the basic strategies of the penal system. The boom today is not accompanied by any real confidence in those institutions. Instead, as Garland remarks, "like the crime it is supposed to deal with, punishment is nowadays seen as a chronic social problem" (1990, 4).

A few years ago it seemed a plausible interpretation of our impasse that we were undergoing a shift in penal thinking from rehabilitation to an emphasis on retribution, incapacitation, and deterrence (Allen 1981). This swing of the pendulum among eternally valid approaches to crime control seemed to be linked to the larger political fortunes of liberal and conservative forces in society. Today, however, the crisis of confidence in punishment appears much more radical indeed. It is the very core of the meta-narrative of modern punishment—the idea that punishment is to be seen primarily as a useful tool of state policy—that increasingly is in question.

Some observers see in this a license for a complete break with modernist ideas about punishment in favor of a purely moral basis for punishment (von Hirsch 1976; von Hirsch and Hanrahan 1979; Newman 1985). Yet it is by no means clear that the crisis of modern punishment is primarily a philosophical one that can be cured by philosophical discussion. On the contrary, correctional strategies attract little confidence because of profound material changes in the economy and social organization of contemporary society. The same developments which have undercut the cultural sensibilities on which the modernist penal regime (in its various forms) relied, deindustrialization of the United States and the emergence of an underclass, call into question the existence of the kinds of morally integrated communities assumed by proposals that just deserts and retribution dominate penal practice.

Flight from Discretion

The confluence of the two themes we have touched on, the growing expectations on the state for security from crime and the crisis in the modernist meta-narrative of punishment, point to a third theme: the problem of how to exercise power rationally under such circumstances. The crisis of punishment as a useful tool of social policy may open our eyes to other cultural motivations for punishment beyond the modernist demand that it be useful (Garland 1990). Yet even if we discover new purposes (or rediscover old ones) the problem remains of how the power to punish can be exercised in a way compatible with the rationality demands made on the modern state.

By "rationality demands" I mean only the degree to which the state must be able to articulate clear ends for its exercises of power and defend these exercises as rational courses to achieving its legitimate ends. The problems of exercising the power to punish have been exacerbated by the rise in the rigor of these rationality demands over the course of the last several decades. The cloak of discretion that once lay over government when it acted to maintain the poor, protect the infirm, and punish criminals has been stripped away by a series of legal and political struggles. The irony is that these developments heightened the rationality demands on the penal system at precisely the same time as the social and economic base that made penal strategies coherent was being eroded.

The resulting crisis is most evident in the absence of any sector of government which wishes to assume a directing role within the penal system. As the demand that the state ensure security clashes with the increasingly difficult task of rendering a plausible account of correctional strategy, a vacuum of leadership is opening up within the power to punish.

One response is the rise of managerial systems which remove discretion from agents of the system. Judges and parole boards have had their sentencing power restrained by more or less comprehensive guidelines. Somewhat less formal guidelines also operate to control the decision making of parole agents, police, magistrates, and prosecutors (Gottfredson and Gottfredson 1984).

A decade ago that process was widely seen as one aimed at correcting the abuses of power in the system (von Hirsch 1976; American Friends Service Committee 1972). Today, it seems less likely that this process is leading to the reorganization of power under a new regime, and more likely that the mechanisms put in place are aimed at compensating for the absence of political will altogether.[9] Often these methods simply redirect power to the bottom of the institutions where the exercise of power takes place below the threshold of legal visibility.

Some Methodological Notes: Narratives and Technologies of Power

It falls peculiarly to non–"normal science" to remain conscious of its role as a piece of interpretive construction. Thus the traditional discussion of sources

---

9. Penal institutions are not the only ones experiencing a flight from political leadership as the recent crises of state and federal financing reveal.

and methods can be usefully supplemented here by a discussion of interpretive strategy.

Power's Interpretation

One of the primary tasks of an institution that exercises the power to punish is to provide a plausible account of what it does, and how it does what it does. These accounts, described here as models or narratives of parole, are ways of attaching the state's power to punish to contemporary social institutions which provide the capacity and coherence for social control. [10] The "model" is only a retrospective creation of the scholar, but the problem, faced by those who actually exercise the power to punish, is the very real one of providing a meaningful background for the effects of punishment. Bullets kill and bars constrain, but the practice of supervision inevitably involves the construction of a set of narratives which allows the kept, the keepers, and the public to believe in a capacity to control that cannot afford to be tested too frequently. The needs of these various audiences may well differ, requiring a narrative structure capable of significant flexibility.

A successful narrative of parole control must include three elements: (1) a narrative of criminogenesis, (2) a measure of its degree, and (3) a set of practices that appear capable of controlling it. Each in turn is linked to broader social and political configurations that set the conditions of plausibility for each component (Garland 1985, 3). Since these may change at very different rates the overall program of parole is a combination of new elements and old ones reinterpreted to stretch around a new ideological demand structure. This makes it misleading to identify clean breaks. Still, it is analytically useful to identify three periods in which quite distinct parole models have stabilized.

From the mid-nineteenth to the mid-twentieth century, industrialization made the discipline of the labor market the most compelling anchor for control. During the 1950s and 1960s, as a deindustrializing U.S. economy rendered the economic position of the unskilled precarious, parole moved toward a clinical model drawn from medicine and social work. Since the 1970s a collapsing inner-city economy and increased legal and political demands for accountability have driven parole toward a managerial model which privileges meeting internally derived performance parameters over the goal of normalization.

Privileging the History of Means

The following account may strike some readers as unusual in its emphasis on "how power is exercised." While that approach is becoming more common today (Foucault 1977; March & Olsen 1989, 18), and has precedents in the

10. What I describe here as an "account" is close to what others have termed an "ideology" (Simon 1988, 775; Cavender 1982, 84).

history of punishment (Rusche and Kirchheimer 1939; Rothman 1971), the tendency to privilege the ends of individuals, classes, and institutions remains. Too often we are embarrassed by means. Yet the means have repeatedly outlived their original ends and gone on to shape new ones. It is through means that institutions bite into real people, not through their ends or objectives. Means require their own history, and their own kind of history (Selznick 1949). This is especially true in punishment which peculiarly relies on its means to define its goals. Indeed, in the history of penal enterprises, objectives often seem to be composed after the fact to justify the installation of new technologies (Berecochea 1982).

The history of means, or genealogy, will by necessity look different than traditional history. The history of ends requires a prioritizing of agents and their intentions. Genealogy eschews that kind of narrative. The reader may find that frustrating. Whole paragraphs and pages go by which do not seem to present the story of people, classes, or interest groups. Especially to those readers who have committed themselves to refocusing history on those who have been excluded from its telling (although not its creation) this kind of narrative may seem insidious, reactionary, and irrelevant to the needs of political struggle.

In its defense I would say to such readers (with whom I am in sympathy) that there are diverse modes of representation which offer different advantages and disadvantages. One does not read a topographic map to find the state capital or the way to San José. Genealogy addresses a different kind of need for refocusing. Finally, while it is often frustrating not to be able to write on a clean slate, it is also liberating. This is not the only history to deal with the issues it covers. Others are available, and cited, which I have used in understanding how the development of means has fit into other kinds of developments.

In analyzing the development of parole we must look beyond those practices which its architects claimed as direct ancestors. Those technologies that coalesce in a practice like parole have their origins in very different concerns. Rather than simply note with surprise the twisting turns of unintended effects in history, the genealogist must attempt to understand the hidden capacities and limitations built into a practice by the logic of its construction.

Against Sovereignty

Punishment should not be seen primarily as a relationship of sovereignty between state and citizen. It is true that the state has claimed an increasing dominance over the exercise of punishment since the Middle Ages, so much so that modern philosophers like H. L. A. Hart (1968, 5) define punishment as a state activity. But how this claim is made and sustained raises more interesting research questions than simply assuming the centrality of the state.

Although the state may take a greater or lesser role in organizing punishments, that state action is invariably found amid patterns of nonstate actions. What we view as a state monopoly in punishment has often been simply the continuation within state apparatuses of relations and struggles that have their origins and ends elsewhere.

The state may well seek to suppress certain conduct with the power to punish, but it does so precisely by invoking other kinds of conduct. People on parole, their families, and other actors in their world use and manipulate the power and resources of the state, even as they are its targets. Thus bringing in the state is important to any study of contemporary punishment, but without the semimystical assumption that its "sovereignty" is an explanation for anything.

Why Study Parole?

Parole supervision, as that term is used here, means a period of criminal custody over felony offenders that follows release from imprisonment. This includes prisoners released through the discretionary action of administrative actors under indeterminate sentence laws, and others released to a mandatory term of supervision at the completion of a fixed sentence less statutorily set "good time" reductions.[11]

Functionally, it bears a strong resemblance to probation and juvenile supervision. In all three, state correctional agents are charged with maintaining contact with, and if possible influence over, offenders who are free to live in the community subject to certain restraints. Typically, these offenders are limited in movement and obligated to submit to surveillance and obey instructions from supervising agents. In all three the agent has power to invoke incarceration should the parolee, probationer, or juvenile delinquent violate the conditions of release. The unique institutional and historical position of parole supervision makes it a privileged site for exploring the power to punish in contemporary society more broadly.

At the border between prisons and the community, parole is a unique enterprise which of necessity manifests in its practice the latent concepts of danger and security, normality and pathology, and social order and disorder, which are often hidden in public policy. Without the metaphor of prison bars to fall back on, parole must provide an account of how dangerous people can be secured in the community, and thus of the relationship among criminal dangerousness, penal technologies, and public safety.

11. Due to changing federal and state sentencing laws the percentage of prisoners released to discretionary parole release declined from almost 72 percent of all releases in 1977 to about 41 percent in 1990 while the percentage of prisoners released to supervised mandatory release increased from about 6 percent of all releases in 1977 to nearly 30 percent in 1990 (Jankowski 1991, 5–6).

Adopted in the Progressive Era, parole also offers us a window onto the changing historical understanding of the mission of punishment. The concept that punishment was a tool of social policy rather than a prerogative of sovereignty had been implicit in modern penality from the start, but the Progressive innovations extended the ideal of punishment as a governmental tool of social regulation. Parole, perhaps more than any of them, exemplified the idea of a penal institution separated from the sovereign claims of vengeance, and wholly given over to regulating the offender and his community.

Finally, parole, along with probation, has become a crucial back-end steering mechanism in a correctional system that is increasingly locked into inflexible policies at the front end. According to the Bureau of Justice Statistics (1989b), on any given day in 1988 three out of four adults under any form of correctional custody were on parole or probation. These sanctions play a critical role in determining who will receive the harsher punishment of incarceration. Offenders who avoid initial imprisonment by receiving probation may end up in prison as the result of violating the conditions of their release. Those sent to prison and then released (even prisoners released by the operation of *determinate* sentences) often remain subject to years of parole supervision,[12] during which they may be sent back to prison for technical violations not amounting to crimes.

The capacity of the penal system to manage the large population of those isolated from the work force and other sources of community social control depends a great deal on its ability to balance public resources and demands for security. Parole as a low-cost custody provider and switching mechanism between different levels of custody increasingly finds itself at the center of that effort (Kelly and Ekland-Olson 1991, 602). Yet the very social and economic developments that are fueling the demand for security through punishment appear to undermine its ability to manage that population effectively.[13]

The Study

Since punishment is by and large an enterprise of state government, it is difficult to analyze a penal institution nationally. I have concentrated on California

12. Historically, the word "parole" has referred to two different practices: the process of setting prison terms administratively after some time of incarceration has passed, and a period of supervision following release from prison. Traditionally they were related, but this is less and less true today, and the number of parole releases declines with no concomitant decline in supervision following release. The percentage of releases from state prisons by parole went down from 71.9 percent in 1977 to 40.3 percent in 1988. During the same period mandatory releases followed by supervision went from 5.9 percent to 30.6 percent while mandatory but unconditional releases remained nearly constant at around 16 percent. Thus, despite the decline in parole release, the vast majority of prisoners released in the United States face some period of supervision in the community (Bureau of Justice Statistics 1989b).

13. This study focuses on parole, but many of the same issues could be explored by taking a close look at probation.

for reasons of convenience and because of its history as a bellwether in correctional policy. The historical portion of the study draws on information from other states as well, while the contemporary portion focuses exclusively on California.

Although somewhat behind the most developed states in adopting parole, it was already considered a leader in parole supervision by the time of the Attorney General's *Survey of Release Procedures* in 1939. In the 1950s and 1960s, California went the furthest in attempting to build a scientifically informed and rehabilitative penal system along the lines of the Progressive vision. In the 1970s it was among the first to repudiate that vision. During the 1980s it had one of the fastest growing prison and parole populations in the country. How California handles the tasks of managing that huge population in the 1990s will likely be a crucial influence on policies in other states.

Part one of this study traces the development of parole from its inception in the 1880s to the threshold of the present configuration in the 1970s. I identify two distinct models of parole, *disciplinary parole* and *clinical parole*. The models are my retrospective effort to reconstruct the narratives through which the power to punish in parole was exercised.

The analysis is based on the published state records as well as periodic public investigations of penal practice which have themselves become objects of historical interest, the *California Penological Commission Report* (1887), articles published in the *Journal of Criminal Law and Criminology*[14] from 1909 on, and the Attorney General's *Survey of Release Procedures* (1939). Part one also has benefited considerably from recent historical studies of parole, including David J. Rothman's *Conscience and Convenience* (1980) and John E. Berecochea's doctoral dissertation *The Origins and Early Development of Parole in California* (1982), and the growing literature on the history of punishment in modern societies.

Part two examines the political and social conditions of parole from the mid-1970s to the present. During this period a new model of parole, what I call *managerial parole*, was organized. Unlike disciplinary or clinical parole, managerial parole does not tie public safety to the goal of reintegrating the offender into the "normal" modes of social life, that is, normalization. It is driven instead by a "technocratic" (Heydebrand and Seron 1990) emphasis on meeting internally set performance standards.

The analysis is based largely on research performed during a year of participant observation of parole with inner-city parole units in San Francisco, Oakland, and Los Angeles. Additional insight was derived from a quantitative analysis of a random sample of 275 parolees initially released from prison in

14. The journal was originally called the *Journal of the American Society of Criminal Law and Criminology*. Since it has changed its name a number of times throughout its history, I will use its current title throughout.

1988 to selected inner-city parole units. Data were collected on their social circumstances and parole actions during their first twelve months.

Part three examines the strains on managerial parole that were just showing themselves during the period of my study. The primary symptom of crisis is the contribution parole is making to the growing prison population. California is in a league of its own in this exponential growth of its prison population.[15] In 1989 more than 40 percent of all felons were returned to prison for violation of parole (Bureau of Justice Statistics 1990a, Tables 6.115 and 6.117). Overall these parolees made up more than half the admissions to prison in California during that year (California Department of Corrections 1991). Other states have a similar problem, although on a smaller scale. This part draws on data from my sample and officially reported statistics, as well as a number of recent quantitative analyses undertaken by academics (Messinger et al. 1988), correctional administrators (California Department of Corrections 1989a), and the California Blue Ribbon Commission (1990).

15. Between 1980 and 1990 California's prison population grew nearly 300 percent (California Department of Corrections 1991, 1–4). The increase for all state and federal prisons between 1980 and 1991 was about 150 percent (Bureau of Justice Statistics 1992, 8).

PART ONE

Parole as Normalization

In the three chapters that follow we will examine the development of parole up to the threshold of our own time. We begin, in chapter one, with some early modern examples of techniques for managing criminal risk in the community. The point is not to trace a direct lineage to parole, but to explore practices in the early modern period that illustrate how the power to punish was organized within the community itself in a period before the modernist penal project took shape. Whether or not these techniques survived as precedents for parole in the modern period, they provide examples of techniques that modern planners had to rediscover or reinvent.

We then turn to the problem of how to manage offenders inside the prison, a problem which arose when techniques of community control were abandoned in favor of heavier reliance on the prison at the beginning of the nineteenth century. Although the rise of the prison marked a decline of faith in the controlling powers of the community, prison planners were faced with creating their own control and looked to the emerging technologies of industrial discipline that were reshaping the community as well.

In chapter two we will examine how the model of industrial discipline, first deployed inside the prison, provided a model for how to deal with released prisoners, and a justification for renewed faith in community control. Discipline, and most especially the discipline of industrial labor, provided a surrogate for personal suretyship in the early modern period because it provided definable and accessible norms for social life that could be enforced by a bureaucracy. The traditional role of personal reputation to stand for one's reliability could be replaced by the normalizing power of the industrial labor market.

Chapter three examines the development of a clinical model of parole prac-

15

tice after the Second World War, in response to gaps in the coverage provided by the industrial labor market. The clinical approach allowed the norms of industrial society, translated into psychological conditions, to be extended by a professionalized correctional apparatus to those increasingly outside the reach of the industrial labor market.

CHAPTER ONE

Surety of "Good Behavior": An Early Modern Model of Community Corrections

From its inception parole has been debated against the background of the prison. Its promoters argued that it could do a better job of reformation by placing the offender in direct contact with the community norms to which he would have to conform. Its detractors argued that it was little more than an excuse to let offenders out of prison early in order to maintain prison harmony, but at the cost of public safety. As it has developed, parole continues to be haunted by these aspirations and fears first laid down during the Progressive Era foundations (Rothman 1980, 51).

At a time when the basic rationality of our penal measures is so much in doubt it is imperative to explore not only our institutions of justice, but also the background assumptions with which we have evaluated them over the years. One way to do that is to produce a different background against which to view the historical development of a social practice. [1] If the crisis we are experiencing is truly one of our penal modernity, it may be most necessary to step outside of the peculiarly modernist frame altogether, at least as a start. This chapter sets out to do that by looking at a variety of techniques of community control in late medieval and early modern Europe.

Before the prison became the central mechanism of punishment, community supervision already had a long history. The heart of these practices was the idea of "suretyship," that is, the assumption by a private citizen of good reputation of the obligation to guarantee the good behavior of another. In the shadow of the more famous scaffold punishments, suretyship played a quantitatively significant role in resolving many cases of less serious criminality,

---

1. This I take to be much of what is powerful about the tradition of the genealogical undertaken by Nietzsche and his more recent followers (e.g., Foucault 1977).

but it also represented a set of concerns that ran through the entire system: differentiating strangers from community members, healing the rifts in personal trust created by crimes, involving the population directly in the administration of justice.

Another significant early modern penal practice was that of confinement. Pieter Spierenburg (1984, 1991) has documented that confinement was already a common practice in northern Europe and Britain by the sixteenth century, well before the prison in its modernist form took hold. But this early modern use of confinement was less a counterprinciple to that of suretyship than an intensification. It aimed to reinforce patterns of community power, not replace them as the Jacksonians imagined the penitentiary would (Rothman 1971).

This chapter looks at both suretyship and confinement and their complex relationship with the economic organization of society with the aim of offering an alternative background for understanding the creation and development of parole. When parole was offered as a supplement to the practices of prison confinement late in the nineteenth century its promoters rediscovered and reinvented some of the logic of suretyship, albeit in a fundamentally new context.

Suretyship and Community Self-Policing

Starting in the 1960s the term "community corrections" gained a currency which it has retained despite great changes in penal rhetoric and strategy. The meaning of community in "community corrections" (as in the more recent talk of "community policing") is always a little vague. It seems mainly to be defined in the negative sense of being an alternative to a more centralized, bureaucratic, and statist corrections apparatus.

Some of the evidence presented in this book will be used to question the thesis that we have ever really had a statist, bureaucratic, or centralized corrections system. Still, it is useful to contrast the largely state-identified corrections system with earlier penal strategies of control that have drawn on the community in much more direct and specific ways. While these may not actually have formed a set of precedents from which community corrections has drawn in the twentieth century, they provide us a model of control technology that is tightly linked to private exercises of power. As used in what follows, community control of punishment means two features in particular: first, a direct and central role for private citizens in actually exercising the power to punish lawbreakers; and second, as a consequence of the first, the impressment of community needs and values on the distribution and effects of penal power.

Frankpledge in Medieval England

In large portions of England from the tenth through the fifteenth centuries the lower orders of free adult males were members of a system of more or less compulsory collective security known as frankpledge. The system imposed on them a legal obligation to report offenses committed by other members of the group and to be financially obligated for any failure to produce the offender at presentment (Morris 1910, 85–86).

The frankpledge system seems to have crystallized out from the earlier and looser practices of "gegild," "tithing," and "bohr" some time in the century before the Norman Conquest (Morris 1910, 22). Gegild was a primitive welfare scheme in which neighbors could be held responsible for the royal taxes due from a family without kin. Tithing was a broad set of community service obligations to which the population was bound in groups of collective responsibility. Bohr was a form of suretyship in which small groups pledged to pay a fine if any among them broke the peace.

Frankpledge also represented the dispersal of the even earlier obligation of feudal lords to assure the peacefulness of their subjects, which before the twelfth century extended well beyond his personal household to include those with any feudal tie. Under frankpledge this duty would become a more general obligation and at the same time more of a relationship between subject and royal sovereign.

The organization of the frankpledge became much tighter in the years after the Norman Conquest. William the Conqueror and his successors seemed to have recognized it as an excellent way to establish controls over a population that could not be assumed to have much loyalty to their new overlords.[2] Indeed, according to Morris, the Norman fear of assassinations led them to intensify a system of localized control for the least reputable members of the community into a system of general surveillance.

> The whole English people, classed like its own malefactors of an earlier time, was thus required to be in collective suretyship. "All villains," says the oldest version of the so-called laws of William (that is to say, all the ordinary men of the vills), "shall be in frankpledge." (1910, 36)

Frankpledge began to disintegrate during the fourteenth century. Morris (1910) attributes this decline to the ravages of the Black Death which made it difficult for groups to retain continuity and leadership. In certain locales it continued to play some role in the administration of justice for decades more. Indeed, one of the more significant documentations of frankpledge processes we have are the records taken at the view of the frankpledge (see below) in the county of Sussex during the late fourteenth and early fifteenth centuries. These rolls show that it retained its shape and some of its functions. The larger strategy of community self-policing continued through such institutions as the "hue and cry" obligation of citizens to assist in the capture of offenders and

---

2. Eric Monkkonen argues that the Norman political agenda permanently disabled the frankpledge system from receiving popular loyalty (1988, 33).

the *posse comitatus* authority to mobilize the population for crime control up to the threshold of modern law enforcement (Monkkonen 1988, 32–33).

Frankpledge offers a picture of the power to punish that contrasts almost completely with our modernist understanding of punishment as a form of state policy and power. The system evolved during the tenth and eleventh centuries through the initiative of what D. A. Crowley succinctly describes as "royal governments wishing to improve public order but commanding few local administrative officials" (1975, 1). It remained an important element in the enforcement of the criminal law through the beginning of the fifteenth century (12), and its vestigial forms survived, albeit largely as empty ritual, until the nineteenth century (Morris 1910, 158).

The ideal frankpledge size was ten, but groups were permitted to grow much larger or remain smaller. The principle of organization varied from place to place with some groups organized along lines of kinship and others not (Crowley 1975, 6). In general the obligation of the group to proceed against any of its members engaged in crime required close proximity. Each frankpledge had a chief selected by the group for terms of various lengths. The chief was responsible for mobilizing the group to perform its duties. More importantly, he was responsible for collecting the amercements (fines) that were imposed on the group for failing to present an offender.

The central ritual of frankpledge was the so-called view of the frankpledge. In idealized form this was a royal review of the assembled freemen of a lordship or village. In its peak years during the twelfth and thirteenth centuries it provided an occasion when virtually the entire male population of the lower classes assembled before representatives of the crown and local elites. With the freemen or their representative chiefs assembled, both royal and local officials undertook to collect taxes and fines, register newcomers, and record the circumstances of the people (Crowley 1975, 5). The frankpledge system integrated crime control into the everyday lives of the common people and local government. Rather than an arm of state power, frankpledge is best seen as a mechanism for mobilizing local power in a manner which was in part constitutive of state power. Like the practices of scaffold punishment, the view of the frankpledge made manifest the mystical body of the king in his people.

Recognizance Bonds in Elizabethan England

In his study of the administration of criminal justice in the English borough of Colchester during the sixteenth century, Joel B. Samaha found that the larger portion of penal actions involved not formal indictments and trials, but the use of a legal device known as the recognizance bond to keep the peace and supervise the dangerous (1981, 189).

Recognizance bonds remain familiar to us through their role in the bail process. In the sixteenth century a suspect eligible for bail might obtain release by submitting to a written examination by two justices of the peace. As community notables, the justices were able to make a determination based on local reputation. Those with strong local ties might be bailed even for a serious crime like infanticide, while a stranger might be held until trial for stealing a shirt (Samaha 1981, 192).

Pre-trial use of recognizance bonds also extended to prosecutors and witnesses. Prosecution in sixteenth-century Britain was almost wholly dependent on private prosecutors—usually, but not always, the victim of crime. Recognizance bonds provided a way to prevent abuse of the prosecution power in the absence of a professional bureaucracy to screen cases.[3] To obtain an indictment, victims needed not only to swear out the facts of the alleged crime before a justice of the peace, but also to enter into a recognizance bond through which they bound themselves to appear at the next court session and prosecute the suspect or else forfeit a substantial fee. Witnesses also had to enter a recognizance bond promising their own attendance.

In examining the Colchester archives, however, Samaha found that forms of recognizance bonding were also used as a final resolution of charges for many less serious crimes. Indeed, these bonds accounted for more of the entire caseload than any other sanction. Several distinct varieties were in use, each aimed at sanctioning and controlling a distinct spectrum of offender.

"Peace bonds" were imposed for acts which could not support full criminal prosecution but which, nevertheless, threatened the peace. They could be initiated by constables or by private citizens who felt threatened by another private citizen. Formally, the bond was intended to warrant the accused's good behavior until, at the next sitting, a court could look into the basis for the accusation. At the same time, they provided a practical means of direct control. The subject had to find two private citizens—called sureties—willing to stand by this promise, with the potential for paying a hefty fine if the bond was violated. Those unable to come up with the bond money or sureties might face preventive detention until the next court session (Samaha 1981, 195–97).

An even broader device was the bond for "good abearing," or good behavior (Samaha 1981, 198). The subject of the good behavior bond was similarly required to find sureties willing to risk payment of the bond to the magistrate should a breach occur, while the peace bond was limited to actual acts or threats of personal violence. The bond of good abearing was expressly aimed at "all them that be not of good fame," a category that included "amongst many others, former convicted offenders who refused to work for a living and

3. Some measure of balance was also provided by the right of defendants to seek civil damages for false prosecution (Hay and Snyder 1990).

persons who had in the past breached the peace, rioted, or barreted" (199). The good behavior bonds were also used against those who seemed to threaten the moral or economic life of the community: transients who might become burdens to the town, fathers of illegitimate children who might abandon them, accused adulterers who might continue to covet other men's wives. Such bonds were even used against irregular church attenders.

The definition of conduct which would break the bond was also wide. Peace bonds generally were broken only by some assault or battery. Good behavior bonds, in contrast, might be broken by "the number of a man's company, or by his or their weapons or harness" (Samaha 1981, 198). They provided a subtle tool for addressing not only crime but a whole range of behaviors that threatened the normative order of the community.

Samaha concludes that this highly flexible device was "essentially aimed at strangers and the poor in the town" (Samaha 1981, 201). In effect, those lacking property or long standing in the community were required to demonstrate the existence of supporters in the community interested enough to come forward. In light of the monetary damages at stake, there was a clear expectation that sureties would go beyond providing a good reference to actively supervising the principal.

The recognizance bond was a way of placing the power of penal exclusion in the hands of private citizens while committing them to a direct role in social control. Rather than placing in a fully public official the authority to exercise public power for public ends, private members of the community were invited to shape the distribution of punishment to their own perception of good order so long as they lent the enterprise their participation and good name.

Private Confinement

In both the British Isles and on the Continent it was possible for relatives and neighbors to obtain public authority to confine troublesome people whose conduct had not been officially adjudged a crime or treated as madness. Indeed, such private "prisoners" constituted a substantial portion of the inmates of the prison workhouses that spread through Europe from the late sixteenth century.[4]

Data on continental Europe show that the people who most commonly made use of these powers were spouses (both husbands and wives) followed by parents and then other more distant relatives (Spierenburg 1991, 235). In France, parents—fathers in particular—seem to have been the usual agents of confinement (Farge and Foucault 1982, 23).

4. Recent research suggests that as many as two or three per 10,000 people in the eighteenth century may have been confined through such channels (Spierenburg 1991, 227). It was used most commonly by the upper and middle classes in northern Europe and may have involved as many as 6 percent of the population of those classes in the regions where the practice was concentrated.

It is possible that these private sanctions were privileged alternatives to traditional criminal punishment or at least served to remove those in danger of soon invoking public punishment (which was considered deeply dishonorable by the elite classes). Spierenburg's research indicates a motive of protecting family honor more generally from rash and scandalous behavior. Although there is some evidence of correctional discourse about reform and redemption, these punishments seem to have functioned for the most part as a kind of banishment and were often followed by actual exile.

Administratively the process of authorizing confinement was handled somewhat differently in different countries. In the Netherlands petitions for confinement had to be authorized by the local courts and magistrates. Terms were lengthy, but inmates could petition the authorities for release, particularly if the relatives who had requested their confinement had died or had a change of heart. In addition they might win a shortened term through acts of cooperation. Relatives could almost certainly obtain earlier release if they sought it, and in some cases they were able to have the confinement extended (Spierenburg 1991, 228).

In France private confinement was regulated through *lettres de cachet*, a kind of royal warrant that allowed private citizens to confine other private citizens in royal custody outside of the regular criminal process (Foucault 1979, 85). In theory they were an order from the king to confine a particular person in a royal stronghold. The most important public decision makers involved were probably local agents of the crown, although the petitions did pass through the hands of royal cabinet officials (Spierenburg 1991, 247). Farge and Foucault's (1982) account of the petitions they studied suggest that they represented a cross section of local disorders, the disobedience of young folk, abusiveness or faithlessness of spouses, conflicts between neighboring property owners, and conflicts of interest among local officials.

Private confinement began to decline in Europe by the end of the eighteenth century. Spierenburg (1991, 249) suggests that the major reasons for its decline were the increasing value placed on individual liberty and the declining stigma of madness as a definitional solution to the troublesome family member. Private confinement was also falling victim to the taint of arbitrariness through its association with royal prerogative. In France it ended altogether with the revolution. In the Netherlands it lingered well into the nineteenth century (252–53).

Some Elements of Community Corrections in Medieval and Early Modern Society

Both suretyship and private confinement contain a double movement. On the one hand, they mobilized private citizens to control other private citizens. This was especially true of the frankpledge and recognizance bonds which required a wide variety of subjects to take legal responsibility for the control of others. Private confinement most clearly served the purposes of family discipline, but it also evidences the existence of a family responsibility for managing the conduct of individuals.

On the other hand, both suretyship and private confinement also operated to make available to private citizens the punitive power of the sovereign. This was especially acute in the case of the *lettres de cachet* which came not from a local official but, at least symbolically, directly from the king. This led antiroyalists to treat them as examples of royal arbitrariness (similar to the way British parliamentarians viewed the Star Chamber). Yet as Foucault points out:

> An abuse of absolutism? Perhaps; yet not in the sense that the monarch purely and simply abused his own power, but in the sense that everyone could make use of the enormity of absolute power for themselves, to their own ends and against others: it was a kind of placing of mechanisms of sovereignty, a given possibility, at the disposal of whoever is clever enough to tap them, to divert its effects to their profit. (1979, 85)

The view of the frankpledge also presents a moment when the figure of king (in the person of his local officers) lent his authority to local hierarchies of power.

In sum, the operation of these practices manifests two important features of premodern societies that affected the power to punish. First, we find the dependence of a central state with limited means for actually reaching people on mechanisms to harness the energies mobilized at the local level networks.[5] Second, we find a community with a widely shared set of interpretive norms with which to distinguish dangerous conduct. Both of these features were reversed by the conditions of modernity.

The Development of Modernist Strategies of Punishment

The basic formula of confining troublesome people and compelling them to labor began to take shape in the Netherlands and northern Europe more generally in the sixteenth century (Spierenburg 1991). During the first two centuries of their operation institutions like the Amsterdam *Rasphuis* or the *Zuchthuis* found in most German cities were mainly devoted to confining vagrants and those committed by their relations as discussed above. From the beginning, however, they held some subjects of criminal condemnation, a pattern which accelerated rapidly in the eighteenth century (Spierenburg 1991). By the beginning of the nineteenth century these places of forced labor were almost completely identified with the control and punishment of criminal offenders.

5. This is an example of what Foucault has characterized as the "deductive" quality of the early modern state (1978, 136).

Despite these continuities the practice of penal confinement underwent significant changes at the end of the eighteenth century when the modernist prison emerges as a distinct refinement of the custodial tradition.[6] The major innovations were in the emphasis that eighteenth-century penal designers placed on the internal layout of prisons and the intensification of controls even to the micro-details of inmate conduct. While the earlier tradition strongly resembled the model of a family or apprenticeship with household-like design and paternalistic control of inmate behavior, the new innovations resembled the logic of the industrial manufactories just then being established with their orientation toward surveillance and precise rules of conduct (Ignatieff 1978, 102–3; Foucault 1977, 6–7).

The practice of imprisonment as it came to be used in North America and Europe in the nineteenth century was exemplified in two U.S. prisons built during the 1820s and 1830s: the Eastern State Penitentiary in Philadelphia and the New York State Prison in Auburn. These two prisons were visited by domestic and international travelers and copied in numerous prisons built elsewhere. Their common practices of isolating inmates from external contacts and enforced silence within the prison defined the ideals of penal planners for much of the nineteenth century. Their differences, likewise, became the central focus of debate on penal design.

Philadelphia's regime consisted of virtually complete isolation not only from the outside world but from other inmates. Inmates were kept separate from each other day and night, thus the name "separate system" which was attached to the Philadelphia model. The inmates lived and worked in large cells into which only official visitors were permitted. Auburn's regime consisted of isolation at night and common labor during the day, thus the name "congregate system" which was attached to the Auburn model.

Most contemporaries agreed that the Auburn system was more economical because it permitted greater profits to be made and thus lowered the net cost of the prison to the state. Private contractors were permitted to lease the shops and the convicts. They supplied the machinery and the technical and supervisory staff, and marketed the products. In contrast, labor at Philadelphia was limited to piecework agreements. Goods were produced by inmates working in their cells and sold at a piece-rate price to a private distributor. Philadelphia's condition that prisoners remain isolated in separate cells made machine tech-

6. The degree to which the penitentiary style of prison was a dramatic rupture with past practice has been a subject of considerable scholarly debate. The revisionist historians of punishment (Ignatieff 1983) have suggested that it was a rather radical break. Foucault (1977), Rothman (1971), and Ignatieff (1978) all tend to emphasize the new innovations in architecture and internal regime and the rapid rise of imprisonment as a replacement for corporal and capital punishments. Others both before (Rusche and Kirchheimmer 1939) and since the revisionists (Spierenburg 1984, 1991) have emphasized the continuities in the idea of confinement and labor as well as the endurance of corporal sanctions.

nology and industrial organization impossible. Production was limited to items, like shoes, that could be made on a craft basis.

Debate at the time turned on the significance of Philadelphia's more complete isolation. Proponents of the Philadelphia plan argued that common work during the day irrevocably compromised the goals of isolation by making it possible for inmates to recognize each other after release and by facilitating illicit communication. Proponents of the Auburn plan contended that total isolation was unnecessarily expensive and, indeed, that it could be lethal to the inmate forced to endure such total loneliness.

While profit level no doubt loomed as an important debating point, the differences in economic organization between the two prisons were more than fiscal. The dispute was also about the role of labor in the penitentiary (Rusche and Kirchheimer 1939, 130; Melossi and Pavarini 1981, 137). The Philadelphia model put the main emphasis on self-reflection and religious conversion. Labor was a supplement, perhaps even a necessary concession, to the worldly needs of men for involvement in profane tasks (as well as the state's fiscal interests). At Auburn, while religious elements abounded, labor was the central practice around which a hope for transformation of the offender was based. Profit was the immediate motive, but the deeper significance was the imposition of industrial discipline as a regime of control for the prison (Melossi and Pavarini 1981, 129).

The form of production at the two prisons also placed them in different relationships to the economic life of the community. The Auburn model permitted fuller integration of the prison into the most dynamic sector of the economy, the still nascent industrial manufacturing sector. By opening up the prison to private contractors, Auburn maximized the opportunity for the importation of industrial methods and industrial disciplines. Philadelphia, in contrast, was linked to forms of craft production that even then were declining.

In this sense Philadelphia represented continuity with the earlier tradition of carceral work houses that Spierenburg traces from the end of the sixteenth century in northern Europe (1991). There, work was probably never intended to be fully profitable or to match the techniques of fully commercial producers. Auburn came to represent a fundamentally new role for labor in punishment, not as part of a moral pedagogy but as a functional mechanism to control the bodies of inmates using industrial discipline.

The factory system then coming into being in Europe and North America was a revolutionary development not simply in the use of machine technology, but in the development of new technologies for managing individuals. The economies of scale which factories hoped to achieve by bringing together large numbers of operatives inside the same workspace would hardly have proved profitable had techniques for coordinating such large numbers not been developed (Foucault 1977, 145). The process by which labor was stripped of its traditional rights of self-control and subjected to a new regime of comprehensive controls from above has been much studied by historians (Pollard 1963; Thompson 1967; Foucault 1977; Ignatieff 1978; Edwards 1979; Zuboff 1988).

Clock towers and factory whistles brought the demands of precise time management right into the homes of workers. Rigid controls over the temporal organization of work were imposed in factories and enforced with fines and dismissals (Thompson 1967, 81). Moralizing campaigns were launched to condemn the evils of idleness, drinking, and virtually all forms of leisure (Pollard 1963).

The idea of bringing the elements of industrial discipline into the prison must have been attractive to penal managers for two reasons. First, it offered a way to efficiently bring order and control over an assembly of potentially troublesome individuals (Foucault 1977; Edwards 1979). Consider, for example, one of the earliest American manufactories to undergo a disciplinary rationalization of labor. The following work rules were promulgated in the 1820s at virtually the same time that the Philadelphia and Auburn prisons were being built.

> Regular accounts will be made out monthly by the foreman and assistants of all work executed by the persons under their charge and forwarded to the Superintendent's office as soon after the close of each month as practicable.

> They [foremen] will make to the Master Armorer weekly and monthly returns of tools and stock used and quarterly returns of all articles of stock, tools, and materials expended and on hand, and semi-annual statements exhibiting the kind and quantity of labor performed by each individual, the amount of tools and material used and the manner in which and to whom the articles have been distributed.

> Fighting among the workmen will not be tolerated, nor any indecent or unnecessary noise allowed in or about the shops.

> Gambling of every description, and the drinking of Rum, Gin, Brandy, Whiskey or any kind of ardent spirits is prohibited.

> [Workmen are] required to give 30 days notice previous to leaving their work in the Armory and the same notice will be given by the Superintendent to them when their services are not wanted.

> [N]o workman leaves his business in the Armory for more than two days in succession or four days in a month without knowing and approbation of the Superintendent or Master Armorer.

> Due attention is to be paid to the Sabbath and no labor, business, amusement, play, recreation, and any proceeding incompatible with the sacred duties of the day will be allowed. . . . The children must cease playing from sunset on Saturday evening until Monday morning. (Hindle and Lubar 1989, 232–33)

These rules speak to us of a time when the general norms of productive labor which are so ingrained in twentieth-century North Americans had not, as such, yet been established. Practices of accounting for time and materials, of restricting interaction among workmates, or of planning ahead and notifying superiors of planned absences are techniques of self-control that were not always a part of life. They were forged in the workshops of early industrial practice in America and elsewhere.

If we can read these work rules both as an aspiration for control over labor and as a response to current social practice, we have a picture of a labor process very much dependent on the individual and group decisions of workers. A disciplinary organization of the workplace, exemplified by these rules, aimed to break apart the solidarity of workers and replace it with hierarchical evaluations, surveillance, and regulation. Clearly workers understood the intent. The first "Yankee" manager sent to Harper's Ferry to impose the new regime was shot, and the workers petitioned the secretary of the army to return to them the power of self-management in the shops that they had long enjoyed (Hindle and Lubar 1989, 232–33).

There were other models available. The military, for instance, offered its own form of discipline, as did the monastic life (which Philadelphia's isolation was designed to reproduce). Industrial discipline offered a strategy that was readily accessible and promised a logical transition between prison and life back in the community for the reformed convict.

By the 1880s "reform" and "industry" were practically synonymous in the discourse of penal managers. To the authors of the *Report of the Special Committee to the Prison Association of New York on Convict Labor,* quoted in the report of the California Penological Commission, industrial labor was a key to the very sustenance of civilized life.

> Industrial labor is not only the most powerful agency of reformation; it is the indispensable instrument, without aid of which reformatory results (except in sporadic instances) are wholly unattainable. Industry is the essential prerequisite of healthy life and progress in all human society; and to such a degree that any community deprived of productive labor must quickly lapse into moral corruption and decay. (California Penological Commission 1887, Appendix, 60)

The power of the prison was understood as a special and intensive case of the power promoted by the course of industrial discipline. The *Report of the Special Committee to the Prison Association of New York on Convict Labor* described this relationship quite precisely in a text which was quoted with approval by the California Penological Commission (1887).

> In a word, it is the aim of reformation to restore the criminal into the <u>likeness of common men</u>; and when that has been effected so completely

that he will lead a law-abiding life through <u>the force of the same habits</u> <u>and motives that govern ordinary men in common life</u>, then the criminal is *reformed*; that which was morbid has become healthy; that which was distorted and abnormal has been made natural and normal. (California Penological Commission 1887, 62. Italics added; underline in text)

While it may have had its origins in the tradition of moral reform through labor promulgated as a cure for vagrants and prodigal sons in the sixteenth century, penitentiary punishment in the nineteenth century adopted an industrial logic of work that was quite different. Work was no longer aimed at facilitating an independent process of moral reformation but an opportunity to subject offenders to the discipline of industrial labor, a development which recognized the distinctive transformations that industrial technique was bringing to labor and social life more generally. [7]

The Philadelphia plan embodied an idea of social order based on the self-regulation of autonomous citizen subjects, or "republican machines" as Dumm describes it (1987, 111). It responded to the problem of individual disorder in a disorderly society by promoting in its inmates a new kind of subjectivity capable of producing social coordination through individual moral integrity. The rapid growth of industrial power in America was beginning to point toward another way of reconstituting social order around a very different strategy of coordination. In contrast to autonomy and integrity, the disciplinary model emphasized coercion and coordination with the machinery of production. The Auburn model picked up on this strategy and became the predominant penal regime of the nineteenth century.

Overwhelming inadequacies in nineteenth-century techniques for tracking criminal careers make it impossible to say whether Auburn's industrial engine of change had a greater crime-suppressant effect than Philadelphia's moral pedagogy, or if either had any effect at all. Since no one really could prove which was more effective, <u>Auburn won out because it achieved a better fit with</u> the broader industrial organization of social control being developed in nineteenth-century American society. As Thomas Dumm puts it:

> The Auburn system did not concern itself with the interior of the individual, but sought to [affect] only the individual's behavior. It inhibited the exercise of free will, but did not make the imposition of its discipline absolute, constraining rather than shutting off automatically the independent judgments of its inmates. It produced timid and hardworking

---

7. Some have argued that the prison played a critical role in forming a disciplined work force for the factory system (Melossi and Pavarini 1981, 163; Dumm 1987, 126–27). They tend to view the prison as having a powerful role in inscribing the new form of industrial power in the populace. It is possible that the penitentiary did play such a role. Situated in a highly visible debate about crime and punishment following the revolution, the disciplining of prisons may have helped promote the model of discipline in the community. The case for transfer in the other direction is, I believe, even clearer.

animals, in the form of people who worked out of habit, not out of a sense
of a self-conscious sense of the rightness of their actions. (1987, 136)

As late as the 1880s, some continued to argue the benefits of the Philadelphia system. In responding to an inquiry on prison labor sent out by the
Penological Commission of California, Philip C. Garrett of Pennsylvania's
Board of Public Charities conceded doubts about the benefits of the Philadelphia model:

> The separate or Pennsylvania system of imprisonment while it has disad-
> vantages peculiar to a solitary life, I believe, on the whole, to be more
> effectual, both in punishing and reforming prisoners, than the congre-
> gate system. I think its spread has been mainly prevented by two
> charges. (1) That it produced lunacy; (2) That it was expensive, because
> economic systems of labor could not be applied to it. I am not absolutely
> clear as to the first allegation, but a comparison of the accounts of our
> Eastern Penitentiary with the Western, where the congregate system is
> in use, does not sustain the second. (California Penological Commission
> 1887, Appendix, 181)

Although the Auburn model became the blueprint for most prisons in industrial states, Philadelphia represents a model of penal practice that has en-
dured as a latent possibility in the penal imagination: a backup program that
emerges when the political/economic situation undermines the link between
penal discipline and economic discipline. Philadelphia, with its emphasis on
conversion and reformation, may rightly be thought of as the progenitor of the
rehabilitative ideal that came to be developed in the twentieth century. Both
stand for the possibility of a penal program based on purely penal methods—
one that did not rely on the vagaries of the market and could fill with professional treatment the gaps in social control left by the economic order.

The very success of industrialism in forging a new social order in America
has left the society peculiarly vulnerable. The question of whether Americans
can sustain any other kind of community, besides the labor market, remains a
frightening but unanswered one which comes to the surface when the cycles of
the capitalist economy bring the labor market to a period of crisis. This is
particularly felt in penal enterprises which must keep large numbers of
healthy young men in a state of contrived deprivation. At such moments the
Philadelphia model continues to beckon us with the picture of a truly moral
and political path to social integration.

Americans in the early nineteenth century looked to the prison to solve the
corruption of the community, and to solve the problem of disorder (Rothman
1971), but right from the start they began to import control from the community in the form of labor contractors. By mid-century, the silent system fell into
disuse, and the principle of isolation was compromised everywhere by overcrowding. The enduring legacy of the penitentiary was the linkage between

labor and penal control. By the Progressive Era the community, disciplined by a half century of industrialization, would shine forth as a solution to the corruption of the prison (Rothman 1980, 118).

The Decline of Prison Labor

The triumph of Auburn's congregate system in becoming the predominant model of prisons in the United States was far from a complete vindication of the disciplinary model. Even at the peak of economic viability, industrial labor in prison never provided a perfect order. Whipping and other forms of violent bodily coercion were frequently relied upon at Auburn and other prisons. Yet these failings might not have motivated fundamental changes in the modernist program had political challenges from the community not endangered the access of prisons to labor discipline.

At mid-century there were two predominant forms of linking prison production to the market. The lease system involved leasing the entire prison to a private contractor who paid the state and ran the prison seeking what profit he could from prison labor. More typical was the contract system, pioneered at Auburn, which left the prison in state hands but placed the prisoner labor force in the hands of a contractor during the working hours.

These systems were the most lucrative from a fiscal point of view since the state received a guaranteed payment up front, but in the most advanced states they came under attack from penal reformers as "detrimental to every practical effort for reformation" (California Penological Commission 1887, 195). These reformers were primarily interested in the professionalization of prison work and saw the contract system as placing too much control in the hands of private contractors with little interest in reform. The California Penological Commission found that "it is impossible, under such a system or prison labor, to effect anything like reformation. All discipline is destroyed. The prison is simply a money-making machine" (125).

The defenders of the contract system tended to be politicians who saw little political gain from professional penology and much to lose in fiscal costs. Some, like Texas Governor John Ireland, seemed almost incredulous at the questions sent out by the California Penal Commission:

> "What is the best system of prison labor?" I hardly know what you mean by system. As far as circumstances will admit, convicts should be kept within walls and required to perform some sort of labor. The labor could be anything that would be remunerative. (California Penological Commission 1887, Correspondence, 183)

Advocates of more professional administration saw virtue in the piece-plan system and the state account system. Under both, the state managed the labor of inmates and then sold the product. Under the piece-plan system, the state put up the capital and sold the product, while under the account system, a private contractor provided the capital and a fixed price. These systems allowed the work of the prison to remain linked to the regular market economy while giving prison managers more direct control over discipline.

Those who condemned the lease and contract systems had no quarrel with the idea of industrial labor. Indeed, the New York Special Commission, quoted in the report of the California Penological Commission, declared earnestly that "the best reformatory treatment involves the assiduous industrial employment of convicts" (1887, Appendix, 62). What they rejected was the power given to profit-oriented contractors. The Commission simply wanted the prison as "money machine" to be replaced by the prison as "discipline machine" which could be achieved through industrial labor.

By the post–Civil War era, contract labor in the industrial manner was the model regime for prisons in the northeast and central parts of the nation as well as in advanced western states like California. Yet, by the start of World War I, prison labor in most of the advanced states had ceased to be organized privately. Where state production took over, many prisons were deliberately deindustrialized and kept out of competition in private labor markets.

These changes did not mark so much the failure of labor to achieve penal discipline as a response to organized political opposition from an increasingly well-organized working class. The nature of this opposition has not been adequately explored in the United States. The standard story is that labor advocates viewed the cheaper production costs of prison labor as a serious obstacle to raising the level of wages. Labor began to exercise greater power at the ballot box, and legislatures in the large industrial states—including New York, Pennsylvania, and Massachusetts—readily adopted limitations on the contract system of industrial labor in prisons. In time, business interests also came to oppose the use of prison labor to produce goods for the private market.[8]

The dismantling of the factory prison took different paths in different states. Many states, California among them, sought to limit production to commodities not otherwise made in the state. California built a jute mill at San Quentin in the 1880s to produce large bags woven from plant fibers for packing use in California's huge commercial agriculture industry. Other states adopted rules limiting production to state use. Prison shops would make printed material and furniture for state offices, as well as some of the services and products (many agricultural) used by the prisons themselves.

This limited the range of activities that prisoners could engage in and almost certainly diminished the capacity of prisons to utilize the most advanced

8. In addition to economic concerns, industrial craft laborers and their close allies among small independent producers may have rejected prison labor out of an earlier tradition which viewed the link to criminals as inherently dishonoring labor (Spierenburg 1991, 163).

industrial techniques now that neither private capital nor managerial skills could be drawn on. Some states reached this stage directly by enacting laws barring the purchase or replacement of industrial machines. As their machines wore out, prisons were being pushed toward craft methods like those that had been central to the Philadelphia model.

Prison managers were understandably concerned about the decline of labor and fought to protect forms of it or to win support for alternative means of organizing prison life. Some prison leaders saw the possibility of a politically sustainable market for prison labor in the state's own needs. This was known as the "state use" or "state account" system. An alternative approach was to use work as a kind of vocational training. Reformers like Zebulon Brockway at the Elmira Reformatory in New York had urged the transformation of prison industries into industrial schools decades earlier.

Rothman (1980, 137–43) casts considerable doubt on whether either mode successfully maintained the role of labor in organizing the penal enterprise. Prison supervision of the shops did not result in very productive labor. State agencies sought ways around the rules requiring them to purchase prison output in order to get better-quality products on the private market. Education was never successful in attracting the interests of inmates or in organizing their conduct during the day.

Some states continued to believe in the potential for prison industries to both occupy inmates and provide fiscal relief. Michigan began building the giant state prison at Jackson with the expectation that it would produce a variety of goods for the private market. Unfortunately, by the time the prison was completed, the Depression had knocked out any hope for employing its huge incarcerated population. Its inmates, housed in a building designed for production rather than surveillance, posed a control nightmare once they were idle (Bright 1992, 44).

The Adoption of Parole and the Transfer of Labor

In the space of several decades, from 1880 to 1914, most of the more industrially advanced states adopted a new panoply of penal practices: probation, parole, juvenile justice. The prison came to be surrounded by new strategies that explicitly rejected isolation and confinement in favor of the saving graces of the community itself. The exercise of power in the prison changed as well. States adopted indeterminate sentence laws which tied the length of confinement more or less directly (varying with different laws and administrative arrangements) to behavior in prison. New programs were added as well which emphasized education and training (Rothman 1980).

These reforms seemed to offer just the opposite of what was allegedly attractive about the prison to its early-nineteenth-century proponents: they took place outside instead of inside the walls. They blurred the lines between the condemned prisoner and other citizens where the penitentiary had attempted to sharpen it. Where the penitentiary had attempted to reform offenders by cutting them off from the corrupting influences of society, the Progressives' vision emphasized the capacity to reform offenders by working with them in the external community itself, either after a period of confinement (in the case of parole), or in lieu of confinement (in the case of probation and juvenile supervision).

The reasons for the wide acceptance of these innovations during the Progressive Era are multiplex. Rothman's (1980, 48–49) study of penal and other reform institutions in the United States during this period stresses the wide appeal of Progressive reform programs to a political culture strained by the momentous growth of a national industrial economy and the immigrant labor it attracted. Just as the penitentiary had appealed to Americans in the Jacksonian Era as a technology which could resolve many of their anxieties about the collapse of colonial social institutions, parole and the other Progressive innovations offered a model of individualized control capable of overcoming the effects of an emerging urban society. The problem was not the corrupting influence of society but its uneven development (Rothman 1980, 51).

Rather than focusing on the opposition between a disordered community and ordered centers of power like prisons and factories, Progressives saw a maturing industrial community that needed to achieve better order both inside and outside specific sites of production and control. The discipline that had seemed a property of specific architectures and carceral locations in the 1830s now appeared as potential of the industrial community itself. Well-placed penal interventions could simultaneously help tie the troublesome individual to the sources of discipline in the community and bolster the community's own forms of social control.

But if the Progressive vision offered a justification for the new techniques, it is less clear that it explains the motivations for such change. John Berecochea, in a detailed study of the origins of parole in California, argues that the need to find a politically expedient method of controlling inmate resentment over disparate sentences was more important to the adoption of parole there than the appeal of Progressive ideas about reform (Berecochea 1982, 74; see also Messinger et al. 1983). Before parole, the only method to relieve such disparities was executive clemency by the governor. As the nineteenth century moved to a close, governors found the exercise of the pardoning power more and more time consuming and politically embarrassing.

As Berecochea suggests (1982, 13), it may be helpful to distinguish between the idea of parole and the problems which led to parole's adoption. The swift spread of parole may be explained by the cogency of the idea or by the widespread nature of the problems it was intended to address. As James

March, Michael Cohen, and Johan Olsen argue in their classic "garbage can" theory of technological innovation, problems and solutions do not follow in neat causal sequences (Cohen, March, and Olsen 1976, 26–27). Often, solutions remain immanent until problems to which they can be applied emerge, and new problems come into focus when a new solution is available. The ideas of Progressive Era reformers may have provided the justifications for parole, but the specific reasons for its adoption in each state had more to do with the political problems of managing increasingly large state prison systems.

In California the problem of rationalizing the pardon power in the face of growing resentment over sentence disparity drove political leaders to consider reforms. Once empowered to do so, they found parole, bolstered by the rising prestige of Progressive reform ideas about government in general, available and well suited to solving the problem. The more credible the Progressive claims for expert knowledge in selecting parole candidates, the more the problem of the arbitrariness of the pardon power stood out in relief.

The problem of sentence disparity, however, was only a part of a larger problem that plagued prisons all over the nation at the end of the nineteenth century, that is, the maintenance of prison discipline in the face of a declining role for industrial labor in the prison.[9] Prison managers may indeed have appreciated the convenience that the promise of parole release would have in winning the cooperation of inmates whom they could no longer hope to contain through exhausting daily labor.[10] At the same time the prison may itself have become a model of the imperfections of industrial society which fired the conscience of the Progressives.

Robert Wiebe (1962) evocatively describes America in the Progressive Era as a "distended society," grown far too unwieldy for its administrative techniques. America's prisons, struggling to keep large inmate populations busy with vocational training and production for state use, seemed the very essence of distended. The flow of benefits it took to keep the prison lid on helped generate numerous scandals of corruption during this era (for Michigan, see Bright 1992, chapter 2).

The relationship between prison labor and parole is, of course, much more complex then the image of replacement conveys. The salience of parole as a

9. Indeed, discipline must have been an integral component of the concern about disparate sentences, for while there were philosophical reasons to reject disparity, it was prisoner resentment, and the threat of disorder, that motivated concern for disparity.

10. The problem of establishing control inside was never fully solved by labor; it only got worse, however, as labor became less available. Even before parole was created in 1893 institution managers had the potential to lengthen prison time by forfeiting good-time credits. Some hint of increasing need for leverage is measured by the increase in both the potential generosity of good-time credits and the discretion of prison managers over them starting in 1868 and increasing several more times until 1889 (Messinger 1969, 38). The fact that no further changes in good-time laws were made until 1929 suggests circumstantially that the adoption of parole in 1893 siphoned off the better portion of this need.

solution was increased by the emerging crisis of labor inside the prison, but that crisis took decades to unfold on a national basis. For California, Berecochea suggests that sentence disparity emerged as a real problem in 1860 when the state took over operation of the prison from its private lessees and began to effectively prevent escapes (which had been a relief valve for prisoner resentment under the lease system) (1982, 29). In 1882 California outlawed contract labor in prison, although it permitted work under the piece price system to continue. In 1887 the first serious proposal to adopt parole was made by a special commission appointed by the governor to study the problems of the prison system (78).

In Michigan parole was adopted by constitutional amendment in 1902 but became much more important in the 1920s when prison managers found themselves in the position of running state use production operations (Bright 1992, 57). Wardens sought to control who would be released as much as possible, and inmates understood that their work records would be an important element in the warden's recommendation to the board.

In most of the advanced industrial states parole laws were adopted a short time after the beginning of serious political limitations on prison labor. New York began a two-decade-long struggle about prison labor in the mid-1880s and adopted parole in 1889. Pennsylvania adopted its first restriction on prison labor in 1883 and its first parole law in 1887. Ohio began limitations on prison labor in the early 1880s and adopted a parole law in 1884. Massachusetts had a rudimentary parole law as early as 1855 but did not expand it to a serious release mechanism until 1880, around the same time that the prison labor debate became important.

While the struggle against prison labor was not equally successful in every state, it was most successful in those large industrial states whose penal choices influenced the whole nation (McKelvey 1977, 126–28). Constrained by laws preventing contact with the real markets for their prison labor, prison managers found themselves without a viable regimen capable of keeping the inmates busy and under control: "To all observers, whether reformers, legislators, or wardens, the prison's greatest failure was its inability to keep inmates employed, to provide steady labor. No goal had been more fundamental to prison from its very moment of inception a hundred years before" (Rothman 1980, 137).

Labor discipline had always been supplemented with directly coercive punishments like whipping, reduced rations, and the like, but without regular employment to occupy their time, inmates in the 1880s must have seemed a far more threatening lot to their keepers. When prison managers saw that political opposition to prison labor was growing, they had powerful reasons for concern. Blake McKelvey (1977, 116) argues that it was precisely the fear over the managerial consequences of the collapse of labor that brought prison wardens together in new national organizations where they could formulate new strategies. These organizations, like the National Prison Association, became points of penetration into the prison bureaucracy for the new class of Progressive social scientists and lawyers who were agitating for parole and other reforms.

Private industrialized labor was the essence of the Auburn system that had dominated prison design for most of the nineteenth century. It provided both ideological coherence and administrative control to the nineteenth-century prison. The movement to ban prison labor, or at least to deindustrialize it, was a stake in the heart of that model. Without the discipline of industrial labor the great virtue of Auburn—its ability to accommodate large groups of inmates at a low cost— was gone. Indeed, without the disciplinary engine of industrial work the Auburn design was hazardous because it brought large numbers of inmates together without an architectural strategy for segregating them (as became clear at the Jackson prison in Michigan; see Bright 1992).

The promise of an early release for good behavior took up some of the slack from the decline of prison labor, but it created its own problem: how to manage offenders in the community. Labor, once again, provided the key. While the lack of prison walls made it more difficult to control the offender, it also made it possible for him to be reconnected with the discipline of the private labor market which had been shut out of the prison. The emergence of parole corresponded to a transfer of penal labor from the prison to the community. Labor would retain its central place as an organizing source of penal discipline, but it would be directly integrated with the competitive private economy.

Conclusion

The creation of an industrial society in much of the United States went hand in hand with the spread of new forms of social control, tied to the discipline of the industrial workplace. This had direct effects on the incidence of violent behavior. [11] It also provided a clear model for how to deal with criminals, mad people, and the troublesome. [12] In the 1830s the best approximation of that ideal was to be found in the closed model of the factory (and thus prison). In the 1910s and 1920s that project was no longer politically viable within the

11. One study of industrialization in an American city found that accidents, homicides, and suicides during the nineteenth century diminished as the population was exposed to industrial discipline (Lane 1979). Analysis of national data suggests that this was a broad trend (Gurr 1981).

12. Rothman, who has little use for Foucault's (1977) *Discipline and Punish* (Rothman 1980, 10–11), seems to miss the significance of industrial discipline for the Progressives' sense that society contained the tools for handling the disordered. He is right to emphasize the importance of the human sciences in the Progressive vision, but he neglects the close nexus between the human sciences and the techniques of discipline on which Foucault and others have elaborated.

prison, but its instrumental and ideological benefits could be accessed outside in the great industrial city through parole and similar forms of community supervision.

George Canguilhem observed that the pathological reveals for the first time the possibility of the normal and gives birth to the enterprise of restoring that which has never existed (1989, 243). It is possible to see somewhat more clearly why the Jacksonians and the Progressives seem so similar in their optimism about reform and their commitment to the model of rational penal policy and yet so opposite in their technical solutions. The emerging patterns of an industrial society were experienced by the Jacksonians as a fall from order into chaos (Rothman 1971, 13). The institutions they invented to concentrate the pathological symptoms of their time clarified conceptually the norms that were being realized more gradually on the outside.

By the end of the nineteenth century the penitentiary had come full circle. Designed to replace the chaos and corruption of the community with rigorous techniques of training and control, penitentiaries now loomed as chaotic communities of the corrupt cut off from the organizing forces of the industrial community. It was in the midst of this stagnation of the prison that parole presented itself as a technology uniquely situated to allow the discipline of industrial society to be deployed upon the pathological elements of society (Cavender 1982, 88).

The big question at the beginning was who should be let out of prison early and how to justify it. What to do with them once they were back in the community was a less salient question. When managers turned to the problem of supervision they rediscovered or reinvented the techniques of suretyship that had been so central to premodernist penal strategies.

It was, however, a much different social order that was being mobilized. A system which relied on the blunt dichotomy drawn by premodern techniques between those with reputations and those without could not function in an economic order that required mobility and thus bred strangers. Moreover, the prison subculture, with its legacy of recidivists (Foucault 1977, 264–68), had come to occupy a permanent space in society. This left parole with the enduring need to provide an account of its capacity to provide control in the community over those defined as dangerous to the community. The legacy of penal labor in the industrial penitentiary pointed the way. As industrial labor disappeared from the prison, it reappeared as the central model of parole control over the felon in the community.

CHAPTER TWO

Disciplinary Parole

Wherever you look in the development of modernist penality you will find labor. Exhort the offenders with religious tracts, but make them work. Subject them to silence, but make them work. Educate them as citizens, but make them work. Treat their pathological features, but make them work. Indeed, whatever the prevailing explanation of crime and its control, work is almost always found as the real content of the myriad reforms proposed or implemented since the eighteenth century, and perhaps earlier. Why has labor never ceased to play such an important role in our penal modernity? Three reasons stand out as paramount.

First, labor for modern Westerners is the essential feature of being normal.[1] While earlier epochs drew sharp social lines between classes who worked and classes who didn't (with the latter on top), modern Westerners have generally expected everyone to work.[2]

Second, labor is punitive. Especially when it is hard, wearing, and low in status, it provides a ready means of causing suffering and marking a disadvantaged class.[3] This was clearly appreciated by the managers of the early

1. The major exceptions to this imperative were women and children of the elite classes. Working-class and rural children were essential elements of the labor force until the twentieth century. After that, education took over as a kind of quasi work which defined normality for them. Since the 1970s work has become a normal experience for women at all class levels.

2. One of the things that repels (or perversely attracts) us about the traditional aristocracy was the fact that they did not work. Today, of course, we have our own elite classes, but we expect them to work and work hard. Indeed, in contemporary times it has become a mark of prestige to work hours that would have appalled nineteenth-century factory workers.

3. This may seem to contradict the first point. How can work be both a mark of status and a form of punishment, an imperative for all and a sanction for the few? This involves two elements. First, a penalty that did not involve work might seem too much like recreation. The offender should work just

prisons who assigned the hardest and dirtiest labor to criminals and vagrants who reoffended while assigning easier work to others and women (Spierenburg 1991). Those confined under private arrangements were not made to work at all.

Third, labor is a potent means of social control. Labor controls by exhausting the time and energy that might otherwise be expended in trouble making. When it is organized around the bureaucratic and disciplinary lines which mark modernity, it also controls by exposing the subject to a precise system of accountability, surveillance, and constraint. The worker in a modern setting must be regular in habits, predictable in behavior, and capable of maintaining a constant level of production over a prolonged period of time.

Above all, labor has stood at the center of modern penality because it overlaps all three concerns and brings together a coherent and plausible account of crime and its control. The criminal is the essential rebel against the modern orthodoxy of work. He refuses to earn his bread through work but steals instead. He refuses to suffer the same burdens as his neighbors, putting himself in an aristocratic position that is both inappropriate to his true station, and largely illegitimate in a middle-class-oriented culture of labor. He refuses to act in a regular and predictable manner, keeping odd hours, avoiding observation, and intending antisocial acts. To work the prisoner is all at once to normalize him, punish him, and control him.

With a repetitiveness that becomes almost obsessional, penal experts and politicians have embraced the model of labor right through to the present. Collecting the opinions of politicians and prison officials in the 1880s, the California Penal Commission was told over and over again of the importance of labor for reformation: "Work, work, work, from the time they enter prison until they leave" was the prescription offered in one (California Penal Commission 1887, Appendix, 201). "There can be no reform without systematic labor, as idleness everywhere naturally breeds crime" asserted another correspondent (Appendix, 185). Over a century later, Governor George Deukmeijian of California assured his audience during the 1990 State of the State address: "I will continue to push for a constitutional amendment that allows all able-bodied prisoners work to help pay the cost of their upkeep, just like the rest of us do" (Deukmeijian 1990).

It is not surprising that forced labor has been the central feature of modern punishment. Whether forced labor actually diminished recidivism was a

---

like any one else to pay for his maintenance. Punishment enters in the comprehensiveness with which work dominates his life. Instead of a domestic realm in which to enjoy the fruits of labor, the prisoner finds that his entire world has been organized on the coercive basis of industrial labor. Only in dreams will he escape the industrial ordering of life. Second, if the work is not compensated at market rates, or not compensated at all, this will transform it from a rational activity to something more like torture.

question that really did not matter (and before the 1960s could not be answered very well). In any event forced labor fit into the larger ideological and strategic order that began to take shape in the early modern period and was considerably intensified by the growth of an industrial culture in Europe and North America. It expressed on the symbolically rich stage of punishment the prevailing ideas about the operation of the economic system in general, and the role of the poor in particular.

Punishment and Labor in the History of the Prison

That punishment practices are related in important ways to practices of organizing labor is hardly a new insight. Sketching the view of this relationship taken by some of the major historians of modern punishment will serve to illuminate the assumptions underlying the analysis of labor in the rest of this chapter.

Punishment and the Mode of Production

In their classic study *Punishment and Social Structure* (1939) Georg Rusche and Otto Kirchheimer traced the history of penal practices in relation to the emergence and modulations of capitalism. In their view this relationship was both instrumental and ideological. It was instrumental in that it operates in terms of the condition of the labor market. In periods where labor has been scarce and valuable, penal law has emphasized the exploitation of offenders for production. In periods when labor is overabundant the penal regime becomes more centered on physical punishments.

The mode of production is also relevant in a more ideological way. The emergence of capitalism transformed the way the human body was understood and used by institutions. As the body became a source of exploitable labor power, punishments designed to destroy or diminish that capacity became problematic.

More recently Dario Melossi and Massimo Pavarini have sharpened and extended this Marxist analysis of modern punishment in their book *The Prison and the Factory* (1981). Melossi and Pavarini highlight the ideological function of the prison. In their account the penitentiary was essentially a machine for producing proletarian subjects. The prison may at times have succeeded in extracting valuable labor from its inmates, but its central mission was to strip the prisoner of the social resources for maintaining an independent identity (independent of the capitalist work contract, that is):

> Ultimately the production of the disciplinary machine has only one possible alternative to his own destruction, to madness: the moral form of

subjection, that is the moral form of the status of proletarian. (1981, 163)

Punishment and the Genealogy of Power

In Michel Foucault's book *Discipline and Punish: The Birth of the Prison* (1977) the practices of punishment are depicted as an essential site for the deployment and development of new technologies of power based on discipline. The replacement of corporal punishments on the scaffold with the prison represented for Foucault not simply a change in the utility of offenders or a new ideology, but a political move to establish controls over the populace that were less expensive in both economic and political terms.

Labor is not central to the meaning of the prison in Foucault's account except insofar as it presents the most compelling vehicle for establishing disciplinary control over the bodies of inmates. Drawing on Bentham's plan for the prison "Panopticon," and related penal proposals from the late eighteenth and nineteenth centuries, Foucault concluded that disciplinary power required architecture that would allow for efficient surveillance on an individual level and a regimen capable of supplying the inmate with precise tasks, the performance of which could be readily observed. Labor, especially labor on the industrial model, was a natural although not exclusive choice. In Foucault's account a disciplinary prison could also have been run on the model of a religious establishment or a military base (1977, 235 et seq.).

Foucault viewed the emergence of disciplinary punishment as related to capitalism but not as simply cause and effect. In his account, capitalism requires the formation of disciplinary technologies of power to realize the potential in the organization of the labor power of numerous workers (Foucault 1977, 174). The prison is a privileged site for disciplinary technology necessary to industrial capitalism, but capitalism does not create or determine the regime of prison punishment.

Punishment and the Moral Imagination of Reformers

Michael Ignatieff in his study of the history of the prison, *A Just Measure of Pain* (1978), concentrated on the overlap between penal reformers and the early developers of industrial manufacturing. Both groups belonged to the Protestant dissenter tradition in England. The relationship between labor and punishment is thus one of shared vision. In imagining the appropriate remedy for criminal proclivity, eighteenth- and nineteenth-century penal reformers drew on the same set of assumptions about the relationship between industriousness and goodness that factory developers had.

David Rothman's analysis of the transformation of social control institutions in the first half of the nineteenth century, *The Discovery of the Asylum*, also emphasizes the continuity in vision between the designers of prisons and factories. What they shared according to Rothman was an understanding of how to overcome the crisis of order in the new republic through the application of new disciplinary techniques (1971, 105).

Punishment and the Civilizing Process

Pieter Spierenburg's work has concentrated mainly on the early modern period well before the threshold of the industrial age. *The Spectacle of Suffering* (1984) argued that public physical punishments did not all at once disappear in favor of the penitentiary but passed a long period of change and reduction coextensive with increasing use of imprisonment. In *The Prison Experience* (1991) Spierenburg explored the practices of forced confinement which developed in northern Europe from the late sixteenth century. Spierenburg contends that prison labor was rarely profitable and acted as more of a tax on the legitimate economy than a spur. The relationship was one driven much more by the assumptions shared by the governing elite that idleness and crime were mutual evils. Drawing on the work of Norbert Elias (1978), Spierenburg sees the development of the prison as part of a long-term change in mentality which has discouraged open display of violence and encouraged a more complicated and autonomous view of the individual subject.[4]

The Present Analysis

There is good reason, as the works of Rusche and Kirchheimer (1939), Melossi and Pavarini (1981), and Ignatieff (1978) show, to believe that the emergence of industrial capitalism provided at least some of the inspirations and motivations for creating the penitentiary (albeit in a way that was blended right from the start with religious and political ideologies, as were the factories).

Some have seen this as a process by which punishment was reorganized to help constitute an obedient work force (Rusche and Kirchheimer 1939; Melossi and Pavarini 1981). The specific relations between the correctional population and the work force have been enormously complicated. In certain extraordinary settings, no doubt, the population under correctional control actually comprised a significant enough subcomponent of the work force to

---

4. A majority of the inmates of the early modern prisons that Spierenburg investigated were vagrants. The changing attitude toward vagrancy represented in the rise of imprisonment is itself a critical influence on the exercise of the power to punish, and Spierenburg's research sheds much light on this. But the close relationship between vagrancy and idleness also suggests that the emphasis on forced work may have been less relevant to the way other crimes were understood.

affect wages for the nonincarcerated.[5] Otherwise, it is difficult to understand
the force of organized labor's opposition to prison manufacturing.

On a historical scale, however, it seems clear that management of the
factory was the predominant influence on prison management and not the
other way around. The discipline of industrial labor, to which millions of
nineteenth-century citizens were subjected in workshops, provided penal
managers a compelling model for controlling the few hundred thousand individuals who passed through prisons in the course of the nineteenth century.[6]
The role of capitalist ideology, however, seems to have been significant in bol-
stering the prison. The picture of a controlled or controllable working class
that seems to have become gradually more accepted among elites in parts of
Europe and North America throughout the nineteenth century probably made
the penitentiary project more successful politically.

The present analysis, however, is least concerned with the question of the
origins of the prison.[7] The relationship with labor seems much more telling in
the problem of managing the prison once it was in existence. Once the practice of confining a large portion of a society's convicted felons in a penitentiary
with the expectation that they would eventually return to society was in place
(whatever its motivations), the problem of how to maintain control over a population in confinement and upon release quickly became the overarching concern.

Both factors are important. Control over a confined population may be pursued through a number of strategies ranging from violent suppression to ac-
commodation. An additional constraint on penal managers was the need to
maintain control in a way that offered a plausible explanation for why an offender released from such an institution was a more acceptable community
member than before.

In solving this problem managers clearly drew on the example of the early
factories in shaping a capacity for control over individuals. The prison factory,
as exemplified in the operation of the Auburn prison, provided a compelling
solution because it offered a way to maintain control inside which also seemed
to promise a greater chance of conformity on release.

When parole itself emerged as a partial solution to the crisis of the prison
factory, the question of how to maintain a plausible account of control spread
from prison to community. The labor market—the real one, not the artificial
situation of the prison—became immediately and remained up to our own
time the most significant part of this plausible account. It is possible to identify several specific levels on which this works.

5. Barbara Yaley makes this claim for California in the nineteenth century (1980).
6. For figures on penal populations during the second half of the nineteenth century, see Calahan
(1986).
7. Eric Monkkonen makes a similar point in analyzing the history of the police (1988, 50).

1. Industrial labor offers a mechanism for disciplining individuals who must submit themselves to the schedule of work and the demands of the machines.

2. The organization of production at a particular time affects how much disciplinary power parole can access in the community. A highly industrialized society offers the optimal environment in which released offenders can be supervised.

3. The tightness of the labor market, particularly at its low unskilled end, has a relatively close relationship with how plausible and effective parole seems to its most immediate audiences, that is, correctional agents, correctional subjects, families, and members of the lower-class community.

The interpretation of penal history in this and the following chapters, then, will depend heavily on the argument that until our own time, major historical transformations in punishment can be understood as efforts to deal with shifts in the way labor is organized, distributed, and understood. Indeed, one of the most striking features of the present is the general acceptance (despite former governor Deukmeijian's enthusiasm for prison labor) that prisoners will be idle.[8] As we shall explore in later chapters, this attenuation of the link between punishment and labor produces overwhelming difficulties for the exercise of the power to punish.

Work as the Measure of Good Men

In the early development of parole far more attention was paid to the problem of selecting those to be released than to supervising them in the community. In California more than a decade passed between the adoption of parole in 1893 and the beginning of a genuine parole supervision apparatus. In this interim stage labor played a central role, not so much as a tool of discipline, but as a marker of whether or not the prisoner was really a criminal by nature. During this phase, parole was used, much as the pardon power had been, to select for relief a few worthy cases, or to mitigate apparently excessive sentences. Parolees were released with little more than a bona fide and approved job, a private sponsor, a list of rules, and a sheaf of monthly reports to be completed.

Parole didn't need to mount a credible supervision effort because it claimed to be releasing men who were not essentially criminal:

> The rules and regulations of parole would *not* be seen as a set of conditions which if adhered to, would *produce* an honorable, law abiding citi-

8. To be sure, it remains possible to invoke the resentment of hard-pressed taxpayers by discussing the coddling of idle felons in the prisons. Yet, especially when seen in the context of a society that leaves large pockets of people outside the effective labor force, the idleness of the prison becomes understandable. Work has become too much of a luxury to reward prisoners with.

zen. Rather, a truly noncriminal parolee would abide by these rules as
a matter of course. Failure to abide by them would mark the parolee
as being a criminal at heart, as might other signs of criminality.
(Berecochea 1982, 118)

So long as it only released a select few with impeccable community connections, parole did not need to establish its legitimacy through its own actions on
the inmate. The challenge was to select the right men; after that, their intrin-
sic goodness or badness took its course.

Labor was an essential ingredient in this arrangement. By obtaining a good
job a prisoner demonstrated a credible claim to being a "normal" person who
had misstepped into crime rather than one who was a criminal at heart. This
spoke to the deep-seated image of the criminal as the opposite of the good
worker. Over and over again in the writings of nineteenth-century politicians,
chaplains, and penological experts, criminality is attributed to idleness—
this being both the cause and best evidence of criminal intent. Thus a parole
system which took into account the diligence of a prisoner at work, and then
ensured that he obtained work before leaving prison, had gone a long way toward separating out those who had committed a crime but were not criminal by
nature from those who were.

The requirement that parolees obtain and retain employment was, in effect,
a continuing character test. As the California Penological Commission put it
in their report recommending adoption of parole in 1887:

> While he is out on parole, he must of necessity be a good man. He must
> show by monthly reports how much he has earned, how much he has
> spent, how many days he has worked, how many he has been idle. If he
> continues honest and industrious during the existence of his parole, he
> undoubtedly will continue so afterwards. (80)

Furthermore, the public could trust the judgment of the employers who acted
as sponsors for parolees. Unlike prison officials who may have had reason to
exaggerate the suitability of an inmate in order to expedite his release, private
employers could be expected to look after their own interests by not hiring a
dishonest person. Moreover, while prison officials might be inclined to over-
look signs of criminality in the recently released parolee to avoid embarrass-
ment, "a reputable firm . . . would not be likely to conceal the person's failure
to be industrious" (Berecochea 1982, 133). Unlike law enforcement agents
who were given responsibility for cosigning monthly reports, employers would
have no reason to accuse parolees of criminal activity prematurely (thus embarrassing the paroling authorities).

From the start there was in the early operation of parole also a strong echo of
the earlier premodern tradition of suretyship. The Board of Prison Directors,
which selected parolees, obtained the opinion of influential people in the prisoner's community prior to considering the application for parole (Berecochea

1982, 133).[9] The community was to be made an accomplice both in the decision to release and in assuring the good behavior of the prisoner while free in the community.

As a result of increasing prison populations after 1900, pressure began to mount from prison managers to increase parole releases (Messinger et al. 1983). In 1905 a committee was appointed by the legislature to look into the overcrowding problem. They pointed to the limited use of parole release and contended that an effort to parole more of the eligible population would obviate the need for prison construction. A law was passed that would have placed the paroling power in a new agency, presumably one that was more committed to using parole as a release valve. Although the governor vetoed the law, the paroling authorities appeared to get the message. Starting in 1907 the number of prisoners paroled increased considerably (Berecochea 1982, 199).

Berecochea argues that it was this growth in parole that stimulated the development of a reformatory ideology in parole (1982, 205). As parole became a less-exclusive club, it became less credible to found parole's legitimacy on the inherent goodness of the erstwhile offender. In 1910 California's first parole bureaucracy came into being: a parole officer, an assistant parole officer, and a clerical worker. Berecochea describes this operation as a "paperwork agency" which reviewed monthly reports and did the paperwork to process for revocation parolees whose violations had been discovered by the police (1982, 213). There was no possibility that the parole officer, located in San Francisco, could make personal contact with parolees spread throughout the state.

Penological expert Frederick H. Wines of New York had written to the California Penological Commission in 1885 that parole "implies the existence of a truly reformatory discipline in prison. Where this is lacking I should doubt its practicability" (1887, 77). But with prison crowding forcing parole rates up, it was necessary to begin building an account of control that could promote the idea that where prison could not be counted on to achieve total rehabilitation, parole would complete the task. While the official ideology remained that the parolee was already reformed before release, penal administrators began to speak of parole as a device that could help effect rehabilitation. Labor remained at the center of this account, now less as a test of character than as a practical method of discipline and surveillance.

Disciplinary Parole

By the end of the First World War, parole laws in many states were being redrafted to encompass a greater variety of offenders, including recidivists and

---

9. Indeed, perhaps the first form of parole was the practice of shortening or sometimes extending the confinement of private prisoners on the petition of family members in the sixteenth century (Spierenburg 1991).

murderers. Instead of being an exceptional measure used to correct errors of judgment at the sentencing stage, parole was becoming a primary method of releasing prisoners. In California the percentage of releases through parole rose from 7 percent in 1907 to 35 percent in 1914 (Berecochea 1982, 218).

A number of states adopted indeterminate sentence laws that made parole the presumptive release mode and allowed paroling authorities wide discretion over when to release an inmate on parole.[10] No doubt this rise in paroles was welcomed by prison managers who saw it as a tool to keep prisons under control by relieving population pressures (Berecochea 1982, 183) and rewarding inmate cooperation.

The interests of prison managers were not, however, identical with the interests of the penal system as a whole. The public was unlikely to be impressed with a program that improved the fiscal and management problems of the prisons by pushing more dangerous criminals back into the community faster. Yet, as the percentage of prisoners released on parole went up, it could no longer be realistically maintained that those being released were completely rehabilitated by the prison.

Reformers helped fashion a case for parole supervision by pointing out that the prison was too artificial an environment. Real reform had to take place in the context of the community, or at least in prisons designed to resemble the community as much as possible. Some advocated changes in the organization of prisons to make them more like the community with which offenders ultimately had to be reconciled. Such changes, which amounted to liberalizing the rules governing prisoner life, were bitterly opposed by wardens who would abide no reduction in discipline. Parole provided a means to satisfy both concerns. The prison would remain a harsh and alien environment that punished the offender and brought him under control. The real work of normalization, reinserting the offender into the effective background controls of the community, would fall to parole.

Although many Progressive reformers looked to the evolving practice of social work to provide parole with a credible capacity for the normalization of offenders, few systems managed even to approach the level of staffing necessary to carry out individual casework until the 1950s. Instead, virtually all states relied on coerced participation in private labor, enforced by employers, local law enforcement officers, and limited central staffs. The parole laws of

10. The indeterminate sentence is often conflated with parole. Indeterminate sentencing systems provide for virtually all prison sentences to terminate in parole, but parole release can also operate to terminate judicially set "determinate" sentences. In California parole was adopted in 1893, but the indeterminate sentence was not adopted until 1917. Under the indeterminate sentencing system, parole was the modal release mechanism, but its rise had begun some years earlier while determinate sentences remained the norm. In the 1970s some states returned to determinate sentences and generally abolished parole release altogether.

all states required employment as a condition of parole. Remaining employed was invariably the most important condition and one of the largest sources of "technical" violations unrelated to criminal conduct.

The mixture of reform rhetoric and labor discipline in the early years of parole was evident in the way California's lone state parole officer described the effectiveness of parole at the start of his biennial reports:

> From a humanitarian standpoint the fact that men who committed crimes have a far better chance to recover their self-respect and become useful members of the community outside of prison walls, than in confinement and association with others of their kind, has been fully established. (State Board of Prison Directors 1918, 107)

The 1918 report of the State Board of Prison Directors, covering the biennial period from 1 July 1916 to 30 June 1918, cited two indicators of the success of parole. First, the report noted that parolees had low rates of recidivism: only 3.7 percent of the prisoners released during this period had been arrested for new crimes, while 19.9 percent were returned to prison for technical violations.[11] In short, most parolees were avoiding crime and even minor infractions of the rules. Second, the report noted that parolees were generally self-sufficient:

> In addition to the humanitarian side of the parole system the practical and financial benefit derived by the state from its operation should not be overlooked. Men who are outside the prisons are self-supporting and no longer a burden upon the taxpayers. The average paroled man earns ample wages to provide for himself all the necessities of life and many comforts. Some of them care for dependents who would otherwise by wards of the community or the state. Ninety percent of them are doing their bit to aid in the financing of the war by the purchase of Liberty Bonds. (107)

Unlike recidivism rates, the second register of success did not conflate the system's effectiveness with the weaknesses of its surveillance methods.

In California employment was virtually the entire program. Although a state parole officer was appointed in 1914, it would be another decade and a half before anything like a field staff would be assembled. In the meantime parole surveillance involved reading the reports submitted by parolees, their employers, and local police. Those states that did begin to develop a cadre of parole professionals used them to help parolees get jobs and to monitor their performance.

---

11. Recidivism statistics in the annual reports must be read with caution not only because they reflect only discovered delinquency, but also because they were calculated using inconsistent bases. Sometimes the base used was those released during the biennial period, while at other times the base used was all who have been released since parole was established.

Looking at the forty-year period from the start of the movement against prison labor to the development of parole, one can see that penal practice followed labor out of the prison and into the community. If offenders could not be subjected to industrial labor inside the walls, new laws would subject them to such labor in the community on pain of reimprisonment.

In the 1920s sociologist Ernest Burgess analyzed a variety of demographic and correctional information on parolees to determine who failed or succeeded on parole in Illinois. Burgess found that work record prior to imprisonment was related to the chance of success following release:

> The very low percentages of parole violation for men with a record of regular employment is eloquent in its testimony to regular habits of work as a factor in rehabilitation. This fact gives new emphasis to the recommendations for the reorganization of the penal and reformatory institutions in order to promote the training of their inmates in trades which they may pursue after their release and that the record of their work progress be considered in granting or refusing parole. ([1928] 1974, 72)

However, the norms of industrial life also showed up in many of the other criteria that Burgess examined, including the social type of the criminal (e.g., hobo, ne'er-do-well, farmboy) and the neighborhood of residence prior to imprisonment, classification of which derived from Burgess's independently famous morphological analysis of the industrial city (hobohemia, rooming house district, furnished apartments, immigrant areas, residential district, etc.) (68–69).

If employment in the private labor market was the primary source of discipline for parolees, evaluating the credibility of employment offers was the primary task of parole staffs. The term *parole* stems from a French military term, *parole d'honor*, for the practice of releasing captive enemy military officers on their word that they would lay down arms. However attractive the phrase, penal managers never looked to honor as a form of control. Criminal parole has always involved the mobilization of credibility. In the beginning, California like many states relied almost completely on local law enforcement to certify the credibility of employment offers. In time the demand for central staffs to investigate offers grew.

Prisoners probably did not find it overly difficult to satisfy the condition that they find a job sponsor. There was in these years a large labor market in the cities for unskilled and semiskilled labor.[12] Moreover, familial and neighborhood associational ties were strong at this time and may have been an additional source of job sponsors. The promise of a job may not have been difficult

12. The years of the Great Depression presented a much different story. Many with formal parole approval were held in prisons for lack of a job. This may have stemmed, however, from increased sensitivity to the availability of work in a time of social tension. A job promise had less surface credibility.

to find. Such jobs may often have been short lived, and the capacity of the system to monitor them was limited.

In California the parolee's monthly form had to be countersigned by his employer and a police officer. This may have worked well in small towns where police could be expected to know all employers and have the time to go investigate them, but this requirement was probably less effective in large cities such as San Francisco or Los Angeles.

Although the parole bureaucracy was created to enhance the credibility of employment, its ability to monitor employment was initially quite limited. California's first office consisted of a parole officer, an assistant, and a clerical worker. They were located in San Francisco and could not possibly have made regular field visits outside of that city, if at all. Instead, they simply collected and processed the self-reporting forms.

The biennial reports of the state parole officer reflected the important role that employers played in the parole process. Virtually every report filed from 1914 until the Depression ended with a paragraph of praise for the state's employers. The 1918 report is typical:

> To make the parole system a success, it has been necessary for the employers of large numbers of men throughout the state to cooperate with this department in giving employment to men released from the prisons, and they have, in most cases, been more than willing to do all in their power to help the men, not merely by giving them employment, but by a kindly, personal interest in their rehabilitation and their welfare. In the large lumber mills, ship yards, iron works and ranches of the state, side by side with his more fortunate neighbor, the erstwhile convict is earning an honest livelihood and regaining his former standing in society and taking his place among the honorable and law abiding citizens. (State Board of Prison Directors 1918, 110)

The reports also stressed the rigor with which the parole system ascertained that employment was bona fide and appropriate: "The employment offer is carefully investigated and if found to be satisfactory and in accordance with the rules of the Board of Prison Directors, it is approved and the prisoner is released to report to his employer" (State Board of Prison Directors 1924, 128). Verification was critical since this was virtually the *only* action parole took to ensure surveillance in the community. If the employer turned out to be a sham, the public had little protection beyond traditional law enforcement to prevent crime.

The reports reflected the importance of the employment requirement by discussing economic conditions and mentioning specific release delays due to such conditions.

> The last half of the biennium, however, was not so favorable, owing to the extreme drought which caused many men to lose their employment.

> Prisoners due for release on parole were detained somewhat longer than the time on which they were due for release, owing to the lack of work to be had for them. In spite of the labor conditions few were detained for any unreasonable length of time. (1924, 129)

The reports throughout this period continue to reference the idea that parole was reformative and linked to a scientific knowledge of offenders, but overall they suggest that, for all practical purposes, the work of parole was work. The First World War appears to mark, at least in California, the full flowering of a disciplinary model of parole,[13] based on forced participation of released prisoners in the private labor market.

War, of course, provided the best possible circumstances for such an arrangement, and many states used the increased demand for labor to boost their parole release rates. Illinois took advantage of the First World War to expand the scope of parole availability in a program appropriately named "Industrial Parole."

> Prior to release on industrial parole the prisoners were subject to careful selection by the prison and parole authorities, and a transitional stage between confinement and liberation was provided for those men whose cases were considered doubtful. . . . If and when the transitional stage was successfully completed, the prisoner was released on industrial parole and put to work in one of the munitions plants. In each case a definite job was found for the prisoner before he was paroled. . . . Supervision over the parolees was exercised both by parole officials and by the State and Federal employment agencies, which at that time were vitally interested in securing labor for war industries. (Attorney General 1939, 26)

It would be an exaggeration to suggest that parole supervision in the first half of the century was defined by employment completely. The theory of parole also stressed the family, community attitude, and the provision of counseling. Perhaps these factors became materially important in limiting cases where a parolee was unable to find work but had supportive kin; however, the official discourse of parole placed greater emphasis on the validity of these concerns than on any description of practice.

In 1939, the Attorney General's *Survey of Release Procedures*[14] stressed that employment was not the only issue of importance to parole supervision:

13. Not all labor was industrial in the strict sense used by labor statistics. As the reports of the California parole officer make clear, many California prisoners worked in the state's large agricultural economy. The term "industrial" was used in the early part of the century to mean labor in general, reflecting perhaps the intensive role that industrial production was playing in the economic growth of the nation as a whole.

14. The survey and report was the most comprehensive examination of corrections on a national basis that had been attempted up to that time and remained the most significant until the 1960s.

It must not be assumed, however, that a favorable employment situation definitely assures successful parole operation. A prisoner released on parole is not bound to make good merely because a job has been provided for him. The success or failure of a parolee is conditioned on a variety of circumstances, both individual and social, as well as physical and psychological. (27)

Yet in its section on methods of parole supervision the Attorney General's report devoted the better part of three pages to a discussion of employment. The family warranted a paragraph. Community received two pages, much of which was devoted to arguing that small town parolees did better than urban ones.

In California supervision was largely a matter of paperwork since there was no real field staff until the 1930s, except for the single parole officer headquartered in San Francisco. In addition to mobilizing employment, this single operative did attempt to work through community contacts to keep the parolee in line. The 1928 report to the legislature remarks on the parole officer's efforts to "salvage" nonreporting parolees through what he termed a "tracer system . . . whereby contact is made with the subject through relatives and friends, and by advising the delinquent to immediately get in touch with the Parole Officer" (State Board of Prison Directors 1928, 86).

By the 1930s, field officers were employed in a number of the leading states including California and New York, but it is difficult to determine what their work consisted of. The Attorney General's 1939 survey reprinted a reporter's log from a day spent with a parole officer in an unidentified city. The log presented several presumably typical functions: finding employment placements and residences for prisoners soon to be released and checking on the location of a suspected parole violator. Employment was repeatedly intertwined with these functions.

To trace the parole violator the agent went to the garage where the parolee had been employed and discovered that he had been seen frequently with a certain woman. The agent visited the family of a prisoner who had been recently granted parole "but who still is being held in the reformatory until employment is found for him. . . . [Agent] [h]opes to get them to exert themselves in finding S—— a job" (Attorney General 1939, 223). The agent visited the young wife of a prisoner to encourage her to look for a home where the parolee could live with her and their child: "her husband can be released from the penitentiary, and get a relief job, if she will make an effort to make a home for him" (223). The team visited a parolee coming up for discharge, who complained that he was having trouble finding a job because "'I can't explain what I did with those 4 years.' Called on J—— D——, placement officer for National Re-employment Service, who will place P——, who has been paroled, but who is being held until work is found for him" (223).

It is true that the study and report were done during the Depression when employment may have loomed as a bigger problem than in other periods. Yet it is clear that for parole to exercise control, a job was the crucial presupposition for virtually every state. Indeed, the authors pleaded for reforms specifically because of the Depression. "[Parole authorities] should not rigidly adhere to employment as a parole condition in all cases, especially under the prevailing circumstances of widespread unemployment" (Attorney General 1939, 186). Yet few states, if any, managed to find a real substitute for work as a form of control. Once parolees left their employment they effectively left the visible realm as far as the parole authorities were concerned. They would become visible, if at all, only if arrested.

In case studies of New York parole violators returned to Auburn prison in 1915 done by prison physician Frank Heacox (1917), the pattern of leaving the job, disappearing from parole, and showing up after a new offense is repeated consistently:

> No. 10 . . . was paroled to a job on a farm, but did not report for work and was later sent to a penitentiary for criminally having narcotics; after serving ten months he was returned to prison. (238–39)

> No. 12 . . . was paroled to work as a carpenter but did not report for work, and began his alcoholic habits immediately; he was out about nine months before he was returned to prison. (239–40)

> No. 14 . . . was paroled to work as a laborer, but finding the work too hard he went into the country to work on farms without obtaining permission from the parole officer; following a spree he was sent to the penitentiary for intoxication, and after serving thirty days was returned to prison. (240–41)

Heacox's summaries contain exceptions as well. Some individuals were apparently paroled without jobs and discovered in short order without the aid of law enforcement:

> No. 16 . . . was paroled to New York City without having a definite job, and left the city apparently without making any effort to obtain one; he was out about one month before he was returned to prison. (241–42)

More typical is the case of No. 26 who "left the job without permission; he was out about four years, before he was returned to prison" (246–47).

The Heacox text is also a testament to the tensions between the disciplinary model of parole and the aspiration of creating a professionalized correctional enterprise. In his statistical summation of the causative factors of parole violation (derived from his case studies) he identifies as the leading factors "Return to previous alcoholic habits; Associating with bad companions; Defective control of sex impulses" (1917, 251–52). Employment problems were not a distinct category, but related categories such as "Employment ill-fitted, Laziness, Ill-treatment by employer, Lack of definite employment" (252) accounted together for more failed paroles than any of the other diagnostic categories except alcoholism.

To a physician like Heacox it probably would have seemed to belittle the problem of parole violation to treat it as a matter of employment. Those who wrote about parole in publications such as the *Journal of the American Institute of Criminal Law and Criminology* (later known as the *Journal of Criminal Law and Criminology*) tended to be interested in defining a task for parole that involved specialized knowledge and complicated decision making. Yet, as Rothman points out about the Progressive penal reformers in general, their ability to invent an impressive language of diagnosis outstripped their ability to offer a program for the operatives of the system (1980, 125). Employment remained the essential framework for parole supervision throughout this period.

There was, however, a compelling logic to the reformers' vision of a more interventionist parole practice. After all, if the labor market held the key to crime and crime control, why did parolees end up in prison in the first place? Since prisons did little to train a person for a better job, and parole agents were unlikely to find a better job for a person than could the parolee's family or friends, why assume that parolees would do any better refraining from crime after their release? Although it was never articulated as far as I have discovered, the answer to such complaints would have been to point out that there was no other alternative, except for permanently removing offenders from society. As defective as work discipline might be, even when backed up by the coercive power of the state, it remained the only path toward normality available in a society which recognized few other foundations for social solidarity.

Was the Disciplinary Model Successful?

Rothman is unambiguous in his summation of parole's ineffectiveness in the Progressive Era and since:

> No sooner does one plunge into the realities of parole than the question of its persistence is further complicated, for one uncovers almost everywhere a dismal record of performance. Neither of the two essential tasks of parole, the fixing of prison release time or post-sentence supervision, was carried out with any degree of competence or skill. Amateurs on parole boards reached their decisions hastily and almost unthinkingly, while overworked and undertrained parole officers did little more than keep a formal but useless file on the activities of their charges. Whatever the reasons for the survival of parole, they will not be found in the efficient or diligent administration of the system. (1980, 162)

The efficiency of parole operatives at this time may have been as poor as Rothman describes. Certainly his view is consistent with that found in many contemporary sources including the Attorney General's survey, and the report of the Wickersham Commission (1931). The very things that parole officials identified as important—accurate predictions of who was rehabilitated and effective supervision by professional agents—seemed to be things that they did poorly. Nonetheless, it is hazardous to evaluate an institution only in terms of its self-identified functions.

Measuring success from the recidivism statistics of that era is highly problematic because of the kinds of records kept.[15] Many parole systems boasted 70 or 80 percent success rates. As the Attorney General's survey pointed out, these rates were calculated from a myriad of different bases (1939, 30). Some rates were calculated by comparing the total numbers of violators to the total number on parole, yielding a smaller figure than would a comparison of the number of violators in each release cohort to the total in that cohort. More importantly, parole authorities were unable to distinguish between successful parolees, who never again showed up in arrest reports or prison rosters, and those complete failures who simply disappeared from the records of the system because of their stealth and success as criminals (237). If the statistics defined failures only as those who returned to prison on a violation, they included as successes all those who absconded and successfully avoided being captured and identified as a parolee.

The negative impression of parole comes in part from taking a national measure of a state-controlled institution. On the eve of the Second World War, parole in the more advanced states had achieved a mark of bureaucratic rationality:

> In States like California, Massachusetts, Minnesota, New York, and Rhode Island where comparatively large staffs of professional paid agents are used, a well articulated program of parole supervision can be carried out. The duties of the agents are clearly defined and policies and methods approximate uniformity. (Attorney General 1939, 211)

Parole agencies in such states were vested with broad powers to arrest and initiate the reimprisonment of parolees on technical grounds, without proving that the parolee had violated any criminal laws, and were organizationally capable of exercising that power. Parolees discovered to have committed new felonies, and many who simply violated one of the technical conditions of their parole, went back to prison. Parole in these states was a success, in the sense that it was capable of operating in a regular, predictable, and rational manner.

Rothman (1980) is surely right that this operation fell far short of the aspira-

---

15. Recidivism statistics have been criticized as problematic even in recent years because of the tremendous amount of control parole agents have over whether or not to report technical violations (Maltz 1984). Prior to the 1960s, recidivism statistics are even more difficult to evaluate because of uneven auditing practices.

tion to maintain constant surveillance, to obtain an individualized knowledge of the parolee, and to effect a rehabilitative influence. But if instead of looking at parole as a relationship between the state and certain delinquent individuals, one views it against the earlier tradition of suretyship, one gets a different basis for evaluating its relative success. To be sure, Progressive reformers envisioned parole as a specialized operation of government and science, above and apart from private power in the community. In practice, it functioned not unlike premodern community corrections, as a kind of public grant of power to the private community and its institutions, primarily the labor market, to exercise power over a class of disreputable members.

The parolee released with a set of conditions broadly defining almost any kind of unwelcome conduct in the community as a violation became vulnerable to the justified or unjustified vindictiveness of his family, employer, friends, and neighbors. These rules defined a level of discipline adhered to by few in the working-class communities to which prisoners returned. As parole critic Hans von Hentig put it in 1942: "In complying strictly with every one of these conditions he [the parolee] would at once draw the attention of his neighbors to his being either a crank or a convict who has been released on parole" (von Hentig 1942, 364).

These rules were defended as an interim condition between prison and total freedom, designed to test the good faith of the parolee (Bates 1942, 437). In actuality they really operated to open the parolee to an almost limitless variety of complaints concerning his behavior or relations with others. Even without a large parole staff, a parole operation that could receive complaints and obtain police cooperation in arresting suspected violators was set up to amplify and carry the power of the community.

Like the *lettres de cachet* available to established citizens in eighteenth-century France, and the analogous practices elsewhere in northern Europe, which enabled a family to confine a troublesome member, parole created a legal status that allowed punishment based on private judgment (see chapter one).

Some of Heacox's (1917) case histories illustrate the effects of this power:

No. 6 . . . out about six months of a fifteen-year sentence, to work for his sister on a farm; was out about eight months when he had an argument with brother-in-law, who requested and obtained his return to prison. (236)

No. 21 . . . was paroled to work on a farm, but changed his work without permission, and was returned as a result of becoming familiar with a neighbor's wife, whose husband complained of him to the parole officer; he was out about fourteen months before he was returned to prison. (244)

No. 22 . . . was paroled to work as a laborer, but worked only three weeks when he was returned as a result of his making threats to his employers. (245)

From the perspective of critics like von Hentig, the parolee became vulnerable to the power of even the weakest members of the community. In one case described by von Hentig:

> [T]he parolee was returned [to prison] because he had been residing with a known prostitute, had been living off her earnings and then had beaten her up when she tried to leave him. Here again the parolee has fallen completely into the servitude of the prostitute who can get rid of him whenever she wants by reporting him to the police. A similar situation frequently arises between the parolee and his wife. Nothing is easier to drop than a parolee-husband; the slightest fight, cunningly provoked, will satisfy the parole agencies. (1942, 370)

Von Hentig found such cases to be outrageous because they flew in the face of social norms that regularly permitted men to commit violence against "their" women. Parole appeared, at least to its critics, a potent grant of power that could be accessed even by those with the least standing in the private hierarchies of the community. Like private prosecutions in eighteenth- and nineteenth-century Britain (Hay and Snyder 1989), parole operated as a vehicle through which the state's power to punish could be used both up and down the hierarchy of private power.

The potential abuse of this power was noted by parole officials and other observers. The Attorney General's report warned that "there seems to be considerable danger of the exploitation of parolees by unscrupulous employers when they are forced to accept any sort of job in order to be paroled" (1939, 186). The California state parole officer noted that "many violations of parole are caused by disagreement with employers as to wages and working conditions" (State Board of Prison Directors 1928, 86). Similar disagreements involving other workers typically were not resolved by reimprisonment of the employee. The danger of abuse was inherent, however, in the powerful combination of the state's power to punish with private networks of social control in an industrial society.

In the end, whether or not disciplinary parole was successful in preventing men from returning to crime may be less important than whether parole was successful in providing a coherent model for how to do the work of corrections. For a society that continued to view criminality through the lens of idleness, coerced participation in the labor market was a plausible account of how to make an offender go straight while also providing the best available means of keeping track of him. It also provided the best available excuse for permitting the offender to return to the community and contribute to its economic production rather than drain resources. California State Parole Agent Edward H. Whyte summarized this equation perfectly when he wrote in the *Journal of Criminal Law and Criminology* that parole did great good "in returning several thousand prospective criminals to the great body of law abiding and industrially productive citizenship" (Whyte 1916, 2).

Rothman (1980) is no doubt right that parole release decisions were haphazard on an individual basis, but individualization was important to the Progressive reform program, not to the disciplinary model which parole operatives used. [16] From the perspective of the latter, success simply required that the prisoner be attached before release to as many networks of private power as possible. The labor market was the most important such network, but family and respected community members could also be significant. Like the Elizabethan recognizance bond, parole made the freedom of the offender both the choice and the responsibility of specific sponsors in the community (Samaha 1981). During some periods, such as the world wars, the economy produced abundant jobs in the large industrial concerns most capable of exercising disciplinary control, and many prisoners could fit into niches of control in the community. At such times, the ideal of the disciplinary model must have come closer to reality than the Progressives' rehabilitative ideal ever did.

The Great Depression and the Limits of the Disciplinary Model

As in so many areas of American life, war production created an ideal environment for refining the system of parole. Under the circumstances of full employment, parole authorities developed a complete schema for conducting parole, including pre-release programming, supervision, and interaction with other social agencies. But this schema was dependent on heightened economic activity. The Depression undermined the foundations of the disciplinary model, revealing its limits and opening the door to the latent potential of professional and reformatory parole practice.

Writing about parole in Illinois in 1936, Henry Barrett Chamberlin acknowledged the effects of the Depression on a parole regime tied to employment, but inveighed against slippage:

> It is realized that for the past years there has been an abnormal employment situation which makes it extremely difficult to obtain jobs for inmates at penitentiaries but, it is believed that stricter compliance with parole regulations should be preserved. (1936, 486)

He went on to disclose evidence of collusion and to call for sanctions against employers who lied:

---

16. David Garland (1985, 14) offers a useful distinction between a system which recognizes individuals and a system which recognizes individuality. During the twentieth century reformers increasingly called for a penal system focused on individuality. Yet until the second half of the century the system largely focused on individuals in terms of their shared traits, in particular their willingness to labor.

Investigation further disclosed that jobs that were waiting for the inmates when they were released on parole, and as verified by the prospective employer in the parole application, were of short duration. Such a
situation arouses the suspicion that there is collusion in this regard. It is
suggested that the Parole Board take steps to have enacted legislation
that will make it a misdemeanor or a felony for employers or sponsors to
make false statements in parole applications. It is further suggested that
in cases where this condition is found that the parolee be returned to the
institutions until such time as a proper sponsor or employer is obtained.
(487)

In California, the decline of employment was remarked upon in the state
parole officer's report:

During the first half of the biennium, employment conditions had
reached a stage where we were beginning to feel satisfied and pleased.
The last half of the biennium however, was unfortunately, less favorable.
This through no cause of those on parole but by a general period of depression that suddenly threw the whole country into a topsy turvy and
chaotic condition, causing wholesale unemployment, affecting not only
our men on parole, but the general public as well and we must consequently be compelled to follow conditions. (State Board of Prison Directors 1930, 98)

The Parole System, like every other organization throughout the country,
has felt keenly the economic difficulties which have been experienced
for several years and especially during the period of this biennium.
(State Board of Prison Directors 1932, 88)

The Parole system as has every other organization of socialogical [sic]
nature, has shown the effects of the existing economic condition, with its
lack of employment and a situation that is prevalent throughout the
country. (State Board of Prison Directors 1934, 94)

These economic conditions were marked in several other respects. The traditional praise of the state's employers as the pillars of the parole system, repeated ritually at the end of reports during the 1920s, was omitted in the
1930s. Instead the report began to discuss, for the first time, the parole field
staff and its effectiveness in maintaining surveillance over parolees. The 1932
report was the first to mention some aspects of parole work besides employment and violations:

A concerted effort is made to create a bond of understanding and a spirit
of friendliness to the subject released on parole, offering him counsel
and every possible aid in his endeavor to maintain the success of his
parole and to reclaim himself as a useful, honest and beneficial citizen.
He is treated by the Parole Officer's department solely as an individual
and not as a class or group; pains being taken by that department to
study his personality and individual makeup together with those charac-

teristics so often peculiar to himself, so that he can be thereby handled accordingly. (State Board of Prison Directors 1932, 87)

In 1936 California created a parole field staff with branches in San Francisco and Los Angeles. With this new expanded staff—eleven in San Francisco and six in Los Angeles—parole became capable of a surveillance that did not rely completely on local employers or local law enforcement:

> The duties of the field men include employment investigations, checking of parolees in the various counties, visiting their homes and places of employment, making inquiries as to their general conduct and manner of living to determine if it is in keeping with the requirements and conditions of their parole, at the same time consulting with sheriffs and police officers of the counties. (State Board of Prison Directors 1936, 107)

The pressure on the parole model was great on the other side as well. With the prison population already at an all-time high in California, there were delays in releasing paroled inmates who could not find jobs. According to the 1937 report of the United States Prison Industries Reorganization Administration nearly half of the prisoners whose parole release was approved by the Board remained confined for lack of jobs on the outside during the mid-1930s. A similar situation was faced in virtually every other state that required employment prior to parole. [17]

The absence of jobs provided an opening for those who wished to encourage the development of a corrections program distinct from coerced participation in the labor market. The rhetoric of professionalism and rehabilitation began to fill the gaps created by declining industrial discipline. The latent promise of the Philadelphia "separate system" model[18]—to make law-abiding and normal citizens through personal transformation rather than by habits of labor—reemerged for a time.

Although temporary, the Depression presaged a time when the correctional enterprise would be permanently cut off from the discipline of the labor market and hinted at the potential for an alternative account of control, based on

17. The U.S. Prison Industries Reorganization Commission issued reports for virtually every state in the country between 1936 and 1939. These fascinating documents contain, in addition to information on industrial and farm production, descriptive information on the organization of prisons, probation, and parole in each state. They also include a heavy portion of prescriptive recommendations embodying for the most part the rehabilitative ideal: individualization of treatment in prison and flexible parole laws that permitted discretion to professionals to release inmates at the earliest possible time. These recommendations were repeated almost exactly in the reports for each state. I have seen virtually no treatment of the Reorganization Commission in scholarship on American correctional history. In the case of California, which it criticizes particularly for the lack of individualized treatment of prisoners, the report's recommendations parallel almost exactly the steps taken after 1944. The possible influence of the Reorganization Commission on post–World War II penal developments there and in other states warrants further study.

18. See discussion in chapter one, pp. 25–30.

professionalism and rehabilitation. This opening was perceived by Donald Clemmer who questioned the viability of the labor strategy in his classic Depression era study of the American prison system:

> As for work placement in this machine age, we must inculcate a doctrine in prisoners that most of them cannot expect to be highly successful as workers. . . . Most of them must be taught that their basic satisfactions of life are not to be found in the field of work, but in the field of leisure-time activities. If we can improve by reeducation the constellation of attitudes which are associated with the usage of leisure intervals, we may make progress in reducing crime, as industrial training prison never has. ([1940] 1958, 276)

Perhaps the Depression did not last long enough to uproot the centrality of labor to the vision of the penal enterprise. In 1941, with the national employment situation beginning to improve greatly, the state of Illinois appealed to employers to hire parolees in a notice published in the *Journal of Criminal Law and Criminology:*

> There exists in our Illinois penal institutions today an appalling situation which we hope by your assistance to correct or partially alleviate. There are many inmates in our State prisons today who have been granted paroles, men who could leave here, but who are unable to fulfill the parole stipulation requiring adequate employment that will pay a living wage. Will you help us to lessen this grave condition by providing employment for one or more of these men.
>
> Because of a condition over which these men have no control, there are several hundred thus being held in our State prisons who are familiar with almost every type of business. (State of Illinois 1941, 561)

The difficulties afflicting the nation during the Depression were viewed as temporary. Even the New Deal, with its introduction of new forms of relief, tied its programming as closely as possible to the weakened but ideologically coherent ideal of labor (Katz 1989). Most correctional managers would probably have agreed with sociologist Ernest Burgess's prescription in 1936 that prisons try harder to develop work skills:

> Because a job is the best single method yet known from getting men to "go straight" I would stress here the importance of providing in every correctional and penal institution the opportunities for work and industrial education which will fit men to get and hold jobs when they are released upon parole. (491)

As war production increased in the Second World War, the disciplinary model of parole was once again functioning fully. An editorial in the *Journal of Criminal Law and Criminology* trumpeted the new ease in securing employment:

> Our parole systems are also playing their part in the war effort. It has become increasingly easy to find jobs for released prisoners, especially

if they have come from an institution where they have been trained, and a large percentage of all parolees are now employed, many of them in war industries. In New York State, 93% of all parolees are now employed. (Editorial 1942, 648)

Indeed, an important part was played by the war itself in taking up much of the disciplinary slack in the penal system. In July 1941 Congress removed a ban on felons serving in the United States Army that had been in place since 1833 (Barnes 1944, 57). This immediately made ex-prisoners eligible for the draft. In early 1942 the army set up procedures for inducting prisoners, parolees, and probationers into the service.

As of 1944 it was estimated that the army took 50,000 ex-prisoners, 20,000 felons on probation, 30,000 parolees, and 2,500 inmates directly from prison (Barnes 1944). The picture of prisoners flowing directly from the institutions into the army fulfilled the logic of the disciplinary parole model even more perfectly than a factory since it included greater controls and less opportunity to return to a previous pattern of idleness. In criticizing the practice of the army to insist on at least some prisoners being paroled for a brief period prior to induction, Harry Barnes invoked the continuity between the two forms of institutionalization:

> Discharged prisoners have been accustomed to strict discipline while in the prison, and this could be continued without any appreciable gap if immediate induction into the Army were permitted. If, instead, prisoners are discharged, with little or no money, and loaf for a month or three months while awaiting induction, there is every incentive, even pressure, to lapse into criminal ways, to get into trouble, and to become disqualified for Army service. (1944, 64)

The reinvigoration that the war provided for the disciplinary model is well demonstrated in the vision of the postwar prison incorporated in Barnes's pamphlet on the prisons in wartime. The end of the war, it was feared, might lead both to a crime wave increasing the demand for punishment, and a hostile attitude toward criminals in a period of patriotic social feelings. Drawing on the wartime speeches of the country's penological leadership such as Richard A. McGee of California, Garrett Heyns of Michigan, and others, Barnes envisioned in response a wave of new medium and minimum security prisons for smaller populations designed to maximize the efficiency of production and the rehabilitative potential of industrial work and education (1944, 76).

The new industrial prison was to be based solely on a rationalized system of state use production in which different states might specialize in products needed by many of them and arrange for cooperative exchanges. The new shops would keep inmates busy while vocational training would penetrate even more deeply into the habits of those Barnes described as "industrially handicapped" (1944, 87). At the same time Barnes's vision extended beyond the immediate discipline of work to the problems of character.

> While most penal and correctional institutions suffer from a lack of concern over teaching industrial skills, too much emphasis can be laid on this aspect of prison administration, if it leads to overlooking character education and the teaching of the virtues of dependability, responsibility, resourcefulness, and adaptability. Though many men are convicted of crime while idle, and perhaps because of being idle, their idleness is due in many cases to lack of the character traits necessary to holding a job rather than to any deficiency of industrial training. (90)

Barnes pointed out that this was especially true in "mass-production and belt-line industries, where little or no technical skill is required [but] the main qualifications for getting and holding a job are the habits of industriousness, faithfulness and dependability, which only good character training can supply."

In the midst of a celebration of the correctional potential of industrial discipline, however, Barnes pointed toward a set of needs outside that model which required psychiatric and counseling technologies:

> Contrary to a general impression, many men are in prison not because of lack of industrial or professional training but on account of personality problems which will be touched but little by any industrial or vocational training program. Such prisoners can only be set straight by psychiatrists and social workers. (86)

While Barnes saw such services as largely supplemental to the new industrial penology, they would increasingly become an alternative center of their own in the decades after the war.

From the end of the Second World War to the mid-fifties, there is little evidence of any disruption of the industrial parole model. The economic recession at the war's end was quickly replaced by full production for the Korean War. The country soon entered a period of economic growth that continued into the 1970s. But by the end of the 1950s, structural changes in both the economy and the prison population began to appear that would ultimately challenge the very core of the disciplinary model of parole.

While the 1950s look today like a golden age of industrial employment, the labor market in many American cities was already beginning a shift from unskilled industrial labor toward service employment with higher skill demands (Kasarda 1985). This shift has had many consequences for American society. The most important consequence, for corrections, was a decoupling of the labor market for low-skilled labor from the economy as a whole. From the late 1950s on, generally low unemployment in the aggregate would disguise considerable slack in the market for those at the very bottom of the skill ladder, among whom are most prisoners.

This not only affected parolees but also the larger lower-class communities to which most of them returned. The ability of parole policies to coordinate with economic conditions in the community was attenuated. In short, the communities most directly affected by the ebb and flow of parole releases entered a period of economic crisis from which they have not recovered to this day.

The second structural factor was the growth of minority populations inside American state prisons. Between 1946 and 1970 the percentage of the prison population made up of African-Americans went from 35 to 43 percent on the national level, and from 19 to 31 percent in California (Langan 1991, 5, 26, 31). This was significant to the viability of the industrial parole model because these communities were among the hardest hit by the retrenchment of the urban labor market. This was true even in California which was enjoying more robust economic growth than any other section of the country in this period.

In 1940 the unemployment rates for white and non-white males age sixteen and older were almost the same at 15 percent for whites and 17.4 percent for non-whites.[19] By 1950 the gap had widened to almost double with whites experiencing an unemployment rate of 7.3 percent statewide and non-whites experiencing an unemployment rate of nearly 14 percent, a ratio which remained virtually unchanged through the fifties, sixties, and seventies. Virtually the same pattern shows up in unemployment rates for the Los Angeles and San Francisco–Oakland metropolitan areas.

While less extreme, a similar pattern is visible in terms of labor force participation rates. In the San Francisco–Oakland metropolitan area the rate for whites and African-Americans was quite close with nearly 80 percent of whites and nearly 78 percent of African-American males age fourteen years and older participating in the labor market. The figures remain close in the 1950 figure, but a significant gap is clearly visible in 1960 with nearly 86 percent of white males over fourteen participating but only 78 percent of non-whites.

Changes of this scale may not have had a strong effect on general perceptions of life and social well-being in the 1950s and early 1960s, but they may well have been noticeable to penal managers. In any economy prisoners are the most marginal candidates for employment. In a slackening labor market they will often remain unemployed. In a shrinking labor market participation pool it may become increasingly difficult just to maintain the pressure on prisoners to locate jobs in the communities to which they will return.

19. Figures are from *Census of Population: 1960*, vol. 1., part 6, tab. 53; *1970*, vol. 1., chap. D, part 6, tab. 164; *1980*, vol. 1, chap. D, part 6, tab. 214. In these figures non-white includes all non-Caucasian races including African-Americans, Chinese, Japanese, and others. Hispanics were counted as white with no effort in this period to break them out. Until 1970 the figures include fourteen-year-olds and up. This probably depressed the labor market participation rate for both groups but should have only minimal effect on the unemployment figures.

It is not surprising then that parole administrators should have experienced, early on, the powerful social consequences of this shift in economic structure. If regular employment, of which the industrial production job was the ideal, could not be found for parolees, the whole structure of supervision was in trouble. This must have been particularly noticeable after the boom years of the Second World War and the Korean War. Both control and normalization needed to be addressed in new ways. Thus some years before sociologists would speak about the coming of "postindustrial society" (e.g., Bell 1973), parole managers began to formulate a postindustrial parole strategy.

The search for ideas did not need to go far. From its inception, parole supervision had been surrounded by a clinical discourse of diagnosis, treatment, and rehabilitation. Yet the actual practices of parole seem to have little to do with these claims. The writings of the Progressives had often invoked the offender as a complex social-psychological subject. But, as we have seen, the reach of practice described a far rougher beast: economic man. With the diminishment of the labor market for low-skilled workers, and especially of entry-level industrial production jobs, the vision of parole success once adequately summed up in the term "industriousness" became inapposite. If few parolees have regular jobs, how can one separate the well-adjusted from the recalcitrant? If finding jobs for parolees is increasingly futile, how can parole agents have a sense that they are progressing?

The vacuum created by the decline of industry made it possible for the discourses of rehabilitation finally to move to the center of parole. But before they could lay hold of practice, these discourses needed a concrete field of emergence: a set of problems, techniques, and technologies that could provide rehabilitation with a body as well as a soul.

Conclusion: The State and the Labor Market

The nineteenth century is typically seen as the time when punishment became a truly state-centered affair in American society. Police went from irregular watchmen to uniformed public employees (Monkkonen 1975; Lane 1967). A host of punishments based on community humiliation, and sometimes physical abuse, were replaced with the methodical practice of the penitentiary (Rothman 1971; Foucault 1977). Yet, when one looks from a distance at the consistent role of industrial labor in the development of the penal enterprise in the United States, it becomes apparent that punishment remained in some fundamental ways a private, that is, non-state, affair.

In the 1880s, when opposition to direct production in prisons arose in the private market, much of the controlling and normalizing functions of the prison moved into the community through parole. The prison still provided walls, but with parole the offender who left those walls could expect months or years of coerced participation in the labor market. In short, penal discipline remained contiguous with the more general industrial disciplining of the urban population.

Yet, from the birth of the prison on, there was a vital, if latent, project to create a penality separate from the private labor market—a penal practice aimed at treating the offender in depth as a subject, whether that subject was considered to be primarily moral/political (as it was for the Quakers) or medical/psychological (as it would be for the Progressives and their successors). As suggested in the last chapter these two strategies were represented in the competing penitentiary models of Philadelphia and Auburn in the nineteenth century. The former deployed labor as a ritual to induce moral redemption, the latter as a functional mechanism of control. But rather than viewing this project as an ideological cover for the discipline of capitalism (Melossi and Pavarini 1981; Dumm 1987), it is possible to see the two as an integrated whole. For nineteenth-century thinkers, there was simply no gap between the idea of reform and the idea of labor.[20] Even in the Progressive Era, when the nascent concepts of the human sciences began to offer a ground for reformers' aspirations, the vision of the "normal" to which normalizing institutions would aspire was always linked to the norms of the labor market.

One may read the story of parole's birth and early years as a bold intellectual departure from the model of the nineteenth-century prison which failed in implementation and survived largely because it served administrative convenience (Rothman 1980). But this is to announce the failure of an institution that never was. Although the Progressives aspired to build a domain of power autonomous from the mainsprings of economic integration, they never really created a state-controlled path to social control. The private labor market remained the only path to social integration in America. Parole, in continuity with the strategies of the nineteenth century, sought to achieve discipline and control by subjecting the delinquent to coerced participation in that market. In the 1950s, however, the availability of labor as a functional tool of control was becoming attenuated even as the ideal of normality defined by labor remained a center of American life. The clinical model, which we explore in the next chapter, offered a way of operationalizing this ideal of normality without as much dependence on labor as control.

20. Spierenburg's work suggests this link is much older, dating at least to the fifteenth century (1991). But it was not until the beginning of the nineteenth century that the combination of labor and confinement (or labor and exile in the case of transportation) seems to have become a master narrative for crime control.

CHAPTER THREE

Clinical Parole

Parole in the heyday of industrial discipline required little in the way of internal elaboration. Formal conditions of parole established a number of general norms to which parolees were to adhere. These ranged from concrete requirements, like employment, to vague standards like being a "good citizen." Parole agents were given broad discretion to enforce these conditions, but where law ended, the community began. If the parolee refused to work, if he was a troublemaker at home, the parole agent could respond to the complaints of employer or family by threatening the parolee or ultimately reimprisoning him. Agents did not need a detailed account of how to supervise parolees because a widely shared understanding of what constituted normal conduct was a feature of industrial society.[1] The community imposed its own requirements. Control and normalization did not flow from the agent but through him. Parole was a three-sided structure—offender, community, and agent—with the most important factor being the community.

The new parole model[2] that began to form in the 1950s could not and did

---

1. As George Fletcher (1978) has taught us, the criminal law traditionally rested on a set of community understanding as to what constituted dangerous and threatening behavior. Modernism in substantive criminal law might well be understood as the effort to place underlying norms of conduct in a framework of analytic concepts capable of interpretation independent of shared social experiences. In punishment the impulse to develop an autonomous discourse of expert knowledge has been counterbalanced by the powerful interpretive norms of industrial society.

2. I refer to models of parole as in the "disciplinary model" or the "clinical model." The reader should keep in mind that "model" here is only a construct. No real blueprint or scheme ever existed, nor would participants necessarily have recognized the concepts as applicable to what they were doing. Parole managers, like most other people charged with running organizations, seek to pull together a cohesive set of practices and discourses that present a plausible account of how to do what they are supposed to do. As used here, the term "model" represents my retrospective effort to describe the underlying logic of these practical ensembles.

not rely on the existence of such a background of community social control. As the market for unskilled labor shrank, as the prison population increasingly came to be composed of minority group members, and as the condition of the urban lower classes became an increasingly important subject of governmental concern, a correctional strategy that relied on focused community self-regulation lost plausibility in the eyes of correctional planners. The triangle broke, leaving the parolee and the parole agent on their own to a much greater degree in determining how to enforce the amorphous parole conditions.

The elements of the new model which emerged in California and other states in the 1950s were strikingly similar to the correctional vision of the Progressive Era reformers, with stress on classification, training, and treatment. As Rothman (1980) shows, the idealized Progressive vision of punishment as a form of social medicine had gradually faded in the 1920s and 1930s. But the new energies for reform unleashed by the war effort and the heightened confidence in government brought by the successful prosecution of the war came together to produce a kind of rebirth of the Progressive penal vision in the 1940s and 1950s.

Like the Progressive reformers, the architects of the clinical model in parole and other penal agencies looked beyond bureaucratic authority to the professional capacity of the individual agent which they hoped would shape a program adequate to the individual needs of the parolee. The reformers of the early twentieth century sought to accomplish this by importing ideas and recruiting personnel from the social sciences and from social work.[3] This helped shape the description of existing practice, but it provided few technologies for changing practice. In California, during the 1950s and early 1960s, an effort was made to go beyond importing expertise by creating specific correctional techniques to achieve the goal of individualized treatment and control.[4]

No doubt the reorganization of California corrections in the postwar years, and the aggressive effort to formulate a new Progressive model, owed a great deal to the existence of political and administrative leaders sympathetic to these ideas. In contrast, the penetration of Progressive reform ideas among penal managers at the beginning of the century was more limited. The development of penal practices cannot be treated, however, simply as a history of ideas or great men. This is especially true when we examine the bottom of the

3. The question of standards for parole officers had been basic fare at professional correctional meetings for decades (although in practice few states succeeded in raising the educational level of parole officers).

4. This was an important distinction between the Progressive Era reformers and their successors in the postwar era. As Rothman (1980, 125) pointed out, the former were long on diagnoses of crime but short on proposing specific measures to address it. This chapter focuses on the experience of California from 1953 through the late 1960s in trying to build a material basis for a new program.

hierarchy where power is ultimately exercised. Operatives at the bottom have a particularly strong stake in making sure that the reigning narrative is flexible enough to create expectations that can be filled. In contrast, those at the top of the hierarchy in an enterprise like parole supervisions can tolerate a larger gap between narrative and practice and have greater incentives to load the narrative with elements attractive for their external prestige rather than their internal functionality.

This is especially true of parole where the exercise of power takes place in encounters that are far-flung and not always visible to managers. Parole had been a classically decentered organization. From the time the first field offices in California were set up in 1936, power over individual decisions came to rest in the local supervisors and their agents. Higher managers could create programs and articulate goals, but they could not exercise effective review over actual decisions. In the early 1960s, this problem was alleviated somewhat by the creation of a regional administrative structure. Five regions were created, under separate chiefs, with the aim of closing the gap between top management and field staff.

Through such administrative reforms and an activist chief parole officer, management succeeded in placing considerable pressure on agents to conform to the new clinical model and its rehabilitative ideology. On the other hand, the agency, and thus its agents, remained ultimately most vulnerable to the charge that they lost control of their parolees, an event usually manifested in some violent or otherwise noteworthy crime.

The strongest insurance against such an event was to construct a credible narrative of control—credibility that lies not in the absence of risk but in the congruence between control and established cultural understandings of criminal dangerousness. The disciplinary model worked, not by preventing all crimes, but by linking action to a widely shared sense that criminals were idlers who needed to be disciplined. As work had done for disciplinary parole, this new model needed to combine three elements: (1) a tactical handle with which to maintain some control over offenders in the community, (2) a stigmatizing quality that satisfied the public's desire to see offenders as deserving and getting the worst fate possible, and (3) a plausible account of how offenders differ from the rest of us which provides the possibility for return and for normalization. The clinical program could succeed only by creating the elements of such a strategy and demonstrating their suitability.

While the clinical model had to be more than a set of ideas, it required them as well. An essential ingredient was a set of ideas that could bridge the disciplinary model and the new clinical model, with a major contributor being the emergence of a body of ideas known as the therapeutic community (Himelson 1968, 70). While much of the Progressive Era psychology focused narrowly on the subjective state of the individual deviant, social therapy (as the name implies) focused on the interactions between individual and milieu combining traditional psychological theories with sociology and social work.

One of the most important elements in moving from ideas to an effective model of action was the creation of a parole agent manual. The manual, which was first published in 1954 and went through numerous revisions, was an effort to set out in an easily accessible format the parole organization's expectations for its agents.[5] As an historical text it helps to document changing understandings of the parole mission, but it should also be seen as a dynamic practice intended to affect the day-to-day operation of parole agents.

A second major source of practical innovation was the research program developed by the Department from the early 1950s on. The Progressives had viewed social science research as the natural base for corrections. While this vision was realized in places like the *Journal of Criminal Law and Criminology*, there was little real penetration of correctional agencies. Statistics on recidivism, of dubious quality, were collected and published by many departments, but quasi-experimental research was absent. Starting in 1953 the California Department of Corrections began organizing such experiments, and in 1958 the Department created the nation's first full-time correctional research unit.

During its first decade, the research program concentrated heavily on the question of whether intensive parole supervision could be shown to have an independent effect on parole outcome. Through a variety of experimental designs, the Division sought to demonstrate that providing agents with more time for each parolee could lower the recidivism rate. The intensive parole studies provided an active program around which to organize parole work and an opportunity to support the claim that professionalized parole agents could make up for the disappearing labor market in keeping parolees under control.

These projects were vehicles for testing the efficacy of proposed supervision methods, and it is a testament to the integrity of the Department's research effort that they were frankly described as failures in many cases. But, apart from their scientific credibility, the research projects constituted significant efforts to promulgate new methods among the staff that provided content for parole practice.

A third major source of development, which also provided a practical base for the clinical program, was the problem of narcotic addiction. The reemergence of public concern with drugs and drug addiction provided a convenient meeting ground between politicians and penal managers. In California the discovery in the early 1950s of a large subpopulation of opiate addicts caused a considerable ripple in state politics. The legislature responded by

5. The Department of Corrections has not shown much interest in preserving a documentary history of its policy development, and earlier manuals may have existed that I have not been able to locate.

funding one of the most ambitious efforts to date to develop a therapeutically effective parole method. Narcotics addiction never yielded to parole methods, and the research unit's reports faithfully reflected that failure. Nonetheless, the problem of the narcotic addict helped bring together a set of practices that would transform parole supervision.

Drug addiction, more than any other problem, exemplified the field in which the new clinical parole practice was taking shape. It brought into focus all of the major problems that plagued parole in its classical industrial guise. It tended to involve members of disadvantaged minorities (primarily Hispanics and African-Americans) and others who lived in the hard-core poverty areas of the cities. The communities to which these parolees returned did not seem well organized enough to provide a context of control, particularly against the potent force of chemical dependence. Only if supervisory action could break the hold of addiction could real integration of the offender into the community take place. A parole supervision effort for addicts obviously had to do more than focus community social control; it had to provide a direct and organizationally driven structure of control over the addict.

The sections below will examine these sources of practical innovation more closely. As before, the focus is not on whether they succeed or fail in controlling crime or treating parolees but on how these methods succeed or fail in constructing an account of the enterprise that is practical, coherent, and plausible.

Historically, the actual effectiveness of a correctional strategy has been only marginally related to its political viability. The absence of tools to evaluate the crime-suppressant effects of specific programs has tended to make their ideological fit a far more important factor. Indeed, one of the crucial vulnerabilities of clinical parole was the capacity of its built-in research component to undermine its plausibility. Where before, parole agents had navigated by the light of private networks of social control, the new clinical techniques were throwing their own light on the parolee and his problems, but that light also made parole practice itself more visible.

The sections below also examine the role of labor in parole during this period. The new practices provided alternative ways for agents to organize their activities, but they did not replace labor altogether. Labor continued to present agents with a compelling model of parole practice which sometimes subverted the implementation of the new clinical programs. When the opportunity to put parolees to work conflicted with the regimens of treatment practices, agents were reluctant to choose the latter.

The Therapeutic Community

If corrections managers were looking for an approach that would be grounded in the normative vision of industrial labor on the one side but that would provide a model of action which could operate independently of the private labor market on the other, they could hardly have done better than look at *The Therapeutic Community: A New Treatment Method in Psychiatry* by Maxwell Jones, M.D. First published in the United States by Basic Books in 1953 the short volume was enormously influential in both the corrections and mental health communities throughout the English-speaking world. Although just a part of a larger movement to incorporate more sociological perspectives in psychiatry and psychology in the 1950s (and lay claim to a greater social role) the book provides an exemplar of how the normativity defined by labor could be abstracted by institutions of control from direct dependence on the disciplines of the labor market.

The "therapeutic community" concept was first developed by Dr. Jones and his associates while working with "neurotic" ex-prisoners of war and sufferers of "effort syndrome"[6] during and just after the Second World War. In both cases the primary functional problem of patients, as defined by the clinicians, was inability to adjust to the normal demands of life, most especially labor. The model they developed had two essential and interrelated assumptions. First, that the most potent source of mental health was the practice of normal life itself. To this end, the regimen aimed at maximum exposure of patients to real-life activities. with labor being the major focus. Second, they assumed that the institution itself and its staff were part of the therapeutic process, whether formally defined as "treatment" or not.

As Jones himself acknowledged, the emergence of this kind of approach was quite dependent on the special economic conditions of wartime and immediate postwar Britain. As in the United States, the tight labor market produced by the war created an interest in reintegrating marginal workers that would not have been there otherwise and a concern for the social and psychological conditions of a population exposed to the violence of war. The shortage of medical personnel caused by the war also contributed to the acceptance of expanding the definition of what could be considered therapeutic both in terms of personnel and activities.

These early experiments were perceived as a success, and in 1947 Jones was authorized to set up what he called (appropriately enough) an "industrial neurosis unit." The patients at the industrial neurosis unit were defined as "chronic unemployed neurotics," people whose main symptom was the inability to retain work. Once again it should be noted how unique this concern was to the postwar labor shortage in Britain. At any other time one suspects such patients would have been written off as "deadbeats" and ignored.

The regime in the industrial neurosis unit explicitly took as its model low-level industrial work rather than the craft specialties that mental hospitals had traditionally offered.

---

6. A condition observed in wartime Britain manifested by the appearance of an epidemic of false heart attack symptoms by workers.

> There is no "occupational therapy" as is commonly understood in hospital practice and we prefer the term "work therapy"; the Unit workshops aim at a normal factory environment so that the man is being prepared for the type of unskilled vocational role which he might follow in normal life. (Jones 1953, 67)

Patients chose among several industrial work options provided either in the hospital or at some cooperative local businesses. They were also exposed to frequent group sessions, films on labor, and another innovation called "psycho-drama" in which patients wrote and produced short plays based on their personal conflicts with family and coworkers.

The therapeutic community had obvious salience for the impasse in corrections in the United States. Like the disciplinary model of corrections the therapeutic community placed disciplined labor as the basic standard of adult conduct to which the client population must be submitted. Yet unlike the disciplinary model it emphasized less the functional control to be accomplished by labor, and more the adjustment to the norms and rhythms of working life. Furthermore, it replaced the intensive focus on disciplining individual bodies with a broader notion of adjustment to the working life, for example, getting along with coworkers and feeling positive about one's prospects. Labor in the therapeutic community showed up as an anchor for social life, not the main purpose of it. Finally, the logic of social therapy moved out from a normality defined by labor to a range of practices that could provide their own validation of normality independent of work, for instance, one's attitude in group sessions or how one treats one's spouse and friends.

It is not surprising then that Jones's book was widely read among corrections planners in California and elsewhere. It won the enthusiastic support of the top leadership in the California Department of Corrections who hired two American psychologists doing similar work to run the research unit and introduced several experimental regimes modeled on Jones's examples.

The Parole Agent Manual

The manual was first and foremost a product of the bureaucratic rationalization unleashed by Richard McGee whom Governor Earl Warren had chosen to head the newly created Department of Corrections.[7] All the elements that comprise bureaucracy—centralization, hierarchy, accountability, etc.—

7. Although the Department of Corrections was created in 1944, as part of a general reorganization of state criminal justice, the parole agency was not initially placed under its control. The Adult Authority, created in 1944 and given authority to act as the parole board, i.e., setting prison release dates and making parole revocation decisions, was given direct control over the parole supervision agency. After a number of years of political infighting between the Department of Corrections and the Adult Authority over parole policy, the parole supervision agency, renamed the Parole Division, was placed under the Department of Corrections in 1957.

require the existence of a manual, and manuals make sense only if there is a central authority that seeks to impose a way of doing things on others. By placing the organization's expectations in a visible and accessible position within institutional practice, a manual creates the anchor for new and far more precise exercises of power.

With the birth of the California Department of Corrections in 1944 and the appointment of its activist director Richard McGee, the development of a bureaucratic organizational culture in the entire Department proceeded at a rapid pace. McGee recognized the importance of manuals in the construction of bureaucracy and produced many of them.[8] Alfred Himelson provides the following list of the manuals he considered most important while working in and studying the Department in the 1950s and 1960s:

> The vehicles for documenting these organizational roles and norms were a series of Departmental manuals. The basic one was the Department's Administrative Manual. But in addition, a series of specialized manuals were also developed. Some of these are . . . Business Administration Manual[,] Inmate Classification Manual[,] Educational and Vocational Training Manual[,] Group Counseling Manual[,] Interagency Relations Manual[,] Parole Agents Manual[,] Personnel Manual. (1968, 25)

The first McGee era parole manual examined is the 1959 edition. The status of the manual before then is unclear because it was only in 1957 that the parole agency was placed directly within the Department of Corrections. References to a 1954 manual suggest that the Adult Authority (California's parole board from 1944 to 1977) probably produced a manual while it managed the parole agency between 1944 and 1957. We can assume that the 1959 edition represented a comprehensive revision, aimed at reshaping the Parole Division along the lines of McGee's rationalization program for the Department as a whole.

Yet, if the 1959 edition signified the advance of bureaucracy in parole, it also illustrated the degree of discretion that was left to the agents. On the very first page of the chapter on parole supervision there is a section entitled "Techniques Used in Parole Supervision," but the agent who looked there would have found little specific guidance. Rather, the section essentially explained why the absence of specific guidance does not disprove the existence of a genuine method: "Since parole supervision is based on individualized

8. The earliest manual to which I have found reference is the 1954 manual. It is possible that before the reorganization of California corrections in 1944 there was no manual. I have attempted to gather as many editions of the manual as possible through veteran staff. Others I have learned about through references in various internal publications. On this basis I believe that complete revisions of the manual were issued in 1954, 1959, 1964, 1977, 1984, and 1987. All of these were designed for constant updating. Pages in the loose-leaf binders were removed as revised pages were sent out. My copy of the 1959 edition contains additions from as late as 1963.

treatment and interpersonal relationships it is impossible to list rules or procedures that will always give adequate answers to the practitioner" (Parole and Community Services Division 1959, sec. 7-00).

What the manual did provide was a picture of parole as a clinical practice. At the core of this practice was what the manual described as an "interpersonal relationship" between the parolee and the parole agent. This is given clear priority over the parolee's relationship to his employer or family: "without such an [interpersonal] relationship which is the 'core' of the total parole supervision process, the [other] efforts will have very questionable value" (1959, sec. 7-00). Much of the program set forth in the manual was designed to foster this relationship. Although later editions would provide specific guidelines, the 1959 edition looked to the relationship itself as the primary source of standards.

In the vision of the original Progressive reformers, the agent's relationship with the subject (deviant, delinquent, offender) was the primary tool of reformation (Rothman 1980, 63–68). The beginnings of professionalized social work at the end of the First World War validated the confidence placed in such relationships. The relationship-centered approach to parole was based on what social work pioneer Mary Richmond called "the casework method" in her book *Social Diagnosis* (1917). Casework permitted the agent to uncover the unique causes or sources of the individual offender's problems through the use of objective methodologies such as interviews, residential inspections, and medical histories.

During the era of the disciplinary model, casework had little to do with the everyday tasks of parole agents. Time was sufficiently and appropriately filled with helping parolees find jobs and making sure they kept them. While employment remains important in the clinical model, its role was moderated by focus on the individual offender. In the disciplinary model, there was no real need for individualization. Any hard and time-consuming job would be adequate. Good agents spent their time drumming up lots of them, not focusing on particular needs.

In contrast, the 1959 manual began to describe a practice that resembled the reformer's vision of a rich personal relationship between agent and felon. For example, one of the few concrete methods proposed by the manual was the initial interview with the parolee who had just been released from prison. The manual emphasized that the primary purpose of this interview was to initiate interpersonal influence; information gathering was secondary: "If the agent goes no further than to use the interview as a means of gaining objective data, he is failing completely in the performance of the fundamental purpose of parole—influencing, motivating, or treating parolees" (1959, sec. 7-18).

This relationship was to be continued and built up through regular contacts between the parole agent and the parolee. The manual's description of these contacts indicated that the parole agent's task was less to enforce the expectations of the community upon the parolee than to help the parolee manage his relationship with the community:

> Such visits enable the agent an opportunity to evaluate the current situation and pressures which surround the parolee as are related to his family, his job, and his environment. Parolees requiring intensive supervision should be interviewed frequently. Those who have demonstrated ability and resourcefulness in working out their problems may require less frequent contact. (1959, sec. 7-06)

Helping implies a kind of advocacy of the parolee, qua client, wholly incompatible with the disciplinary model of parole. In the clinical model, supervising the parolee no longer meant coercively utilizing the power of parole to impose a standard of behavior defined by the parolee's community. The approach of the manual to the issue of child support and other financial obligations illustrates this point. Before 1956 the requirement of employment in the California parole conditions included the advice that "you should make every effort to support any dependents you may have" (Star 1974, 22). The 1928 State Parole Officer's report specifically mentions these considerations as part of the parole procedure:

> In cases of prisoners having children to support or other obligations to comply with, arrangements are made, whereby he is to contribute a certain amount, consistent with his earnings toward the support of his dependents. This money is forwarded to the Parole Office, from where it is sent to the parties for whom it is intended. (State Board of Prison Directors 1928, 87)

Debt collection fits tightly with the disciplinary model of parole. The model's goal was not simply to subject the parolee to the discipline of labor, but to use the sovereign's power to punish, in order to perfect the reach of private norms. This increased the power of those in relationships with the parolee while tightening the network of surveillance and pressure on the parolee to stay employed as much as possible.

After 1956 the work requirement remained in effect but was no longer linked to a broader notion of economic responsibility (Star 1974, 22). Indeed, the 1959 edition of the manual makes explicit that the parole agent was not to act as an enforcer for debts (with the exception of funds lent from the Parole Division to the parolee), or for child support payments (Parole and Community Services Division 1959, sec. 7-12).[9]

9. I cannot determine how many people, if any, were returned to prison for not making what a parole agent believed was a sufficient effort to support their dependents. Interestingly, the state was getting more rigorous in its efforts to collect on delinquent child support payments in cases where welfare funds were going to the dependent mother and child. The parole manual required agents to cooperate fully in providing information on the whereabouts of parolees, and it instructed the agent to exhort the parolee to pay, but it prohibited the use of reimprisonment on a parole violation as a threat to coerce payment.

Instead of drawing on the web of private obligations to anchor the parolee, the manual pointed to internal parole resources for intervention. In Los Angeles the Division had established the Parole Outpatient Clinic, described as "the first psychiatric unit to be made a part of parole service in this country" (Parole and Community Services Division 1959, sec. 2-05). The function of the clinic was to provide evaluation and treatment for parolees referred by their parole officers. Although access was limited by resources, the clinic was supposed to be a general resource, not a specific program for the chronically mentally ill as it became in later years.

Also illuminating are the practices the manual rules out. Parole agents traditionally had utilized jail as means of drying out alcoholic or drug-addicted parolees or of delivering an intermediate sanction to parolees whom the agent wanted to punish but not reimprison. The manual discouraged casual use of jail and established firmer procedures for monitoring parolee custody.

> The power of arrest is to be used by the agent when necessary. Arresting a parolee and housing him in jail without justifiable cause, either as punishment or implied benefit of instilling fear, is contrary to parole policy and will not be allowed. It is intended that the parolee will remain in free society as long as there exists a likelihood of his making a satisfactory adjustment without danger to society. (Parole and Community Services Division 1959, sec. 7-02)

In other words, if someone was locked up because they violated parole, the agent had better be in the process of filing a report to the Adult Authority for formal suspension. Limited exception was granted for "men held pending the completion of an investigation, further clearance with other agencies, [or] to work with serious alcoholic and/or narcotic problems" (Parole and Community Services Division 1959, sec. 8-04). These rules clearly left room for agents to utilize the jail, which they continued to do, but linked its use to the panoply of new programs and procedures. The agent was now required to construct an account of his actions compatible with the clinical model of control.

The pressure from management to conform to the clinical model exerted through the manual and other processes faced two sources of resistance. One source was the friction of trying to fit that model onto the task of managing parolees, a problem that would have to be addressed through the creation of real clinical practice options. The second source of resistance was the pull of an alternative model of how agents could fill the gap left by the decline of the labor market as an anchor for the exercise of power, that is, law enforcement. Against this resistance the manual set out a range of expectations that would make it difficult for agents following it faithfully to transform themselves into police officers.

Many parole officers and supervisors in this era came directly from law enforcement work and thus had a ready-made program. Even those that did not could hardly have ignored the fact that law enforcement provided a model for dealing with parolees that was both coherent and politically viable. In the early days of California parole, before a regular staff had been created, local law enforcement was expected to assist parole by checking the validity of employment offers and keeping an eye on the parolee once he was back in the community.

The manual affirms cooperation with law enforcement but rules out imitation. Guns were barred. The use of parolees as informers was discouraged, and a long list of specifically police-like activities was ruled out of bounds:

> It is difficult to list all activities that are not compatible with the philosophy set forth. Among these, but in no manner limited to, are the following activities incompatible with the normal professional parole functions:
>
> (a) The "stake-out" by a Parole agent—the watchful waiting in concealment . . . after which the intent is to arrest the parolee.
> (b) Acts such as crawling through windows or breaking doors to gain admission to premises.
> (c) Routine search of the premise of a parolee . . .
> (d) Routine search or inspection of the parolee . . .
> (e) The performance of police duties for law enforcement agencies when such agents do not have the legal right to take such action. (Parole and Community Services Division 1959, sec. 7-04)

The manual defined a parole strategy involving interpersonal relationships established through in-depth interviews and sustained through regular contacts. Employment, family, and community were treated with diminished importance. The parole agent was not to spend all his time pursuing parolees, and he was not to allow pressure from these sources to disrupt his relationship with the parolee. Finally, the manual discouraged adoption of police techniques, although these methods must have been very tempting to parole agents attempting to pursue control as the changing economic and social situation made employment a less viable program.[10]

In his forward, Director of Corrections McGee provided a sense of how he viewed the manual. First, it was to be treated only as a link in a chain of command that ended at the center and top:

10. This is a point where it is useful to remind ourselves that a manual establishes a basis for the exercise of managerial power, but it does not guarantee its successful deployment. Veterans of the California Department of Corrections uniformly testify to the enduring influence of the law enforcement model manifested primarily in the agent's reliance on the negative threat of arrest as the most significant tool of parole work. Parole Chief Milton Burdman made an all-out drive in the mid-1960s to overwhelm the law enforcement commitment of the parole agents by applying pressure directly on unit supervisors to reduce their rate of returns to custody. While this drive was successful in reducing return rates for some years, it never managed to establish itself through ongoing mechanisms and remained dependent on the cruder and less consistent exercise of prerogative from above.

Departmental policies and procedures are set forth in the Administrative Manual and in other source materials. It is not intended these would
be repeated in this Parole Agent's Manual. This is a supplement to other
sources of policy and procedural statements. (Parole and Community
Services Division 1959, v)

Second, it was to be a vehicle for two-way communication in the Department:
"If change to the manual is required, provision is available to make such
change. The staff is encouraged to bring to the attention of the Chief of the
Division areas that should be examined for possible modification." But until
such modifications were made, it was to be the authoritative guide to action:
"Each employee must be aware of all the contents of this publication, keep it
current at all times, and adhere to the policies and procedural requirements
contained herein" (v).

The 1959 edition left much to the discretion of the parole agent in conjunction with the field supervisors. This discretion, no longer filled by expectations of the parolee's family, employers, and creditors, was to be guided by a
growing body of clinical knowledge on the part of the parole agent. The manual itself did not contain this knowledge or even a very concrete procedure for
getting access to it. Instead, it pointed toward other programs, such as narcotics control and the parole outpatient clinic, that appeared to be likely
spawning grounds for a clinical practice. Over the years the revised editions of
the manual would offer more procedures for more contingencies, but until the
1970s it remained a heavily philosophical document.

The manual provides a picture of the aspirations of the Parole Division's
elite as well and an anchor for real strategies of power. There is also a practical
content which the manual almost surely provided, the importance of using the
manual itself. Consulting the manual became a part of doing the agent's job,
and meeting its standards a significant strategy for defining that job as compe-
tently executed. Although it provided few specific techniques for practice at
the beginning, it established a channel through which elements of a clinical
practice could be passed into parole work. Like the community in the disciplinary model it offered not so much an answer as a place to look for answers
when the exercise of power (as it inevitably did in parole) ran beyond the guidance of formal rules.

Intensive Parole Supervision

In the model of disciplinary parole, the agent established control over the
parolee by fixing him in a web of private relationships and obligations—
primarily that of employment. The clinical model started from the presumption that parole had to provide its own foundation for control. It is not surprising that the first place to look for such a foundation was in the parole

relationship that the manual touted. The most obvious ways to make that relationship more effective were to give it more time—something which could be accomplished by reducing caseloads—and direct it more precisely, something that could be accomplished by classifying parolees.

Reformers began to talk about the need for smaller caseloads from the very start of organized supervisory systems like parole and probation as well as service functions like social work. Somewhere in the early twentieth century the ratio of fifty clients to one agent or caseworker developed as a standard of professional excellence and has been repeatedly invoked up to the present with no obvious basis in research or theory. Regardless of its inherent slipperiness, the size of caseloads served as the perfect excuse for the failures of parole wherever it was established: if only we had smaller caseloads, the real efficacy of supervision in the community could be established. The first important effort to verify experimentally the effectiveness of intensive parole supervision in California was a series of programs known as the Special Intensive Parole Unit program (SIPU). Four different phases of the study were carried out between 1953 and 1964. Parolees in California at this time generally were released to caseloads of around ninety men. The studies focused on the effects of releasing them to much smaller caseloads of fifteen, thirty, or thirty-five.

The major dependent variable considered was parole outcome after one or two years, defined by a continuum ranging from "no arrest" to "minor arrest" to "major arrest" to "return to prison." The results of the first two studies provided no support for the hypothesis that small caseloads increased the effectiveness of parole. [11]

Investigators felt that the lack of success in the first two studies might have stemmed from two complicating factors. First, the time for which the parolees were actually exposed to the intensive supervision was brief—three months in the first study, six months in the second. Second, the exigencies and pressures to maintain balanced workloads (for reasons of personnel policy rather than a research protocol) led to high turnover of parole agents in a number of experimental units.

If the point of intensive parole was, as suggested in the manual, to build interpersonal relationships, rapid turnover in agents would surely undermine the effectiveness of the system. As the investigators put it: "SIPU Parole

11. The first study showed some advantage for the experimental group during its first year. On reanalysis, it turned out that the experimental group included a disproportionate number of parolees who were already identified as good risks on the basis of the Department's statistical risk prediction instrument (the Base/Expectancy score). Although the research report does not comment on the source of bias, it is likely that the leadership's interest in showing the utility of intensive parole encouraged subordinates to stack the deck. The first two phases of SIPU were carried out before the research had been organized into an distinct unit within the Department.

Agents became, in effect, intake workers. The Agents themselves felt they were not given enough time to develop meaningful relationships with their parolees" (Havel and Sulka 1962, 3).

Phase three was intended to tighten procedures and extend the duration of exposure. Experimental groups were formed of parolees released to thirty-five-person caseloads as compared to a regular caseload of seventy-two (the regular caseload had been reduced by administrative negotiation). The intensive supervision lasted for a full year. At its conclusion the investigators found that the data did support the hypothesis that intensive parole supervision could make a difference in parole outcome. When the SIPU experimental group was compared with the control group with respect to offenses committed a year after first release, a statistically significant difference was found in the expected direction.

After five years of experimentation, the Division and investigators for phase three were clearly relieved to be able to say that intensive parole had a measurable effect. The idea that the parole agent could influence the parolee to avoid criminal activity was consistent with the evidence that the best results were achieved with medium-risk parolees. Some parolees might be too deviant by the time they were released on parole for supervision to make much difference. Others were perhaps likely to succeed even without the assistance of parole. If supervision could make a difference it would be with those wavering between these two poles.

Like the manual, the intensive parole project made no real effort to define or structure supervision. Supervision remained a black box. For a decade the project sought to show a statistical advantage to small caseloads on the assumption that smaller caseloads would give parole agents more time to work with parolees, but the project had no control over what the agents did. In fact, it had no way of knowing if the supervision was qualitatively different in any way.

Phase four, initiated in 1959 before the results of phase three were in, offered something new. Instead of assuming that some kind of generalized supervisory effect came from providing more time, phase four explored the role of different parolee personality types and their relation to different styles of parole supervision.

Phase four was the first to be organized under the new professional research unit that the Department created in 1958. The first head of that unit, J. Douglas Grant, was a clinical psychologist. Grant and his collaborator (and wife), Margaret Grant, had formulated a theory of delinquency focusing on stages of maturity. Like Jones and other psychologists in the postwar period the Grants were interested in the interaction between psychological factors and social settings. They developed a five-stage scale of maturity development and theorized that delinquents were either individuals with stunted maturity development who resolved their problems in a manner consonant with their limited capacities for self-management, or higher-maturity individuals whose environment did not encourage the appropriate adjustment. Progress might be expected either by raising maturity levels or by helping higher-maturity delinquents confront their inappropriate strategies for dealing with the world (Grant and Grant 1952, 130). In their first experimental test with "nonconformist" military inmates serving time after court martialing, the Grants found that inmates with high maturity levels did better after being restored to duty, but only if they were in therapeutic groups supervised by a team of nonspecialists who had been rated more effective by the experimenters. The potential for adjustment might be inherent to the difficult-to-change maturity of an individual, but this potential required the right technique to actualize it.

In setting up the phase four experiment, the Grants developed this model further. They hypothesized that parolees with the lowest maturity levels would do best when supervised by parole agents whose supervision style was "external," that is, "concerned primarily with factors external to the parolee." In contrast, more mature parolees were hypothesized to do better with "internal agents," who "[focus] more on what is happening inside the parolee" (Havel 1965, 4). Since immature parolees have a weak sense of self, exposure to supervision which emphasized the encouragement of internal reflection would only generate confusion and resistance. Likewise, the mature parolee would chafe under the rule-oriented supervision of an external agent. If these cross effects were operating, then intensive supervision may have produced real effects that were masked in phases one through three.

Unfortunately, the new data provided no confirmation of this hypothesis. The investigators stressed the design and implementation problems which were indeed formidable. They did find reason for some satisfaction, however, in their additional analysis of caseload size factors. These data supported the same effect as had been shown in phase three, that there was a limited benefit to caseloads smaller than the regular size (but not the smallest tested), especially for parolees regarded as moderate risks.

Some years later, in a highly critical 1969 memorandum entitled "It's Time To Stop Counting," James O. Robison (a member of the Department's Research Division, Bay Area Unit) summarized the project in terms that implied its focus on caseload had become irrational and perhaps even obsessional:

> Caseload size has been more exhaustively studied than any of the other methods of reducing recidivism. Hopes attached to caseload reduction have justified numerous demonstration projects. The bulk of evidence available today, however, does not show superior efficacy for smaller caseloads. (1969, 49)

The lengthy career of the SIPU experiments testifies in retrospect to the importance the management of the Division placed on documenting that parole supervision provided control effects quite independent of community-based factors. From the perspective of creating an effective and plausible account of control in parole supervision the modest effect documented in phases three and four was critical. The empirical validation that the Department pursued promised not only a means of sharpening parole practice, but of demonstrating to the public that, given enough resources, parole itself could handle more released felons in the community despite decreasing background support.

The SIPU experiments were also an investment in the creation of an infrastructure for clinical practice. Much time, money, and personnel were devoted to these experiments. The first three phases were huge, absorbing virtually every parolee released in the state as either an experimental subject or control. Agents all over the state were placed in special units with the opportunity for more intensive work.

The limits of the SIPU in constituting clinical parole in California were marked by what it did not include. Agents and parolees were subject to the same employment requirements as before. Fulfilling these requirements took considerable agent time. Parole agents with fewer parolees might find more time to develop methods of interpersonal communication, but they might simply spend more time looking for violations, a result that could lead to a worse, rather than a better, recidivism rate in the experimental units. [12]

One of the problems with building up the notion of parole supervision along the SIPU lines was the absence of a link between activity and parole outcome. SIPU created a space for clinical parole, but it stopped short of delivering a program. The boldest effort in this direction was the Grant personality modification strategy used in phase four. The research provided no support for its classification scheme, let alone for the hypothesis that coordination of parolees and agents according to the scheme would make any difference in the success of parole.

However, as SIPU wound down, the Division arranged to institutionalize its basic mechanism. The Work Unit Program inaugurated in 1964 sent half of the parole releases in the state to small caseload units where they were to receive more intensive parole. Rather than being offered primarily as an experimental program, the now "proven" effects of intensive supervision were offered as a means of controlling parolees with increasingly tenuous economic support. [13]

12. Indeed, several years later the Chief of Parole decided that agents were misusing intensive supervision to do more policing and thus to send more parolees back to prison. The chief toured the state instructing supervisors that the aim of intensive parole was finding ways to keep the parolee in the community, not send him back to prison.

13. Robison (1969) suggests that there was some dispute between the legislature and the Department of Corrections over how much of the parole population would be covered (the Department wanted all) and whether the program would be experimental (the legislature wanted evaluation). The resulting

Narcotic Addiction and Control

Narcotic use, addiction, and sale have been national concerns since the First World War, but the intensity of that concern has varied (Musto 1973). An initial flurry of interest in the 1920s was followed by a period of relative quiet during the 1930s and 1940s, then the narcotic problem captured public attention in the 1950s. In California it became virtually a panic. In 1948, 3,000 felony narcotic arrests were made in California. Three years later the number had grown to 5,264 (Himelson 1968, 6). In Los Angeles alone arrests had gone from 295 in 1940 to over 1800 in 1950 (Burkhardt and Sathmary 1963, 1). These figures may indicate either growth in the use of illegal narcotics or growth in demand on law enforcement to act against narcotics. Both seemed to have been at work in the 1950s.

Addiction in the 1950s was associated with two demographic characteristics that may have helped raise the salience of a clinical approach. Increasingly, addiction was viewed as a condition of the young and of minority group members living in depressed urban enclaves (Musto 1973, 230). These features, which would become part of the more general image of crime in the 1950s and 1960s, suggested that social discipline alone could not be counted on to control the offender. Since drug users belonged to communities that were already marginal to the labor force, independent measures were required.

Narcotics also offered a singular pathway to the elusive core of a clinical regime, the psychological subject. The figure of the addict, locked in the mortal grip of his individual need, popularized in novels like Nelson Algren's *The Man With The Golden Arm* (1949), haunted the imagination and helped clarify the picture of the individual deviant. More importantly, the fury over narcotics in the 1950s provided a bridge between politicians anxious to cultivate and service moral panics and the California correctional management's drive to intensify its professionalism and reputation as a leading innovator in rehabilitative methods.

The apprehension with which California correctional officials began to look at drugs is captured by exconvict author Malcolm Braly's description of his commitment to the Department of Corrections as a second termer after burglarizing a medical office in search of amphetamines while on parole in the early 1950s.

> Any advantage I had my first time in Quentin was now sharply reversed. Every detail served only to draw the net tighter. For one thing, the briefcase we carried contained a small bottle of morphine sulfate. We had

---

program, which ran for more than a decade, placed half of all parolees in small caseload units and half in regular-sized ones. Evaluation was performed, but Robison claims that assignment bias eliminated any experimental validity. Prisoners prone to violence, as well as those with the best prognosis, were placed in the work units.

taken it because it was a glamour drug. Neither of us had ever taken morphine, or any opium derivative, nor did we know anyone who did. It was with a number of other drugs, and we took it because it was there.

The morphine became critical. It was then what heroin is now, and the prison Establishment was alert to the implication that morphine could be both a symptom and a cause of criminal behavior and it was, in significant addition, a politically loaded issue. Several state senators were basing their political lives on the fight to make sales of these opiates punishable by death. (1976, 217–18)

In retrospect it seems as if the narcotic addict was the perfect figure around which to reconstruct the penal project in the 1950s. The broad strategy of rehabilitation pursued by Department head Richard McGee drew heavily on the medical analogy of patient to prisoner, an analogy that clearly strained the credulity of staff, let alone the public, in a way the disciplinary model never did. The addict seemed to fit right on the line between illness and crime—a subject compelled to break the law by the power of a medically recognized pathology. Moreover, it seemed possible that the traits underlying far broader forms of delinquency might be brought to light in plumbing the depths of the abnormal personality structures that made people addicts. This represented a major shift in the centrality of addiction to the imagination of crime.

Prior to World War II the addict had been viewed in much the same way as other criminals were, primarily against the counterexemplar of the industrious worker. The following passage from a 1926 California Senate Report captures this sensibility:

Drug addicts as a class are idlers and not workers. The majority of them depend upon petty larceny, stealing, begging, drug peddling, prostitution, and other illegal methods of obtaining money to satisfy their craving. Our narcotic officials estimate that approximately 80 per cent of our California addicts become criminals, either because of their abnormal personality or to satisfy their craving for the drug. (quoted in Himelson 1968, 56)

Writing in 1917 in the pages of the *Journal of Criminal Law and Criminology*, Philadelphia's U.S. Attorney, Francis Fisher Kane, prescribed labor and isolation as the cure for addiction:

Drug victims must be cut off from old surroundings, removed from the temptations to which they succumbed, and this separation must be maintained for a long period of time, under strict discipline at first, relaxed afterwards by degrees as they regain self control and not taken away suddenly. Occupation meanwhile is a prime necessity. Mind and body must have work. Idleness does not supply the alternative required. With idleness no cure is possible. (Kane 1917, 506)

Himelson[14] described the opposing forces debating narcotics control policy in California during the 1950s as belonging to two basic camps. One viewed narcotics addiction as intractable and proposed prolonged incapacitation through extended sentences. They attacked judges for handing down light sentences and called for new legislation aimed particularly at the narcotics user. In 1958 the state Elks lodges sponsored a petition calling for a mandatory thirty-year sentence for narcotics peddling which obtained over a million signatures (Himelson 1968, 12). The other camp viewed addiction as a treatable condition. Increasing punishment would do little to solve the underlying problems that led people to use opiates. Moreover, chemically dependent people were the least likely to respond to deterrence (1968, 13).

The proposal that ultimately was adopted by the California Legislature implied compromise in its very name, the Narcotic Treatment and Control Program (NTCP). It offered a treatment-oriented program, but with the promise of incapacitation for those who failed to respond. The program included smaller caseloads to permit parole agents to address the underlying personality problems that led to addiction, a testing process that would permit the discovery of opiate use within a two-day range, and special confinement units lodged at state prisons but designed to provide treatment for those that failed to stop using drugs. Finally, the whole program was to be organized experimentally to document scientifically whether or not treatment could work.

Small caseloads were supposed to free up the agent's time to do more in-depth work altering the personalities of parolees. Yet the available methodologies were thin. Agents were to lead group counseling sessions (most agents rejected the term group therapy). Some in the Division believed that a kind of psychotherapeutic transfer would take place between the parolee and the parole agent in the course of sustained personal contacts.

Group counseling had been in use in the California prisons since the early 1950s. Malcolm Braly described one such group at Folsom:

> By the time we were all gathered, sitting in a circle on wooden folding chairs, usually ten minutes of the therapeutic hour had already gone by. Our circle here, like Arthur's table, was supposed to have no head, for the remaining fifty minutes we were all equally free to say anything we liked, but naturally we polarized toward the therapist. His equal voice might be heard by the Adult Authority. We all knew that the Adult Authority took special interest in these programs. (1976, 245)

As Braly's quote implies, the potential interest of prisoners in the benefits of therapy was inextricably tied up with the perceived institutional advantage of

14. Himelson was a member of the Department's research unit and coauthor of the experimental analysis for the Department's major narcotic treatment program (discussed below). He drew on these experiences for his fascinating study of the politics of scientific failure, "When Treatment Failed," his Ph.D. dissertation in UCLA's Sociology Department.

cooperating to impress the Adult Authority, which had the power to set prison terms for California prisoners within extremely wide margins (Messinger 1969). This interplay between coercive punishment and the exposure of therapy would rapidly become a major target of criticism from the left (Mitford 1971).

Beyond group counseling, ideas on treatment were scanty at the start. The program relied heavily on the idea that agents and supervisors would meet in their own group sessions regularly and begin to build a shared practical knowledge of addiction control. This took place in the early part of the program. Himelson describes the staff as generally enthusiastic (1968, 125). The NTCP philosophy and its administrative autonomy from the regular units also created conditions that fostered parolee-parole agent rapport in a way which was crucial to the manual's call for interpersonal relations, but was generally precluded by the normal course of supervision.

One element of the program which promised to lend it the medical credence to fit with its clinical ideology was a method of chemical narcotic detection known as "nalline testing." Nalline (N-allylnormorphine) is a synthetic morphine derivative. When subcutaneously injected into a person who has used opiates in the last forty-eight hours it causes dilation of the pupils. The basic format of testing required parolees to attend a "nalline clinic" where their pupils were measured by a doctor. They were injected with nalline, and approximately fifteen to thirty minutes later a second measurement was taken. A person who had not used narcotics within the last forty-eight hours should show constriction of the pupil; if the pupil was the same size or dilated, opiate use was indicated.

The documentary record of the NTCP program indicates that nalline testing was built up as far more than a mere test. It was referred to as an "anti-narcotic drug that has the effect of counteracting the physiological [actions] of morphine, heroin and other morphine derivatives" (Burkhardt and Sathmary 1963, 6). In fact nalline provided no direct therapeutic benefits. Its counteraction of the "physiological" actions of opiates involved measurable but therapeutically irrelevant physiological effects like pupil dilation.

The ideological association was furthered by the reference to testing centers as "clinics." Because the testing involved injection of a drug, medical doctors were required to be present. Yet neither the presence of doctors, nor any other features of the clinic, offered techniques for combating addiction.

Parole agents assigned to NTCP were required to attend the clinics on a weekly basis. While medically irrelevant, the clinics might have served as the perfect environment for the invention of a clinical practice, but only if real incentives to innovate had been created. Some agents did attempt to organize activities like group counseling sessions for the parolees, but the demands of the traditional parole agent role never really lessened. In general, however, Himelson describes the clinic duties as having been a time-consuming requirement that took away from the agents' ability to concentrate on their assigned caseload (1968, 152).

A far less complicated and time-consuming test was available. The program could have relied on chemical tests of urine to detect metabolites of opiates. Urine samples could have been collected anywhere a bathroom was available and did not require the involvement of physicians either in collecting or analyzing the urine. (The latter was done in commercial labs.) Yet nalline was enthusiastically supported by the Division's leadership which evidently bought into the "clinical" allure of the program. Urinalysis was used, but only to confirm opiate use when the parolee continued to deny use.

There is no question, however, that nalline was effective in discovering narcotic use. A year into their parole nearly half the experimental subjects undergoing nalline testing were discovered to be using opiates. In contrast a control group of addicts not receiving nalline testing revealed only 31.7 percent using opiates (Burkhardt and Sathmary 1963, 19).[15] Yet this success of nalline in detecting drug use created a crisis for the program. Agents had been led to believe that the small caseloads and the treatment-oriented supervision would rapidly "cure" addicts. Nalline was proving them wrong. The strong inclination of the staff was to revise their assessment and assume that several relapses might be necessary before a full cure resulted (Himelson 1968, 128). Yet such action flew in the face of the control promises made to the legislature.

During the first year of the program the agents had considerable discretion over what to do with parolees who were shown to be using narcotics. They could continue them on parole in the community. They could send them to the Narcotic Testing and Control Unit which was a confined treatment setting on the grounds of the California Institute for Men, a state prison located in Chino, California (a second one was eventually opened at San Quentin for northern California addicts). If the situation suggested intractable addiction, they could report the matter to the Adult Authority and let it determine whether to suspend the parole as violated.

This created an intolerable situation for the management of the Parole Division. The program was hailed as a way of suppressing narcotic use, yet program staff were leaving narcotic users in the community, or returning them there even after they had received inpatient treatment and failed. Narcotic use was associated with criminal activity in the minds of the public. Allowing someone using narcotics to remain in the community appeared to be inviting crime. When news spread that parolees were not being reimprisoned after

15. An additional control group received nalline but not the intensive supervision. They turned up as many positive tests as the experimental group, which suggested that nalline was responsible for the entire effect.

drug use, there was an outcry in the legislature. The inpatient clinic was referred to as a "revolving door" because of the practice of sending parolees there two and even three times. The policy was revamped after the first year. From then on, a parolee who was documented positive on the nalline test was immediately sent to inpatient confinement if there was no other evidence of criminal activity. Those who failed a second time were sent back to prison.

The new regime had two immediate consequences. First, any chance that the parolees would view the nalline centers as treatment facilities disappeared. If they came in and were detected positive, they were taken into custody immediately. The rapport between agent and parolee which had been so central to the whole clinical model was undermined. Indeed, on several occasions large-scale fights between agents and parolees erupted at the clinic while arrests were being carried out.

Second, the nalline procedure began to drive the agents' allocation of time. One of the reasons that agents had favored keeping parolees on the street was that it saved them the paperwork involved in sending the parolee to the inpatient clinic or in reporting the matter as a violation. Now there was little escape from an escalating paperwork cycle that ate up time while arrests were being carried out.

Third, the program's emphasis on the parole agent as clinician making individualized assessments about the parolee's condition and dangerousness was fatally undermined. Instead, a rigid policy coupled to an automatic testing procedure reduced the agent to arresting parolees and writing reports.

The new policy may also have discouraged one of the hidden utilities of the nalline program. John Irwin discovered through interviews with parolees in the mid-1960s that while the clinics often provided a convenient place for drug sellers to meet buyers, many parolees had found the nalline program beneficial in controlling their drug use. The program called for scheduled weekly testing and one random test a month (a test scheduled less than forty-eight hours in advance). The regularity of testing meant that a person could use drugs for a few days after the weekly test but then had to clean up:

> He may go for months following this pattern. He can continue to live a relatively normal existence while using drugs because having to use drugs intermittently prevents him from becoming addicted and, therefore, having to increase his dosages. The nalline clinic, while it has helped to induce and entice him into drug use, serves as a control on his habit. (1968, 146)

The monthly random test meant that such controlled use would lead to eventual discovery. Those with controlled use may have been parolees whom agents wanted to leave on the streets. As long as the agents had discretion they could distinguish between those who appeared to be fully readdicted and those who were doing well and maintaining a controlled life. The new policy

raised the stakes on any positive test. Nalline could be either a tool for enforcing abstinence if drug users were sent to prison, or a tool for controlling drug
use in the community, but it could not, apparently, be both.

The nalline clinic had actually succeeded in doing something quite relevant to the new situation parole found itself in, that is, creating an alternative
stabilizing structure for people whose disintegrating communities provided
fewer and fewer niches. The agents may well have appreciated this function,
but nothing in the prevailing drug ideology of the day would have lent support
to this kind of tolerance of controlled drug use once it became visible. Visibility, of course, came with the research function which was consistently monitoring and reporting what happened to parolees who were discovered to be
using drugs.

The part of the program that came closest to realizing the clinical model was
the Narcotic Treatment and Control Units (NCTUs). The clinic staffs were made
up of true believers who were mainly newcomers to corrections. They operated
explicitly on the therapeutic community model developed by Maxwell Jones.
The ideal was an egalitarian and communitarian group of staff and patients
based on mutual respect and open communication. This was in striking contrast to even the most progressive prison administration at the time, although
few anticipated conflict at the outset.

The basic method of the inpatient clinic was intensive group meetings to
discuss any and all subjects, including details of personal history and day-to-
day problems of custody. A large group of the entire unit, including staff and
inmates, met weekly to discuss matters of discipline, work problems, and
housekeeping (Himelson 1968, 197). Smaller groups met every other day to
engage in intensive group therapy. The idea was to confront the addict with his
own behavior and make him responsible for it.

The clinic's model was ultimately undermined by conflict between the
clinic staff and the regular prison staff over two issues that highlight the differences between the industrial and clinical models in corrections. Inside the
prison, labor was viewed within the traditional disciplinary model, entirely as
a matter of output. The clinic staff, in line with the emerging clinical model in
corrections, believed that the goal was to develop a proper psychological attitude toward personal responsibility.

Prison discipline was also a matter of conflict. In the prison the staff were
responsible for identifying and prosecuting infractions on an adversarial
basis. The clinic program utilized the group meetings to bring up and discuss
disciplinary problems in a community context. In the end, the Department
sided with the prison staff, and the clinics were brought into line.

The second source of resistance was inmate culture. The therapeutic community model presupposed that patients accepted the staff's account of them

as people in need of psychological help. Himelson reports that inmate resistance eventually broke this down (1968, 203). The staff, confronted by this resistance, actively sought to foster a counterinmate subculture which shared staff values. The results of this effort were, however, dismal.

As an innovation seeking experimental confirmation the program was a failure. In the first two years experimental groups were compared to two kinds of control groups: one with nalline testing and one without. Both control categories utilized standard parole supervision procedures and maintained standard caseloads. The investigators looked at two dependent variables to assess the hypothesis that NTCP made a difference. They examined the percentage of subjects detected using drugs, and the percentage who received jail sentences or prison terms.

The first fell conveniently on the central ambiguity in the program between treatment and control. If the data showed fewer cases of drug use among the experimental group it might suggest that the program was working. If the data showed more cases of drug use among the experimental group, it might suggest that the program was a good way to find drug users and control them. When, in fact, the experimental group was compared to both controls, it appeared that the only benefit was the discovery of more drug use and that this was attributable to the nalline testing, not the program (Burkhardt and Sathmary 1963, 19).

In analyzing the second variable, cases ending up in jail or prison, the investigators dropped the control with nalline testing altogether and compared the experimental group to the control group without testing. The best that could be said for the program on this basis was that fewer went to jail or prison. On other hand a significant percent were sent to the inpatient clinic for having used drugs (Burkhardt and Sathmary 1963, 19). Himelson and Thoma, explaining an analogous finding in phase three of the experimental program, argued convincingly that this factor probably accounted for the difference (1968, 44). Parolees locked inside the inpatient clinic for three months, and in some cases six months, were simply less exposed to the opportunity to get caught committing a crime.

NTCP phase three was also a failure. At the time it began in 1963, the Department was well aware that the previous study had shown no positive effects. Himelson, who along with Blanche Thoma acted as the principal investigator on phase three, argued that the project was continued simply because the Department was stuck with a legislative grant with over two years to go (Himelson 1968, 164).

NTCP continued to have enthusiasts in the Parole Division, and phase three was the most ambitious part yet. Experimental groups were arranged in four combinations. Half of the total were sent to the inpatient clinic prior to release. The other half were sent to NTCU units upon their regular parole date. The whole was divided in another respect. Half were sent to caseloads of fifteen, while the other half were placed on forty-five-person caseloads. None of these variations made any positive difference. In fact, the parolees sent to the NTCU prior to release did significantly worse regardless of what size caseload they went to afterwards.

Although the NTCP research program ended after 1964, the nalline program has continued in various forms to the present. With the clinics operating independently of the parole agents, drug violation detection became institutionalized as a force in parole and likely a major cause of returns to prison. While the testing clinics displaced some of the agent's control over the parolee, they also played a tremendous role in organizing the work of parole agents. Instead of focusing on finding employment for parolees, agents could work the large and growing private drug treatment world. Finding a placement in a treatment program for a troubled parolee using drugs (a task that did not exist before the early 1960s) had become a bona fide way of doing their job well.

A narcotics program of even larger scope which utilized a similar approach to NTCU was created in 1961, but without the experimental emphasis. The California Civil Addicts program was available as an alternative to prosecution under the criminal code for those accused of some narcotics offenses. Diversion into the program resulted in dismissal of criminal charges and the entering of a kind of civil commitment. Addicts entering the program were confined for seven to fifteen months in the California Rehabilitation Center (CRC), a prison which had been reorganized as a treatment center for addicts. Confinement was followed by up to seven years of supervision. After release from CRC, "outpatients," as parolees in the program were described, were supervised in special thirty-two-person caseloads and subject to regular urine testing for drugs. An outpatient detected using drugs or committing other violations could be returned for up to six months at CRC by the action of the Civil Narcotics Board (which functioned analogously to the Adult Authority in parole revocation matters).

During the program's most active period, from 1961 to 1972, almost 18,000 individuals passed through it, and scores of parole agents were assigned to Civil Addict duty (Anglin and McGlothlin 1984). The program remains in effect, but its population dropped precipitously in 1977 when the new determinate sentence law made prison a more attractive alternative for many drug offenders because of its fixed duration. A series of analyses and follow-up studies of the program, conducted during the 1970s by William McGlothlin and Douglas Anglin of UCLA, have showed that the program was at least partly successful in lowering the crime and readdiction rates for participants (McGlothlin, Anglin, and Wilson 1975; Anglin and McGlothlin 1984). More importantly from our perspective, it helped build an infrastructure for the clinical model in corrections. The Civil Addict parole units were known as the most innovative in the state.

The Pivotal Role of the Research Program

During the decade in which SIPU and NTCP were running there was hardly a parolee or parole agent in the state who was not in an experimental or control group at one time or another. This means that they provided in themselves a practice to structure the parole agent's exercise of power. Despite the modest success enjoyed by SIPU experimentally, and even the failure of NTCP, the experimental program worked as an engine for the infusion of new techniques and ideas. The small caseload, the drug-testing program, and the custodial treatment units all survived the dismantling of the larger experimental program to become fixtures in parole to the present. The world of the parole agent which for so long had been organized primarily around employment services became far more diverse, and while research did not yield any magic bullets, it provided a whole new set of tasks and programs around which supervision could define itself.

The new clinical model that emerged following the Second World War also held a certain coherence and fit with the assumptions of the new class of citizens trained in universities to believe in the capacity of the social sciences to generate solutions. For reasons that require further study the war itself did much to mobilize the powers and prestige of the social sciences. Creating a professional research staff within the Department and building it into the parole program offered a powerful way of elaborating the model and the promise of legitimating it, but it also placed a burden on the clinical parole model that was entirely different from that which had faced the disciplinary model.

No other correctional program had ever committed itself to the kind of research effort that was made during the 1950s and 1960s in California. Corrections had always produced statistics, but most were considered far below the standards of academic social science. The effectiveness (or lack thereof) of the various programs evaluated by the California research unit was consistently and accurately presented. Yet the paradoxical consequence of the research program was to undermine the plausibility of programs that conceptually fit with the prevailing social ideas about crime and disorder. So long as researchers made parole outcome a visible object, parole supervision would lack a secure anchor. Not surprisingly, the most important components of the clinical model, intensive supervision and drug treatment, soon separated themselves from the strictures of the experimental method.

After the big research programs wound down, the research unit did not fold up. Instead, it began looking closely at the very fabric of parole decision making, a path likely to even further damage the plausibility of parole. By the late

1960s the research unit became the source of some of the most critical appraisals that any penal institution anywhere (and perhaps any bureaucracy of any kind) has ever undertaken of itself and allowed to be published.

Particularly striking was the work done by researchers at the Bay Area research unit, many of whom were associated with the School of Criminology at the University of California, Berkeley.[16] Researchers like Paul Takagi and James O. Robison began to demonstrate that the whole concept of success in parole was captive to the enormous discretion in the hands of parole agents (Robison and Takagi 1968). Recidivism rates were the stuff of parole evaluation, but by deciding whether to report a violation to the Adult Authority the Division could effectively influence its recidivism rate.

After 1968 the unit began to be whittled away. Its budget was severely cut, and by the early 1970s it survived only by finding temporary assignments for its staff in other units and through occasional research grants. The Department continued to collect and publish statistics on its populations, but the experimental drive was largely eliminated. There is no question that the research unit's critical edge helped lead to its demise. Yet its focus on internal procedure helped, in the end, to point parole toward an entirely different model, one based on measures of parole staff effort, rather than parolee outcome. That model, still developing today, will be considered in part two of this study.

The Enduring Role of Employment

Through the manual and the research programs, the Division tried hard to shape a model of parole supervision that depended on the interpersonal skills of the parole agents in relating to the parolee rather than on their ability to secure the parolee to networks of private social control in the community. Securing employment remained important, but its official presentation reflected its decentering within the ensemble of parole practices and discourses.

A comparison of California parole conditions from World War II to the early 1970s, undertaken by Deborah Star, suggests that while employment continued to be a formal requirement, its practical significance was declining. In 1949 the conditions stated: "It is necessary for you to maintain steady employment and any change of employment must be approved by your Parole Officer" (Star 1974, 22). That formula remained in effect throughout the 1960s.

By the 1970s African-Americans and Hispanics constituted a majority in

16. Founded in the late 1950s as to aid in the professionalization of California law enforcement and corrections, the School of Criminology was phased out in 1976 after becoming famous (or infamous) as a center for left-wing critiques of the U.S. legal system. Its rise and fall is worth a study of its own. The influence of the School on the Department of Corrections in the 1960s was significant. Many of the Department's research staff came directly from the School.

the prison system. The strains on the employment base of the disciplinary model in the 1950s were now full-scale fissures that could not be denied. Perhaps in recognition of this the language of parole conditions practically did away with the requirement of work and limited the parole agent's power (and responsibility) to governing the parolee's economic choices.

Amendments in 1971 eliminated work as a specific requirement: "I agree to report to my Parole Agent upon parole and to keep him continuously informed of my residence and employment locations." In 1973 some emphasis on employment was restored but not as a requirement: "I will make every effort to remain gainfully employed and will not change employment without approval of my Parole Agent" (Star 1974, 22).

Rather than ceding power from parole agents to parolees the changes at the start of the 1970s probably reflected an understanding of the futility of enforcing a labor requirement on a population increasingly excluded from the labor market. No doubt, as the 1973 change suggests, the image of gainful labor was still an important symbolic part of parole, but maintaining it as a bona fide requirement had exacted an enormous toll in organizational tension and deceit.

Paul Takagi presents an in-depth view of the tensions within California parole caused by the parolee employment problem during the mid-1960s in his 1967 doctoral dissertation, *Evaluation Systems and Adaptations In a Formal Organization: A Case Study of a Parole Agency*. Takagi wanted to study what happens inside an organization when evaluation criteria are disjoined from the ability of those being evaluated to effect the criteria purposively. One of the tasks which most exemplified this dynamic was that of ensuring that men scheduled for release from prison had employment arranged as required by the conditions and the agency's manual.

Release on parole in that era required two steps: first, formal approval by the Adult Authority of parole, and second, approval by the Parole Division of a plan of release including an offer of employment and a residence. For prisoners who arranged an offer of employment on their own, the parole agent assigned to the case had only to verify the existence and the appropriateness of the job. Far more problematic were the majority of prisoners, who had no standing job offer. In those cases the parole agent assigned the case by the regional parole administration had the burden of arranging employment.

The description of this process in the 1959 manual leaves little doubt that it was considered burdensome:

> Some cases will be referred without residence or employment leads. These may appear to offer less optimistic prospects for adjustment than others. Each district must assume its share of such cases. If, after a real effort to place has been made, satisfactory placement is impossible, the

Parole Agent will set forth all details in a report to the Supervisor of the Placement Unit at the earliest possible date. The Department of Corrections will not tolerate evidence on the part of any staff member being selective on the basis of his personal bias and prejudice towards the parolee nor reviewing the action of the paroling authority. The concepts, attitudes and philosophies governing the acceptance of cases by all district offices must be uniform. (sec. 6-02)

When an agent could not place a parolee there were two options open. As illustrated above, the agent could report the lack of success to the regional administration. This practice, known as letting a case become "overdue," was explicitly if ambiguously approved in the manual: "If satisfactory programs cannot be arranged, the retention of inmates beyond such dates is not inconsistent with the intent and philosophy of the Adult Authority or the policy of the Director of Corrections" (sec. 6-01).

Takagi found that in practice letting cases become overdue was unacceptable. When a case became overdue the regional administration applied direct pressure on the agent in the form of phone calls and letters demanding an update on the situation. When Takagi asked parole agents how often they would let a case become overdue if they could not "formulate a satisfactory program," half answered "almost never," and only 23 percent said they would "almost always," or "most of the time" (1967, 59).

The other option open to the agent when a parolee proved difficult to place was to approve a program without employment. Despite the language of the parole condition this was sanctioned by the manual:

> Release without definite employment offers will be permitted in those instances where in the opinions and judgments of the Parole Agents such individuals will not be unduly dependent upon the Division or other public agencies and where the personality structure and/or crime pattern does not contra-indicate release without employment. . . . This is not to be construed as a license to release without offers of employment except when the conditions previously set forth exist. (1960, sec. 6-03)

While the language in the manual suggested such a practice was unusual and to be undertaken with caution, Takagi found that it was, in fact, frequently done. Reviewing the total release cohort of a six-month period during the mid-1960s, Takagi found that 51 percent of the releasees had no jobs to report to on release. Of those that did have a job on release, only one-third remained so employed two months after release (1967, 59). Agents apparently looked the other way at the frequent practice of an inmate's family or friends coming up with a fictitious job. When Takagi asked agents if they agreed with the statement that "under our present system of pre-release procedures . . . the agent is sometimes forced to deviate to get the job done," fully 68 percent agreed either strongly or moderately, and 69 percent of the supervisors agreed that their agents often had to deviate (1967, 60, 69).

Parolee employment was not, however, an empty shell for the agents. Takagi points out that supervisors viewed employment as second only to avoidance of law violations in their evaluation of how parolees and thus parole agents were doing. Many of the supervisors in this period had been trained in the forties when the disciplinary model of parole was at its peak. They tended to view their job as one of establishing relations with civic leaders, participating in voluntary associations, and making the acquaintance of local employers, all in the interest of generating parolee job placements.

This task was of course far easier in middle-class neighborhoods where the local economies supported a larger labor pool. In the depressed inner-city enclaves that were becoming more and more the modal home of parolees the situation was far more difficult. Not surprisingly assignments to middle-class or traditional working-class neighborhoods were considered plum jobs to be earned.

By the mid-1960s one avenue of relief was opening for the parole agent, the expansion of the social service network of private and public-funded agencies organized to aid residents of poverty-stricken areas. Where parole agents in the industrial era would have spent most of their time working the local factories and businesses, the parole agent in the mid-1960s often concentrated on building connections with people in this service sector. A pre-release program that called for a parolee to be in a training program, or in a placement service run by the Salvation Army or the Society of St. Vincent De Paul, was considered fully acceptable.

Conclusion

While the research programs helped to disseminate new styles of parole supervision, they never succeeded in completely replacing the traditional role of employment. Often the two clashed. Agents in the NTCP attempted to keep parolees on the street after discovering drug use if they had jobs. This was unacceptable to the top leadership of the Division, but it probably reflected the wisdom at the unit level that employment was still the best way of keeping a parolee under control.

The endurance of the disciplinary model of parole testifies to the powerful hold that labor has on the idea of normality. America was only beginning to discover that normality for the middle class and the traditional working class was no longer normality for the emerging underclass in the ghettos and depressed urban enclaves. Poverty areas had always been part of the American urban scene, but social planners in the first half of the twentieth century had seen them largely as way stations on the path to economic integration (Park and Burgess [1925] 1967). If the poor sometimes got bogged down in slum pathologies, the Progressive reformers were ready to intervene more directly in their fate through settlement houses and social workers; but reformers recognized that these were only ways to facilitate entry into the only realistic path of integration, the labor force.

Since its inception, parole has been in the business of managing the risks of returning felony offenders to the community. Parole models survive not because they are effective in reducing parolee crime, but because they are coherent, because they jibe with pretheoretical understandings of the crime problem and avoid generating obvious anomalies. Effectiveness at reducing recidivism has always been part of coherence, but as researchers began to understand in the 1960s, recidivism itself was as nebulous and manipulable a concept as other, more apparently ideological elements of correctional programs.

There is no particular reason to believe that industrial parole worked very well in reducing crime. Placing parolees in jobs may have had no relationship to whether they committed crimes when they left work, or after they absconded completely from parole. Parole agents often found jobs for parolees and then lost track of them until they showed up in jail on new arrests. Malcolm Braly's first meeting with his parole officer after being released from San Quentin in the very early 1950s was cursory:

> My parole officer, a former cop, had no interest in me. I signed papers, received the balance of my release money, and was told, "Good luck."
> "Where should I live?" I asked.
> "Get yourself a room in a cheap hotel. You've got a job waiting. When you get paid you can look for something permanent. Look, you and I aren't going to be any trouble to each other if you remember just one thing, get your report in every month by the fifth." (1976, 201–2)

In short course Braly left the job he had been found, got himself another one, and never saw his parole agent again until after his arrest for a commercial burglary.

The defenders of parole in that era demonstrated its effectiveness using statistics that could not in any significant way distinguish between real successes and total failures. It is true that parole in those years was constantly being pilloried in the press based on the individual notorious case. Yet the model survived because its internal plausibility was so high. Its defenders had no problem articulating why the individual failure did not disprove the model, and the audience of those in a position to influence policy were persuaded for more than a half century.

The creation of a clinical model of parole represented one of the first institutional responses to the emergence of what we today call an "underclass." In the late 1950s and the 1960s, they were understood by policy makers as a class of people who could not be integrated by moving them into the labor force; indeed, they were considered a class who must be altered before they could be moved into the labor force.

This entailed a far more complicated task for social institutions responsible for normalizing the most troubled members of the poor. Where once parole could satisfy its aim by reinforcing the disciplinary capacity of the community, parole in the 1950s and 1960s attempted to develop a model of supervision that could operate independently of the community. If under the disciplinary model parole was like a back porch attached to the great house of the industrial community, under the clinical model parole more closely resembled a tent pitched on a swamp.

It is likely that correctional officials were some of the first social managers to become aware of the degree to which America was separating into two societies—the mainstream, a highly stratified work force which despite its heterogeneity of privileges would share in the general increase in American wealth through collective bargaining agreements, social insurance, credit, and pensions, and an underclass locked out of the economic expansion of the postwar era altogether.

By the middle of the 1960s this problem had become an object of considerable attention at the highest levels of government. Starting in the Johnson Administration the federal government began to promote actively the construction of a remedial structure to prevent the disintegration of life in the underclass. In 1968, as this "war on poverty" reached its peak of expenditure, the Kerner Commission wrote ominously of the costs of not spending even more:

> The rising concentration of impoverished Negroes and other minorities within urban ghettos will constantly expand public expenditures for welfare, law enforcement, unemployment and other existing programs without arresting the decay of older city neighborhoods and the breeding of frustration and discontent. ([1968] 1988, 398)

The growth of government service efforts in the late 1960s gave new life to parole supervision. The thin network of institutions created within the underclass communities provided some kind of structure to which supervision could attempt to attach the marginal individuals in its charge. While these new services fit with the clinical model's emphasis on helping the inmate adjust to the community without the labor market, there are significant differences. In this model, parole acts as only the first link in a new chain of agencies aimed at providing a basic structure for communities abandoned by the traditional structures of civil society.

The description of parole supervision in the 1964 manual seems to hint at a subtle turn away from the purely psychological model of clinical parole, fashioned in the 1950s, toward a broader social service perspective:

> Parole supervision is an integral part of the correctional process. It is by this means that the true purpose of parole is satisfied. Every effort is made to protect society from further transgressions on the part of the offender; while at the same time, attempts are made to assist the parolee in becoming [a] self-sustaining, law-abiding, and contributing member of society. Through the medium of supervision, agency staff is able to develop case information that is used in future evaluations and decisions as the parolee moves through the parole experience. The information gathered is frequently of great value to other agencies which may become involved from time to time in reaching decisions in reference to their particular interests. (sec. 7-00)

This vision continued to influence parole during the 1970s when a bold effort (described in the next chapter) was undertaken to reorganize parole on much more of a service delivery orientation.

The aspirations of the war on poverty were summarized in what the Kerner Commission called an "Enrichment Choice" to fill in the thin network of welfare structures with a massive reinvestment in the urban enclaves of the poor:

> The Enrichment Choice would aim at creating dramatic improvements in the quality of life in disadvantaged central-city neighborhoods—both white and Negro. It would require marked increases in federal spending for education, housing, employment, job training, and social services.

> The Enrichment Choice would seek to lift poor Negroes and whites above poverty status and thereby give them the capacity to enter the mainstream of American life. ([1968] 1988, 395–96)

The Commission understood that this proposal stood in contrast to the prevailing emphasis on integration because it focused on building up the poor communities rather than dispersing them. In a like manner the clinical model of corrections emphasized the idea of transforming the offender as a person in the hope that he would then be able to fit into the main organizing institutions of social life rather than directly integrating him into the community through labor force participation. Both the Kerner Commission's Enrichment Choice and the clinical model in corrections represented an effort to maintain the centrality of a common norm to life, so long embodied in labor, by building an alternative infrastructure of normalization. Neither approach turned out to be enduring.

Despite the importance welfare has played in modern American society, it has never succeeded in laying down a claim to normality. As Daniel Patrick Moynihan, no enemy of welfare, wrote in the late 1960s:

> The principal measure of progress toward equality will be that of employment. It is the primary source of individual or group identity. In America

what you do is what you are: to do nothing is to be nothing; to do little is to be little. The equations are implacable and blunt, and ruthlessly public. (Kerner Commission [1968] 1988, 252)

The viability of clinical parole decreased in the 1970s along with the welfare structure as a whole. Faced with an escalating crisis of public confidence, correctional managers once again thought to reformulate a credible model of what they do to provide security for society. Clinical parole had been a total failure in terms of creating a form of supervision truly based on interpersonal relations between agent and parolee apart from the community. Yet many of its elements—drug testing, special caseloads, short-term reconfinement—would remain fixtures of parole in the 1980s.

Like the clinical model, parole in the 1980s was faced with constructing a form of parole supervision capable of standing on its own with little or no external sources of stability. While clinical parole had built self-standing structures, it continued to tie its criteria of success and failure to recidivism. The parole model that began to emerge in the 1980s cast off this measuring rod in favor of a system that increasingly measured its own output in assessing its effects.

Where the law ends in parole there is space for discretion in which decisions about risk, security, and punishment must be made. Once this space was filled by the discipline of the labor market and the normative order of the community. Later the professional parole agent of the clinical model sought to build a body of expert knowledge to ground those choices. With these gone or going in the 1970s, parole faced a crisis in the rationality of its powers spurred by collapse of the very idea of normality.

PART TWO

From Normalization to Management

Parole supervision should not be treated as a generic type of state control, the unchanging significance of which can be read off from its founders' declarations. It is most usefully seen as a discontinuous series of power configurations involving both public and private actors.[1] These networks provide a more or less successful basis for maintaining knowledge and influence over the least reputable class of people in society, that is, released state prisoners.

A narrative of criminogenesis became vital to parole as soon as it ceased to be a pardoning mechanism in the business of releasing from prison people who should not have been there to begin with (Berecochea 1982, 131). As a surety of good conduct, parole had to have a narrative about what marked the return of the parolee to crime, an ethno-theory of good order and its decline. As has been emphasized, narratives consist of both practices and discourses.

From the middle of the nineteenth century to the Second World War, labor, especially industrial labor, provided the most attractive model of how to discipline criminals. It was more compatible with the predominant social and political institutions than competitors like military or religious models of discipline, and it was sufficiently available to offer hope of keeping pace with the burgeoning urban population.[2] Crime, a constant source of challenge to the sense of order, was readily imaginable in terms provided by the model of labor discipline. Since the sixteenth century it had been understood as an extreme

1. As Douglas Hay and Francis Snyder have recently argued with respect to the history of prosecution, "important continuities in organization can none the less accompany important changes in functional emphasis and hence social significance" (1990, 9).

2. It is far from the case that all or even most prisons or penal systems successfully modeled themselves on industrial discipline. Some remained organized around quite different forms of labor, as in the South where plantation-style agricultural labor was predominant. Industrial discipline, not surprisingly, became predominant in states with developed industrial economies.

form of moral decay resulting from idleness (Spierenburg 1991). While confinement offered the most potent tool for dealing with such individuals in the eighteenth and nineteenth centuries, the increasingly social discipline brought on by the factory system made it possible to imagine controlling such idleness in the community itself by the turn of the twentieth century.

The account of criminality must also provide a visible register on which the otherwise invisible process of criminality might be tracked. "Work history," as it is often called in correctional discourse, provided a comprehensive, if inexact, picture of criminal degeneration or its arrest. As it was applied in parole supervision, labor was not just a matter of hours worked, but of the norms of class-specific discipline. These norms gave parole agents a practical set of factors they could go after to stay on top of the exoffender. What are his working habits? Does he drink on the weeknights? Does he plan purchases wisely and save money from his paycheck?

Finally, labor discipline provided an implicit strategy of crime control. If crime arises from idleness and resistance to the discipline of labor, it can be controlled by making sure that those vulnerable remain coercively locked into the labor market.

After World War II the disciplinary model remained coherent but was rendered less reliable by the declining opportunity structure for low-skilled, urban, and minority labor. Parole's narrative of control began to shift toward a clinical model that could fill the gap opening between the ideal of industrial order and the condition of the communities from which offenders came.

Criminality, in this account, was not simply idleness, but a maladjustment between the individual and the institutions of the community. The arrested or malignant status of a parolee's criminality could not necessarily be determined from his status in the labor market, but instead had to be traced in the signs of psychological disturbance perceived through the communicative relationship between parole agent and parolee. Such degeneration could be halted by counseling and treatment which addressed the underlying pathologies that discouraged identification with conventional norms.

By the middle of the 1960s the disciplinary model needed more than gap-filling. The requirement that parolees have jobs went from being a plausible and inexpensive way to impose order on their lives to a burdensome task that exposed the incompleteness of control, undermined staff morale, and compelled a good measure of organizational duplicity.[3]

This was especially true for the fast-growing African-American portion of the prison population in the 1960s. The unemployment rate for all African-

3. Paul Takagi shows that verifying the acceptability of the prisoner's release program, a requirement for getting him out on parole, was one of the major sources of organizational tension during the 1960s. Many agents resolved it by making verifications that were well understood to be with one eye closed (1967, 61).

American men was 116 percent that of white men in 1940, jumped to 190 percent in 1950, and has remained around 200 percent through the 1980s. By 1980, before the Reagan Administration, it reached 225 percent.[4] In the meantime African-American men went from 11 percent of California prisoners in 1942 to 40 percent in 1980 (Langan 1991, 22, 38).

This might have made the clinical model more vital than ever. Indeed, in the course of the 1960s the Department and the Division experimented with some fairly dramatic efforts to create a genuine and effective clinical milieu. Still, from the perspective of the 1990s, it is clear that in its own way the clinical model of corrections was, like the disciplinary model, bound up with the existence of a labor market for unskilled labor and a culture of working-class virtues. Both accounts of control depend on a shared sensibility that the task of corrections was to return the offender to a condition of "normality," whether that be understood in industrial terms, like the venerable adjective "industrious," or in psychological terms like "well adjusted."[5] In this sense they follow the master correctional narrative of normalization which Foucault (1977), Garland (1985), and other revisionist historians of punishment have identified at the heart of modern punishment.

In addition to the social and economic developments that undermined the role of labor, community, and clinical practice, a series of important political and legal developments directly attacked the legitimacy of the clinical program in corrections. In the course of a decade between 1968 and 1978, courts found important due process restrictions on parole decision making, and many states, including California, restricted administrative power over prison release. These movements, although very different, nonetheless jointly undermined the status of normalizing parole by questioning the arrangements of power and knowledge that made it possible. Similar developments eroded the foundations of other social service enterprises including mental health, schools, welfare, and juvenile justice.[6]

The end of that normalizing program might logically have marked the end of parole. Indeed, in the late 1970s, during the legal and political dismantling of indeterminate sentencing and other normalizing enterprises like the mental hospital and the reform school, the total elimination of parole was considered.

Parole has survived, and in the 1980s grew to a larger and more expensive

4. Calculated from 1980 *Census of Population*, vol. 1, chapter D, part 6, table 214; 1970 *Census of Population*, vol. 1, chapter D, part 6, table 164; and 1960 *Census of Population*, vol. 1, part 6, table 53 (includes 1940 and 1950 data).

5. On the most abstract level it may be that the very notion of "the normal" is peculiarly linked to a highly mobile society undergoing rapid economic expansion. Once societies settle into stratifications that are seen as enduring or permanent, the idea of a common norm is as meaningless as the calculation of the mean for a multinomial variable.

6. On mental health, see Brown (1985); on welfare, see Katz (1989).

enterprise than at any previous time, but its survival has required changes in function, in organization, and in strategy. Faced on the one hand with a community far less capable of providing control and a meaningful set of normative distinctions upon which judgments can be made (such as working/not working, stable family/unstable family, lapse into reuse/readdiction), and on the other hand with greater demands for visibility and accountability, parole has turned inward.[7] Wherever possible parole now seeks to establish both structures of control and frameworks of evaluation that it can access without relying on the power or interpretive license of the community.

Since the mid-1970s parole has been reshaped along the lines of what might be called a "managerial model." The outlines of this model were already visible to Donald Cressey, one of the greatest scholars of modern punishment, in a 1959 article criticizing the then-ascendant clinical mode. Cressey argued that corrections in the 1950s had sought to follow the path of rationalization of other skilled service occupations like law, medicine, and engineering toward "professionalization" which involved most essentially "the development of specialized knowledge and an ethical code" (1959, 3).

Professionalization in corrections might follow three logical courses on Cressey's analysis. First, all correctional workers might be included in a new corrections profession. The problem with that approach was its assumption that all tasks in corrections could be linked to the same base of specialized knowledge and subjected to the same ethical norms (ibid.).

A second alternative, which Cressey saw as the dominant one at that time, aimed at increasing the significance of an existing profession within corrections, specifically social work. This alternative closely matches what we have called the clinical model of parole. Cressey argued that this approach wrongly assumed that all tasks within corrections could be brought within the social work base of knowledge and ethics (a variation of the first path) and that social work was itself a coherent profession (1959, 4). A good example of this was the 1959 parole manual discussed above in chapter three. It sought to link all parole action to a unified base of knowledge and ethics based on the social work ideal of individualized casework, but ended up providing little specific guidance to agents.

In addition to these dubious assumptions Cressey forecast organizational problems with professionalization along the lines of social work. By virtue of its commitment to a disease model a social-work-oriented corrections would emphasize the needs of the deviant individual. But this would make it vir-

7. Diana Gordon notes that the intensive supervision programs being touted as the "intermediate" punishment of the future redefine policy goals to make the system performance more central than social adjustment (1991, 119). The argument here is that such adjustment while always "elusive" has now become incoherent.

tually impossible for the decisions of individual correctional workers to be controlled by the center.

> Since the needs of individual clients are different, a precise system for administering treatment to clients cannot be specified by an agency chief. He cannot make a list of punishment-enforced administrative rules to be followed by the workers. (1959, 9)

Instead, the coordination of activity would depend on the development of a shared "professional theory and ideology." Even if such development took place Cressey foresaw that corrections on this model would clash with two essential external factors. First, corrections deals with criminals, and an ideology of client service so important to professions like social work might well appear perverse to the general view of crime in our culture. Second, correctional workers are government employees who must be accountable to politically set standards rather than those set by an autonomous association of professionals. As we shall see, both tendencies helped undermine the clinical model in parole.

Cressey's third alternative was a highly prescient forecasting of what is called the managerial model:

> This alternative would follow the broad trend toward professionalization of many specialties, including management, in American industry as a whole. In this instance most technical specialists in correction would be organized in special branches of existing professions rather than as members of "a correctional work profession." (1959, 4)

Cressey argued that the model of industrial management, rather than the professions, would allow a successful integration of knowledge and power in corrections. This would not depend on the difficult task of inventing new knowledge but of coordinating existing knowledge necessary to efficiently carry out the tasks of the correctional system whether that be custody, treatment, or simply administering.

The consequences Cressey foresaw for the organization of corrections fit closely with the operation of parole in the 1970s and 1980s in several respects. First, Cressey foresaw increasing separation between the knowledge of front-line workers, like guards and parole officers, and higher-level managers: "We do not expect an industrial manager to be trained in all the things factory employees do, we do not expect the factory's night watchman and its personnel supervisor to be members of the same profession" (1959, 6).

Second, Cressey foresaw that administrative skills were central to the practice of corrections and would become more so. The model of professionalization if accepted would doom these tasks to be performed by those primarily skilled in social work rather than management, and reward skilled social work professionals by placing them in administrative positions that did not utilize their professional skills.

Cressey was writing in a professional journal of the National Parole and Probation Association and was consequently more concerned with spelling out the implications of his analysis for practitioners rather than for its theoretical sociological significance. But his vision of how the correctional field might undergo further rationalization fits well with much more recent theoretical work in the sociology of law.

Wolf Heydebrand describes current rationalization in the court system as forming a "technocracy," which he defines as

> A system of social control based on scientific technical knowledge and instrumental rationality in decision making. It involves highly systematized and codified forms of knowledge ("science") and their systematic application in terms of technology, social engineering, information processing, decision making, and work procedures. (1979, 32)

In a recent book Heydebrand and Carroll Seron (1990) suggest that technocratic rationalization is distinct from both professionalization and bureaucraticization, although it includes elements of both. While both professions and bureaucracies center around social objectives which they purport to intensify, technocratic systems operate on the basis of goals internal to the specific organization.

Heydebrand and Seron (1990, 229) reject a global story of unidirectional rationalization; instead they suggest a dialectical model where organizations respond to external challenges by absorbing aspects of their structure. Thus, they suggest that courts as centers of professional power were challenged by new bureaucratic forms of rationalization at the turn of the century. But rather than abandoning professionalism they harnessed bureaucratic elements to advance their overall power (38). A similar framework seems to fit the genealogy of parole agencies, only in different order. Parole grew up with bureaucracy as its predominant mode of rationalization. This rationality fit well with the disciplinary model of control. Both emphasized the legitimating power of uniform and hierarchical regulation. While the rhetoric of professionalization was around throughout the era of industrial discipline, it was only when the disciplinary model began to falter in the 1950s that elements of professionalism really penetrated into the practices of parole.

Currently the drive toward technocratic rationalization in parole is fueled by the same processes that Heydebrand and Seron (202–6) detect in their analysis of courts. Both institutions are beset by the double challenge of a changing economic structure and a changing vision of how power should be exercised in a democracy. Heydebrand summarizes this combination as follows:

Pressures for efficiency, productivity, and rational control emanate not only from managers, experts, and technocrats, but also from cost-conscious and vote-conscious politicians as well as from counter-cultural, ecology-conscious or populist critics of bigness, waste, formalism, and irrationality. (1979, 52)

The next three chapters will describe in more detail the political and economic pressures on organizations which exercise the power to punish, and the development in response of a parole model that corresponds well with both Cressey's forecast for corrections, and Heydebrand and Seron's theory of technocracy. This "managerial model" involves a diminishing role for discretion and professional sovereignty, increased integration of production functions and functions that monitor performance, and a tendency to transform substantive evaluations (is he dangerous?) into formal procedures (is his drug test positive?).

CHAPTER FOUR

The Legal and Political Environment of Contemporary Parole

A newly hired San Francisco parole agent in the early 1950s would have found himself part of an operation with five agents and approximately two hundred parolees in the city. The nature of the job was well understood: the agent did his best to make sure that the parolee obtained and remained at approved employment and residence, leaned on the parolee whenever the occasion arose, and hoped the parolee did not do something illegal, at least not something that the newspapers would pick up.[1]

The agent might sense some ambiguity as to the vocabulary he should adopt in constructing a narrative of his actions and the parolee's behavior ("Am I chewing the SOB out for leaving his wife, or counseling him?"), but any significant interpretive slack was taken up by the powerful figure of the unit supervisor who dominated all the important pathways of visibility and control. Central administration could set out general policies, but functional decision-making power was in the hands of unit supervisors who presided over large territorially based domains.[2] The supervisor interpreted the significance of parolee behavior against a background shaped less by criminology or the substantive criminal law, than by the norms of class-specific discipline in industrial society.

Many of them were products of the urban working-class culture, with strong ties to industrial employers and unions and reputations out in the neighbor-

---

1. From the inception of parole, newspapers have found it a favorite target to blame for perceived increases in crime. The fact that the indeterminate sentence law often resulted in longer terms than offenders faced under earlier laws never undercut the basic indignation that newspapers (on behalf of their readership) expressed at the idea of a prisoner being allowed to leave prison before their maximum allowable term.

2. In the mid-1960s the creation of a regional administrative structure over the units allowed the leadership to intensify its oversight. After that supervisors lost some, but not all, power to set the policies for their unit through their reputations and characters.

hoods where the poor lived among the working classes.[3] A regional staff member who was an agent in the 1950s remembers the supervisors of that era as "benevolent despots" who found jobs for parolees but expected paternalistic deference: "They might find you a shitty low-paying hard job and threaten to lock you up if you started showing up late for it. Then they'd expect you to thank them for it every time they saw you."

There were holes in the system, of course. Parolees left their work or their wives without permission. Sometimes the agent's efforts to browbeat the parolee, drive him to job interviews, or threaten to take away his driving license failed. Lots of deviation was certainly ignored. When an agent decided to get tough he could place the parolee in jail for a weekend as a warning. As a last resort, the parolee could be returned to prison, usually for having been convicted of a new crime. From the end of World War II through the 1960s this recourse was used in only 10 to 20 percent of all cases (Messinger et al. 1988, chart 5).

An agent starting in San Francisco in 1992 would find five active units consisting of some fifty agents presided over in person by five supervisors and a district administrator. This parole complex is responsible for supervising approximately three thousand parolees in the city. There are no clear parameters for how to do the job. That does not mean there are no clear objectives or obligatory routines. Agents must get reports done on time and meet the minimum specifications for contacts with their parolees. These expectations offer a guide for how to stay busy but do not really permit a sense of control over the task, let alone the parolee.

There is less dispute today over the right vocabulary to use because no vocabulary claims very much. Rather than there being a surfeit of explanatory words, there is a lack. Increasingly, the job does not require much language since checklists and boilerplate language suffice. Interpretive validity does not reside in a powerful charismatic boss, but in a complex set of procedures and routines.

Employment and family stability remain vital concepts, but they play a greatly diminished role in mediating the exercise of power over parolees, so the flow of relevant input from the community has been reduced to drug use and crime. When the agent seeks to respond within this narrowed universe of possibility, there is little sanctioning power available except for returning the parolee to prison and initiating formal revocation charges.

Indeed, imprisonment is a readier response than ever. In the past, revocation of parole usually followed conviction for a new crime. Only a small minor-

3. For an analysis of how changing urban morphology affects working class culture and politics see Hobsbawm (1989).

ity of parolees revoked in 1988 were convicted of a new crime by the court
system. Returns to prison, mostly taken at the initiative of parole supervision
staff, have been climbing steadily since 1977 (more on these in chapter
seven).

The transformation of parole supervision has been driven by changes in
scale and in the social and economic circumstances of parole. It has also come
from the legal context in which parole's power to punish must be exercised.
That context in California remained much the same from World War I to the
1970s. The essential elements were an Indeterminate Sentence Law (ISL,
adopted in 1917 and amended frequently; see below) which provided broad
administrative discretion over how long convicts spent in prison, a nearly
complete absence of review by courts or any other independent agency of decisions to release or revoke parole, and an organizational structure that permitted most power over parolees to be exercised by local parole supervisors
without significant interference from statewide parole authorities.

This context permitted a parole strategy directed from the local level and
attuned to the mosaic of local social control networks such as local law enforcement and employers, families, and neighbors of parolees. These local
sources of social control, not legal process regulations, were the primary external check on the application of a broad power to punish.[4] The parole agent,
subject to the powerful local supervisors, wielded the power to return parolees
to prison for violating conditions of parole that covered virtually every aspect
of adult life. It is not that the central administration had no interests. It clearly
was concerned with the crowding of prisons and with publicity about crime
(considerations that cut both ways in revocation policies). What the administration lacked were structures capable of overseeing those interests at the local level.

Starting with the creation of California's Department of Corrections in
1944, a number of efforts have been made to create greater bureaucratic control in parole.[5] One important strategy of centralization was a growing research program which placed local practice under the scrutiny of centrally set
experimental protocols. Another was the parole agent manual which contained a full statement of administrative policy on a vast range of practical

4. "Check" implies a concern with overuse, but in many respects the primary problem in parole and
other social control systems is the invocation, rather than the limitation of, the exercise of power. The
emphasis on limiting an otherwise expansive power has dominated much of legal thinking on discretion (see Davis 1969). A more sociological perspective gives equal attention to problems of invoking
and limiting power.

5. During the 1944 reorganization of California corrections the parole supervision function was
placed under the administrative control of the Adult Authority (the parole releasing agency). In 1957
parole was transferred to the agency responsible for administering California's adult prison and work
camps, the California Department of Corrections, and became known as the Parole Division (or just
the Division).

judgments that a parole agent was likely to be called on to make. In 1964, under the administration of Chief Parole Officer Milton Burdman, a regional administration structure was set up which placed independent regional administrators over the local units.

These changes were limited in their ability to penetrate the world of local parole decisions. The experimental programs did not go very far in setting specific demands on parole action. The manual consisted largely of philosophy rather than precise expectations. The regional structure helped remove some bottlenecks in the review of local actions deemed problematic, but the identification of an action as problematic still relied too often on the happenstance of publicity. Neither the regional structure nor any of the internally based rationalizing efforts in the 1950s and 1960s closed the vitally important information and control gap between administrator and parole actions. Central policy initiatives still had to be mediated through local supervisors. For more direct control to develop, the very nature of parole practice on the micro-level would have to be transformed.

Starting in the 1970s, pressure to regulate and routinize parole practice at the micro-level accelerated dramatically from political/legal centers outside corrections.[6] Parole was far from the only public institution to come under heavy criticism during the 1960s and 1970s. Just about every institution that exercised power over citizens, whether for their own interests, or for those of the public, became the subject of intensive pressures for reform. Parole, however, was uniquely situated to catch the full range of dissatisfactions.

The major reform initiatives to hit parole during this period include the following.

1. In the 1972 case of *Morrissey v. Brewer*,[7] the Supreme Court held that due process protections applied to parole and probation revocation hearings. While leaving the substantive power of parole intact, due process reforms encouraged the establishment of centralized controls over local practices including arrest, detention, and decisions to revoke, rescind, or grant parole.

2. In 1977 California adopted a new sentencing statute, the Determinate Sentence Law (DSL) which eliminated discretionary parole release for all but those sentenced to life in prison for murder. All other felons are sentenced by a judge at the point of conviction to a specific term derived from a presumptive range set by a legislatively created menu of offenses and circumstances. Once fixed, the sentences are lessened only by the operation of statutorily created "good time" credits.

6. All of these developments involve reworking of the rules through which power is exercised in parole: some originated in courts, others in the legislature or in the administration. Most developments involved all three. Each is so clearly an act of both politics and law that it does not pay to differentiate.

7. 408 U.S. 471 (1972).

The new law was perceived by all observers as deeply hostile to the philosophy which had guided parole in California for a quarter century or more. It explicitly rejected the relevance of rehabilitation and declared the purpose of imprisonment to be punishment. Uniformity replaced individualization as the watch word for penal decision making. Parole supervision was not formally included in these sweeping changes, but few inside or outside parole failed to read them as a warning for parole to adopt itself to new standards of regularity and accountability in the exercise of penal power.

3. To shore up what they perceived as weak public support, parole managers initiated an administrative reform program of their own dubbed the "New Model." The approach was strongly influenced by "operations research" approaches which had become increasingly influential in public administration since the 1960s. The New Model broke parole supervision down into its functional components and sought to reassemble them as an integrated system. The resulting approach, with its emphasis on setting specific procedural standards and then auditing the results, fit well with the accountability and uniformity values expressed by *Morrissey* and the determinate sentence law.

In this chapter we will explore the effects of these changes in the political and legal demands made on the exercise of the power to punish during the 1970s. In aggregate they permanently raised the cost of that power and are relevant to explaining the impasse in corrections today, but, of course, not in a vacuum. The reader should keep in mind that these institutional reforms were taking place at the same time as important changes in the social environment of parole that will be explored more fully in the next chapter.

Parole and Due Process

Between 1972 and 1975, federal and state courts imposed an array of procedures on a postconviction criminal process which had historically been a zone of unreviewable discretion. While the Supreme Court had begun to review procedural justice by the states starting in the 1930s, they concentrated on errors and abuses of the arrest and trial process. Even during the 1960s when the Court created bold, bright line rules for police and provision of legal counsel,[8] they maintained a "hands off" rule with regard to what happened after punishment began.

Starting in 1972 this hands-off doctrine disappeared as the Court struck down the death penalty as practiced in the states and began to review prison

8. See Mapp v. Ohio, 367 U.S. 643 (1961) (requiring the exclusion of evidence collected by the government in a manner which violates the Fourth Amendment from use in the prosecution's case-in-chief); Gideon v. Wainwright, 372 U.S. 335 (1963) (establishing a right to counsel for all criminal defendants facing felony charges).

conditions and the procedures for changing conditions of prisoners (such as parole release). While a continuation of the criminal procedure revolution, the Court's new approach might also be seen as part of its growing concern with dependent and vulnerable populations. [9]

Parole was a natural target for due process. Few other administrative processes exercised such massive power over the lives of people possessed of citizenship (qualified, of course, by their status as felons). Indeterminate sentence laws, in place by the First World War in many states, empowered administrative agencies (usually known as parole boards) to determine the length of punishment within wide boundaries. Parole release was strictly conditional, and the boards could revoke parole for good cause with little opportunity for the parolee to participate in or challenge the proceeding.

This power was justified by the expertise the parole authorities possessed by legislative decree. Under the theory of indeterminate sentencing the time of release was set by the board after an individualized evaluation of the prisoner's social and psychological condition and the likelihood of criminal conduct if returned to the community. Paroled felons remained vulnerable to parole revocation and return to prison if they violated the "conditions" of parole, long lists of requirements which left individual agents broad interpretive power. [10] This placed the parolee in a most precarious position. Practically any private citizen with a grievance against the parolee, and the ear of the agent, could potentially bring down the full force of incarceration.

Hans von Hentig, Director of the Colorado Crime Survey, described the vulnerabilities as seen by the parolee in a 1942 issue of the *Journal of Criminal Law and Criminology:*

> The prisoner thinks that in general the release practice cannot be complained of very much, but that our return methods spoil everything. The more formally wrong he is, the more he is embittered, and the more he feels trapped between the clear words of the written parole agreement and the enormous disproportion of cause and effect when he happens to violate one of the parole conditions. This conflict of formal right and factual wrong works day and night on his mind and renders the returned parole violator a peculiarly society-made problem. (369)

Indeed, until the United States Supreme Court acted in *Morrissey v. Brewer* courts found no basis in either state or federal constitutions, or state law, to

---

9. The Supreme Court's decision in Goldberg v. Kelly, 397 U.S. 254 (1970), finding a due process right to a hearing prior to the termination of welfare benefits, is often considered the first important precedent in this wave of heightened standards for administrative action affecting dependent populations.

10. In fact parolees generally learned from their parole agent just what the real operative ground rules were. While the ground rules may have been more or less consistent, they could be easily bent to deal with new pressures on the parole supervision staff (see Takagi 1967).

require *any* particular procedures for either parole release or revocation.[11] California and many other states provided hearings, but these were largely ceremonial, taking place months after the parolee had been reimprisoned and generally ratifying the earlier decision to recommend revocation taken by the local parole supervision unit. They were considered a matter of grace or sound policy and not a right to be expanded by the courts.

The predominant legal theory was that of constructive imprisonment. In California the courts ruled that parole, being a continuation of a period of imprisonment imposed lawfully, required no independent adversary process for denying, rescinding, or revoking parole:

> The notice of a hearing was given and required to be given in the proceedings which resulted in the original conviction and the imposition of a sentence that was indeterminate, and until fixed, amounted to a maximum sentence provided for the crime in question. When the [Adult] Authority reduces a maximum sentence, its action, in the very nature of things, is tentative and may be changed for cause.[12]

In 1972 the Supreme Court decided in *Morrissey* that the revocation of probation on parole without a hearing and a meaningful opportunity to contest the violation charges offended the Fourteenth Amendment's due process clause. Chief Justice Burger wrote for the Court that constitutional due process required parole revocation procedures to include written notice of violations, discovery of evidence, the right to confront and cross-examine adverse witnesses, a preponderance of the evidence standard of guilt to be determined by a "neutral and detached" hearing body, and written statement of the evidence relied on and reasons for the revocation.[13] One year later in *Gagnon v. Scarpelli*[14] the Court found a limited right to counsel where the factual or legal issues in the case were unusually complicated or the parolee or probationer was particularly incapacitated.

In both cases the Supreme Court adopted a moderate tone, stopping far short of calling the rehabilitative ideal or the competence of administrative decision makers into question. Yet the hooks on which it hung a right to adversary procedures poked two deep holes in the legal ideology of parole. First, it acknowledged that the parolee had a legally protected interest in remaining out of custody, notwithstanding the validity of his conviction. Second, and

11. *In re McLain*, 55 Cal. 2d 78, 87 (1960); *In re Schoengarth*, 66 Cal. 2d 294, 304 (1967); *People v. St. Martin*, 1 Cal. 3d 524, 538 (1970); *In re Gomez*, 64 Cal. 2d 591 (1966).

12. *In re McLain*, 55 Cal. 2d 78, 85 (1960).

13. At 489. As Judge Burger of the District of Columbia Circuit, the Chief Justice had, almost a decade earlier, upheld the absence of parole revocation procedures in a classic and influential statement of the old jurisprudence. See *Hyser v. Reed*, 318 F.2d 225, 237 (1963).

14. 411 U.S. 778, 790 (1973).

more damaging, the Court questioned what interest was served by the absence of adversarial procedures.

The Court reasoned that, just as in a criminal trial, the state's legitimate interests could only be advanced by a process that clarified the actual truth of the matter. The criminal process analogy had been articulated as early as von Hentig's 1942 article, and by Sanford Kadish's influential 1961 article, "The Advocate and the Expert-Counsel in the Peno-Correctional Process." The *Morrissey* package, as developed in later decisions, stopped far short of the trial ideal. The hearing was to be a pragmatic one aimed at enhancing the production of truth, but not of honoring the ritual innocence of the accused: no rules of evidence, no high burden of proof, and most importantly, no lawyer for most of those accused.

Looking simply at the outcomes of formal revocation proceedings the development of due process appears to have done rather little. In California the rate at which the parole revocation recommendations are denied has gone from 30 or 40 percent before *Morrissey* to less than 5 percent today (Star, Berecochea, and Petrocchi 1978; California Department of Corrections 1988). Such outcomes, of course, are driven by multiple causes. The system eliminates legally problematic cases prior to the hearing stage more readily. The stream of alleged violations that moves through these improved procedures is not the same (see chapter seven). The determinate sentence law (discussed below) has reduced the stakes limiting the absolute length of revocation terms. Still, in practical terms the *Morrissey* rights, at least without counsel to support them, appear to have done little to improve the parolee's chances of fighting revocation successfully.

The more significant institutional effects of due process, however, lie in the fundamentally changed role of the parole staff in the revocation process. Formerly the hearing had just included a presentation before the Adult Authority, often some months after the parolee had already returned from the community. Now the parolee, and the agent, would both be expected to participate. While before, the agent was present only in a cryptic written recommendation and summary of the parolee's failures on parole, now the agent must be there and answer specific questions from the hearing officers and from the parolee as to his actions and decisions.

The most important effect of these procedures was not on the balance of legal power between parolee and agent but on the distribution and circuitry of power within the parole agency. The hearing rights created by *Morrissey* required a major administrative effort where there had been little before. Under the old system, when the agent and the local supervisor determined that the parolee had violated one of a number of specific provisions established by the Adult Authority requiring a revocation report, or simply that he was a danger to the community, they initiated revocation. If the parolee was not already in custody, a warrant was put out, and he was returned to prison. The agent would file a report signed by the supervisor with the parole board, and let them decide how long he should remain there.

Now under *Morrissey* the parole agency had to notify parolees of the charges and their rights, evaluate any application for counsel, and arrange for a reasonably prompt hearing with witnesses. Just as importantly, it had to do each step in a way that was traceable should it be called to account in judicial review.

In California these effects played out in the following ways.

1. *Morrissey* mandated a focus on visibility and accountability long central to lawyers and legal thinking but an altogether new kind of concern for correctional professionals. Until *Morrissey* the California Department of Corrections had no lawyers of its own, and no lawyer in the attorney general's office specialized in corrections. Correctional officials had little exposure to, or interest in, the peculiar reflexivity required by due process. Most of them had learned the business in an age where keeping the lid on the prison population and keeping parolees off the front pages were the prime concerns. In short, they were used to worrying about the substance, not the formal regularity, of their decisions.

2. The *Morrissey* rights also required the development of new operating procedures to get the work done. Each right translated into a series of new responsibilities for the staff to take on that had to be set into the ongoing business. It was, in effect, a problem of industrial design not unlike that faced by a factory which must incorporate new safety or antipollution procedures into its production process.[15] If a parolee were to receive notice of the reasons for a parole hold, someone had to go to jail and present him with a copy of the report. More importantly, the system had to make sure it happened every time, not just when parole agents found time to get to jail. To this end the Department set up a new staff of hearing agents working out of regional administration headquarters and responsible for arranging notice and all aspects of the hearing.

The hearing agents are responsible for reviewing the report and discussing the charges with the parolee. They also work with the parole board in deciding whether a revocation is reasonable and in making an initial screening offer to the parolee.[16] Formally, hearing agents are charged with facilitating the pre-

15. The Department of Corrections hired the man who had set up the welfare department's response to *Goldberg v. Kelly*, 397 U.S. 254 (1970).

16. A screening offer is a proposed revocation term which the parolee will receive if he agrees, in effect, to plead guilty to the charges without benefit of a hearing. The terms are generally considered to be shorter than a sentence likely to be handed down after a hearing. A large majority of revocation charges are settled in this way.

sentation of the parole case, but practically, they exert pressure on units to screen their own revocation choices against charges that appear too trivial or difficult to prove.[17]

3. Perhaps the most significant organizational effects are those which reduce the room for maneuver of those most involved in case decision making—the agents and their unit supervisors. *Morrissey* required not only an adversarial hearing but a timely one. The language of *Morrissey* actually suggests two separate hearings: review of whether there is probable cause to hold the parolee in custody, and an eventual hearing on the merits of the violation. Both are required to be carried out by a body independent of the parole supervision staff. Since 1977 California has provided only a single hearing to take place within forty-five days. That time limit, set in the Board's administrative regulations, has been viewed as a guideline by the Department rather than as establishing a personal right of the parolee.

Parolees and their legal advocates have argued that the current practice of a unitary hearing violates the right both to a pre-revocation hearing and to a timely revocation hearing.[18] The Parole Division contends that two hearings in the community are simply not feasible given the current crowded conditions of county jails. Further, they have contended that parolees seeking habeas relief must show prejudice from delay.[19]

17. The hearing agent position is also considered a significant pathway to promotion. It is an opportunity to demonstrate management potential because it requires coordination of numerous processes and individuals. Through the normal requirements of the job, the hearing agent contacts and considers the situation of the local units, the local prisons which absorb revocations, and the parole board. The nature of the position encourages a conception of the agency quite different from that developed by the classic line of advancement from field agent to supervisor and beyond. In a system where all administrators were once supervisors, leadership starts with a local orientation and then adds an awareness of the problems of the system. In contrast, the hearing agent is trained from the start to be attentive to the needs of parole as an integrated system.

18. Litigation has also involved the closely related problem of whether the hearing must be held in the community. *Morrissey* specifically requires a hearing proximate to the location of the alleged violation so that evidence and witnesses can be easily obtained. If parolees could still be held in county jails indefinitely (as was once the case) this would not be a problem. Chronic overcrowding and court orders against it in county jails have severely curtailed state use of these facilities. In San Francisco and Oakland the limit is three days before the jail will automatically release parolees unless they are picked up and transported to a state facility. This has produced a major logistical problem, one that would be doubled if the state brought every parolee back to the county for their hearing. Thus far they have balked at doing that. The Board's policy is that the hearing may take place at a state prison so long as it is within fifty miles of the location of the alleged violation.

19. Two California Superior Courts have ruled for the parolees. In *In re Pittman*, San Bernardino Superior Court Judge Rouse ruled that prejudice was not an issue where the Department had failed to act in "good faith" in complying with *Morrissey* since the average delay from the time of the parole hold to the filing of the habeas petition was seventy-eight days, which the court took be violated under any conditions. In *In re Cooperwood*, Solano County Judge Ely ruled that where a hearing is not held for sixty to ninety days after the hold is placed, prejudice can be presumed. The court went on to set a limit

In the view of many managers the ironic result of the timeliness right is a rush to press forward with a full revocation.

> One of the reasons the revocation rate is so high is that the courts have criticized parole for taking too long. The period between hold and filing of charges has gone from 13 to 4 days. We are taking away the discretion of the agent to find alternative dispositions.[20]

The short time allowed them encourages agents to invoke the revocation process rather than risk that an alternative program in the community cannot be set up quickly enough.

> The bottom line is that keeping people in the street takes more work than writing Board reports. Most parole agents aren't willing to do that kind of work. . . . Currently if a person is placed in custody by the police he stays there. The agent on duty just automatically approves holds when the phone call comes. To the agent the process is then set: leave the hold on, get a police report, write a violation report, send him back. What we need is some investigation.

Lawyers for accused parole violators vigorously contest that reasoning. They point out that the time limits run only so long as the custody hold is on. If the agent and supervisor believe that an alternative to revocation can be found, they have the power to lift the hold and release the parolee to the community without losing their ability to file for revocation and rearrest.

Dropping a hold is currently unimaginable to many parole agents and supervisors who feel that if they cannot guarantee control over parolees in the

---

for thirty days in the case of a unitary hearing. No statewide decision has yet been handed down.

Even under the forty-five-day standard set by the Board, the initial decision at the unit level to submit a report to the Board must be made very quickly. To ensure time for coordinating the hearing, the Division's internal rules require a revocation report to be sent to the hearing officers within thirteen days. This means that the parole agent must determine his recommendation within four or five days to permit the supervisor time to review the matter. The thirty-day limit for a unitary hearing, which is now in effect in several counties as a result of *Pittman* and *Cooperwood*, would squeeze that period significantly.

See *In re Cooperwood, et al.*, Super. Ct. Solano County, no. 19907 (1986); *In re Pittman, et al.*, Super. Ct. San Bernardino County, WHC No. 03 (1987). Judge Ely's thirty-day limit may be considered dicta since the actual relief was release of the prisoners who had been held past the limit. The statewide law is in doubt because neither side has appealed. In a recent case in Marin County, *In re Clark*, the Superior Court judge found for the state, and the plaintiffs did not appeal. It was clear to one of the attorneys representing the plaintiffs in the Marin County case that the Department had improved its performance significantly in response to the *Pittman* and *Cooperwood* cases, thereby making appeal less promising.

20. Unless otherwise noted all quotations from parole staff are from interviews conducted by the author.

community, they have no business keeping them there.[21] Many parole managers who can see the effect this is having on the prison population would like to reverse this, but doing so is difficult in the context of a parole model that offers little instruction for how to maintain dangerous people in the community.[22]

4. Revocation is attractive because it has been so intensively routinized. The pressure of complying with timeliness and the other rights has made the revocation procedure, from the agent on up, the most attended-to aspect of parole. In no other action is the individual parole agent more subject to close review of her technical performance, and in no other action is the system more set up to define and enforce good performance.

Although it may take only a few words on a violation report to continue a parolee on parole despite a violation, it is far more difficult to construct a "program" that promises to reduce the risk of leaving the parolee in the community. In practical terms that means a residential drug treatment program, job training, or something more than a hope that the parolee will not get involved in crime. It also means construction of a narrative about what the parolee is doing and why the intervention will make a difference.

In contrast the revocation guarantees that the parolee will be secured during the time of incarceration and doesn't require any more in the way of explanation than a detailing of the facts supporting the violation. Indeed, many agents view the hearing with relief as a means to transfer the burdensome power to decide among public safety, the parolee's freedom, and the Department's overcrowded prisons. In fact, the Board revokes parole in 95 to 98 percent of the cases before it (California Department of Corrections 1988, 25).

Due process was intended to advance the level of rationality in parole decisions by requiring higher standards. But it is formal, rather than substantive, rationality that has followed. Indeed, as the conditions in the community that permitted a kind of substantive rationality in parole decisions have eroded, parole has found itself more and more dependent on the formal structure of rationality which due process requirements have compelled them to formulate.

21. Since release from prison is no longer a matter of discretion in California (more on this below), parole staff do not feel they must or can assume control in the community. But once a parolee comes to their attention for conduct in violation of the law or parole rules, the staff feel responsible for any subsequent decision to keep him in the community.

22. With little real programming or private employment with which to respond, the only plausible alternative is an increase in surveillance to meet the increased risk indicated by minor violation behavior. But that would require a dramatic increase in the already rapidly growing parole agent staff. Even then the claim of control is dubious. Doubling the contacts per month of even a high control agent would still amount to little more than one fifteen-minute contact per week. Working out a program in the community takes time, resources, and creative initiative.

Parole and Sentencing Law

While parole had been possible in California since 1893, and accounted for nearly half of all releases by 1917 (Messinger 1969, 44), the power to establish the length of custody (time in prison and on parole) remained a function largely of the trial courts. The indeterminate sentence law adopted in 1917 by California shifted authority to set the complete sentence (prison and parole) within wide statutory minimums and maximums. Through a variety of amendments that law governed California imprisonment for a half century.

The theory of indeterminate sentencing in California, and in much of the nation, was that an administrative determination of when to release the offender was to be based upon an expert determination that rehabilitation of the offender had been effected (Rhine, Smith, and Jackson 1991, 24).[23] To this end, the administrative decision maker could consider virtually any evidence about the offender's life, criminal record, and prison experience.[24] The courts interpreted the indeterminate sentence law as requiring only that the administrative decision maker act with cause in deciding whether to release a prisoner on parole or return him to prison on a revocation.

The tendency of the law was to move toward maximum administrative discretion over both the full length of custody and when in that period the offender should be released on parole. While California was not the first to adopt indeterminate sentencing, by the 1940s it had taken indeterminacy as far as any other state (Messinger and Johnson 1980, 952).[25] Not only did California's law give the administrative decision maker maximum flexibility in these choices, but after 1931 it also gave them full powers to reconsider. A prisoner with a term set by the Board could have the order rescinded for misconduct (or any other good cause) before ever being released. More typically

23. *In re Lee*, 177 Cal. 690 (1918). This was true of parole supervision as well as initial release (Robison et al. 1971).

24. This power was vested in several different bodies over the course of indeterminate sentencing in California. Terms and releases were set by the Board of Prison Directors from 1917 to 1931, the Board of Prison Terms and Paroles from 1931 to 1944, and the Adult Authority from 1944 until indeterminate sentencing was abolished for most offenders in 1977. After that the power to release life offenders was exercised by a body known as the Community Release Board and after 1979 as the Board of Prison Terms. Other bodies have had similar authority over juveniles, women, and narcotics addicts. For a comprehensive discussion up to 1968, see Messinger (1969).

25. Initially the law permitted the administrative decision maker to set the total length of time most offenders would serve under legal custody (both in prison and once released on parole) after they had served a judicially set minimum sentence. In 1921 an amendment gave the Board discretion to set the sentence after a year. This was adjusted to six months in 1931. Many felonies, such as murder, rape, robbery, and burglary, had a maximum sentence of life which gave the administrative decision maker the widest imaginable powers to determine both custody and imprisonment (Messinger and Johnson 1980, 954). For a full discussion of these legal changes see Messinger (1969, 40–48) and California Penal Code, sec. 213 (West 1972).

changes took place after revocation of parole. The Board (or Adult Authority as the California parole board was called after 1944) could reset the term to the maximum and delay fixing a new parole date and term for a year or two (Conrad 1975).[26] Thus, in the most extreme cases, a parolee within months of completing the term initially set could have their parole revoked and begin what was in effect a new term of life imprisonment. All of these decisions were made by the same administrative decision maker with no right to notice, hearing, or counsel, and no requirement of proof that a new crime had been committed.[27]

The theory of indeterminate sentencing as developed by penologists and reform-minded prison managers involved three assumptions. First, that the response to crime should be individualized as much as possible to the specific qualities of the criminal. Second, that since the purpose of correctional custody was rehabilitation, the length of that custody should be responsive to the actual success of custodial treatment. Third, that supervised release into the community was an essential feature of rehabilitation and an essential safeguard of the public. California's indeterminate sentence law appears to have embodied all three of these assumptions (Messinger 1969, chapter 2). But in fact the law itself provided no guidelines for parole release decisions, or for revocations and recisions. The intent of the law, as interpreted by the California courts, was seen as permitting release upon evidence of rehabilitation. No statutory language or judicial gloss defined this state or how it was to be determined,[28] save that the actions of the Board be for "cause," that is, that it be rational.[29]

From the start both public and elite opinion have been skeptical about all of these assumptions. Examination of the practice of penal decision makers under the indeterminate sentence law suggests that even the nonskeptical would have trouble believing the project was being effectively realized. Even in the states most committed to penological ideals, parole board hearings were always extremely brief affairs, lasting no more than five to ten minutes, in some states only two or three (Rothman 1980, 165). The concerns raised by parole board members to the inmates resonated with rehabilitative themes, but they provided no clue as to what, if any, systematic standards for rehabilitation were applied (Rothman 1980, 165–75).

This is not the place for a more sustained discussion of the indeterminate

26. After 1941 no notice or hearing was required for inmates or parolees although a presumption of good cause remained (Messinger 1969, 65).

27. The power of the administrative decision makers was made complete by a series of court decisions which gave the Board virtually total discretion to grant good-time credits which had previously automatically been deducted from the maximum sentence for set periods of good conduct (Messinger 1969, 50). They already had the power to take them away after 1889 (38). While credits continued to be granted they operated (and were viewed as operating) solely to extend the discretion of the Board.

28. *In re Lee*, 177 Cal. 690 (1918).

29. California Penal Code, sec. 3063 (West 1972).

sentence law in practice or theory. What is critical from our perspective is understanding how its operation affected the control of parolees in the community. How, if at all, did it change the way power was exercised?

The first thing to note is that tendency of the law's development to increase the salience of parole control. Sheldon Messinger argues that changes in the California indeterminate sentence law from the time of its adoption in 1917 reflected "the growing concern of the prison directors with the control of parolees, as well as 'prisoners' in the older and narrower sense" (1969, 47). Their concern is understandable. The extent of their public responsibility for controlling the parolee was now extendable practically indefinitely. Pressure to extend through earlier release dates was doubtless a constant force emanating from those responsible for managing the prison population. The dilemma, of course, was how to do it in a way that made control in the community effective or at least plausible.

By maximizing administrative discretion the indeterminate sentence law had brought a fundamental tension into penal administration. The managers of prisons were principally concerned with preventing escapes and riots, and thus with inmate morale. Those making the decision to release on parole were fundamentally concerned with maintaining security in the community. This conflict moved into active status with the division of this authority and responsibility into three major fragments in 1931: power over the prisons, power over paroles, and power to release onto and to revoke parole (Messinger 1969, 56).

Messinger has traced the fascinating struggle for power between these bodies up to 1968 (1969, chapter 2). Suffice it to say here that this dynamic influenced the exercise of power in parole in several ways. First, it clearly resulted in a somewhat smaller and more selective stream of releases from prison than would have been the case had prison population pressures not been counterbalanced.[30] Second, it raised the importance of coherence in the overall parole model. The releasing agency seems to have worried extensively about its public face. This meant putting public safety first (1969, 62). Third, the releasing agency had far more incentive than the managers of operations (parole and prison) to develop an account of parole that fit ideologically even if it did not map onto the practical tasks of parole very well. That is, whatever model of parole was dominant, the release authority could be expected to demand the most conformity to it.

From the late 1960s on, the indeterminate sentence came under both political and legal attack (Mitford 1971; Zimring 1983). One legal ground for attacking

30. That would be true even if the two functions remained formally in the same agency. Messinger points to the tensions of release delays during the early years of the Great Depression as evidence of this during a period when the boards were still essentially the same (1969, 62). The development of practical separation intensified it.

indeterminacy was the due process clause of the Fourteenth Amendment. Some judges argued that a prisoner's or parolee's interest in being free was too significant to allow him to be stripped of an opportunity to challenge the basis and support for that decision.[31] Following *Morrissey* this view became predominant, but the courts using due process stopped well short of dismantling the entire structure of indeterminate sentencing, parole release, or much of the revocation and recision power. While the Court created procedural standards for the latter they never attempted to regulate its substantive standards under a due process theory.[32]

The California Supreme Court went a good deal farther in dismantling the indeterminate sentence under the Eighth Amendment's prohibition against "cruel and unusual punishment" in *In re Rodriguez* (1975).[33] While declining to "consider the wisdom of the Indeterminate Sentence philosophy," Chief Justice Wright required that the Adult Authority administer functionally determinate sentences by setting terms on the basis of crime severity and doing so soon after first arrival at prison.

In fact, the release agency in the early 1970s was implementing administrative reform along the same lines, a process that became more rapid when Raymond Procunier took over as head of the Adult Authority early in 1975 (Messinger and Johnson 1980, 959). During Procunier's earlier tenure as director of the California Department of Corrections he had come to view the indeterminate sentence as irrational, from an organizational, rather than a constitutional, perspective. Waiting to set a presumptive term until a year or more into the prisoner's stay made population planning in the Department of Corrections far more difficult. Keeping prisoners guessing about when they were going to get out was unfair and caused resentment. Moreover, while director, Procunier had experienced frustration at the release authority's willingness to hold prisoners longer out of fear of the political reaction against crime.[34]

Both the constitutional and administrative reforms rejected at least two of the three assumptions underlying the indeterminate sentence system. They rejected the idea of maximum individualization, and they rejected the link between performance in prison and the earliness of release. The third assumption, that some period of parole was vital and that it should be as early as possible, was not explicitly attacked by either of these programs. Under the administrative reform model, the releasing agency should stop operating as if

31. *In re Tucker*, 5 Cal. 3d 171, at 209 (1971), Peters, J., dissenting: "So great a curtailment of freedom cannot be swept aside on the theory that the prisoner, while on parole, is subject to restraints and thus has no freedom to lose. Although in the search for simplicity and order there is room in the law for some fictions, this fiction is so divorced from reality that it cannot be tolerated by any fair minded man."

32. *Greenholtz v. Inmates of Nebraska Penal and Correctional Complex*, 442 U.S. 1 (1979).

33. 14 Cal. 3d 639 (1975).

34. Although parole boards have often been viewed as pressure release valves for prisons, they can just as easily allow the pressure to keep building.

it were predicting how offenders would behave in the future. Sentences were to be determined as soon as possible after the offender's commitment to prison. Crucially, however, both reforms left term-setting power in the hands of a centralized state agency.

It is not difficult to believe that given a few more years there would have been a successful convergence of administrative and judicial intent on the organization of the sentencing function. The time turned out to be unavailable. In 1976 the legislative track suddenly opened as the most promising for sentencing reform, and by September of that year the state had adopted a law which formally eliminated indeterminate sentencing for all but those prisoners with life sentences (generally murderers). The new law fundamentally reordered the way prison and parole terms had been set since 1917. In place of broad sentences, such as five years to life for robbery, the statute established low, medium, and high terms within fairly narrow ranges for each offense, with the middle term presumptive unless the judge finds aggravating or mitigating factors present.

Once set, the prison term could be reduced only through the operation of a good-time credit mechanism which established day-for-day reductions for prisoners engaged in work or educational programs, subject to good behavior.[35] Thus there was no longer a significant administrative power to set release dates for felons serving their judicially imposed terms.[36]

Effective in July 1977, the determinate sentence law shared with the judicial and administrative proposals for reform an emphasis on uniform offense-based prison sentences. Where it differed dramatically was in removing control over sentences from a state agency. The legislature essentially took back the power to fix prison sentences, while the power to place the individual offender within the schedule lies with the county criminal courts. In practice a great deal of this power has moved to prosecutors who largely determine which sanctions will apply by their charging decision (Lagoy, Hussey, and Kramer 1979, 229).[37]

35. Good-time credits have played a role in the length of time served in prison in California more or less continuously since 1874. Under the indeterminate sentencing system these credits were somewhat less consequential, yet they were important enough to be the subject of considerable organizational conflict between the releasing authority and the administration of the institutions (Messinger 1969, chapter 2). Today good-time credits are virtually the only way to shorten a judicially imposed prison and parole sentence. A small percentage of inmates are conditionally released several months prior to the completion of their terms to halfway houses for the Department's work furlough and mother/infant programs.

36. The one exception to this was first-degree murder, punished either with the death penalty or a life imprisonment term. Prisoners sentenced for life may be released by administrative action of the Board of Prison Terms, the successor agency to the Adult Authority.

37. Lagoy and his colleagues found that compared with the role of the prosecutor in all of the other determinate sentencing systems in existence in 1979, "the prosecutor in California has the greatest share of available discretion." However, they discounted this power because they found that the relative leniency of California's penalties undercut prosecutorial power (1979, 229). The years subsequent to 1979 have resulted in a considerable expansion of many statutory terms in California.

When the law went into effect in July 1977 parole supervision found itself in the odd position of being set in a dramatically different environment but with little if any legislative directive as to how it should operate. The determinate sentence law explicitly repudiated the rehabilitative ideal that had been the primary public purpose of indeterminate sentencing. Prison was to be for punishment.[38] In the period leading up to the new law the system had been severely criticized for permitting grossly unequal punishments for offenders who committed the same offense. Interestingly, it did not mandate punishment as a purpose for parole supervision or define uniformity of treatment as a goal, as it did in sentencing.[39] Yet it clearly offered a paradigm of how penal power ought to be exercised that parole officials could ignore only at their peril.

The swift passage of the law left corrections in general, and parole in particular, in a defensive posture. Although no published draft of the law included a provision eliminating parole supervision, the widespread belief in the Division was that parole barely survived.[40] Cut down to a year of supervision in most cases, and a maximum of six-month penalties for violations, parole managers were hardly unjustified in thinking of the institution as an injured branch. Many, inside and outside parole, wondered if it would not wither and fall off.

The original 1977 act set a parole term at one year for felonies other than those with a life sentence. Those with a life sentence were sentenced to a three-year parole term following their release. Parolees who were found responsible for a violation of the conditions of parole could be returned to prison for a maximum of six months, or eighteen months for lifers. Originally the time spent incarcerated on a parole violation counted against the total maximum parole term of a year. Following amendment in 1977, the time spent incarcerated stopped the clock, leading to a maximum eighteen month parole period. The period of supervision was extended to three years by amendment in 1979. Rather than a one-year transition from prison to freedom, parole was now a period of state supervision for as long as four years (three years plus the first twelve months of revocation), a period longer than most prison sentences, and a good deal of that time could be spent back in prison on revocations. In time this extension has gone a long way toward creating a new indeterminacy. As one veteran parole official explained it:

38. California Penal Code, sec. 1170 (West 1993).

39. "It is in the interest of public safety for the state to provide for the supervision of and surveillance of parolees and to provide educational, vocational, family and personal counseling necessary to assist parolees in the transition between imprisonment and discharge"; California Penal Code, sec. 3000 (West 1993).

40. Most legislators seemed to have agreed that some supervision in the community would only add to public security. This may have been exacerbated by fears over the initial wave of ISL prisoners sentenced under the DSL which, it was feared, included incorrigibles whom the Adult Authority had kept beyond the normal time for their offenses. There was also institutional lobbying from corrections not to lose such a large portion of their staff.

In 1978 the law was very specific with a one-year parole. No real discretion. Once you have issues of discharge discretion comes back in. It was never absolute. Discretion stretches like a rubber band.

The original 1977 law left most of the power over length of imprisonment to prosecutorial discretion at the charging phase. The 1979 amendments had the effect of redistributing a large share of that power to parole discretion to lengthen sentences through the back door of revocation.[41] Consider that in 1989 over half of all prisoners released had served less than a year (Messinger and Berecochea 1990, table 10), while that same year almost half of all parolees spent time in custody for parole violations. It is clear that, for many state prisoners, parole officials will control a significant portion of their total time in incarceration.

Despite this power the Board and the Division have been left in the defensive posture by their 1977 scrape with extinction. Like a person afraid to drive for years after a bad auto accident, both institutions seem to have been left with a programmed reluctance to exercise judgment over the risk posed by parolees in the community. Both have responded by resolving doubts in favor of incarceration. The Division reported approximately 46,000 violations to the Board in 1987; only 11,000 of those violations were required to be reported by Board regulations.[42] The Board for its part revoked the parole and sent back to prison 98 percent of the reports it considered that year.

Like due process, determinate sentencing was a critique of a certain mode of exercising power associated with the rehabilitative ideal and characterized by broad and unreviewable discretion of correctional officials over the lives of individual offenders. Together those critiques pierced the overinflated claims of the rehabilitative ideal, but they never provided an alternative way of organizing the exercise of the power to punish. Yet the parole process continues to wield a significant power over the distribution of incarceration both in the aggregate and for individuals who may serve more prison time on revocation than during their initial sentences. Discretion over the power to punish remains, but it is shaped by neither the community, legislatively established substantive purposes, nor any alternative rationalizing principles provided by legal reforms.

The New Model

The traditional stance of corrections officials toward politics had been to remain as invisible as possible, relying on the unpopularity of criminals and on

41. Instead of guessing whether inmates will commit new violations if they are paroled, the new logic of parole increases their sentence after they commit a violation.

42. These figures were estimated by the Department based on projections of 1986 proportions on 1988 raw totals (California Department of Corrections 1988).

their presumption of expert authority to ensure public legitimacy. The turmoil of the late 1960s and early 1970s changed that forever. Corrections would have to justify its costs and powers by opening its books (so to speak) and documenting its product.

In 1974 Arlene Becker, a new parole chief appointed by Governor Jerry Brown,[43] initiated a task force composed of younger administrators to create a new design for parole supervision. The shock of *Morrissey* and *Gagnon* was still resonant, and discussions of eliminating the indeterminate sentence were already underway. The leadership of the Parole Division understood that the survival of the institution was dependent on its ability to project a capacity for effectiveness untainted by the political liabilities of the clinical model.

The design, which was adopted as policy by the Parole Division in 1978 and dubbed the "New Model,"[44] combined several elements then becoming more popular in many areas of public administration: classification into specialized caseloads through statistical instruments; auditing procedures to coordinate and document decision making about problems; and a systemic emphasis which highlighted the functioning of the organization as a whole.

Beset by radical changes in the organizational environment, the leadership of the Parole Division showed itself to be responsive rather than reactive. In a report that was widely circulated the Parole Division directly acknowledged the importance of providing a coherent narrative of parole that would establish clear and achievable expectations for staff, parolees, and the public.[45]

The heart of the New Model, in the place that industrial labor and clinical treatment had occupied in earlier periods, was the idea of continuous assessment of the parolees' risks and needs. The risks and needs would initially be calculated using a semiformalized process partly based on actuarial calculations and partly based on the judgment of the individual assessor. The New Model aimed at allowing a more precise individualization of treatment than had been practiced in the past, but as against the clinical model's emphasis on the parole agent, the New Model introduced a more comprehensive coordination from the top.

Action plans for each parolee were to be regularly drawn up on the basis of a risks and needs profile. The plans would operate to specify, justify, and memorialize case decisions. The risks and needs score would also determine the classification of each case. The New Model called for three specialized caseloads: control (for parolees with a high risk score), services (for those with a high needs score), and minimum supervision (if the parolee posed little risk and required few services). Rather than vague guidelines, the New Model

43. Becker was the first woman and first African-American to hold that post in California.

44. At the time of its implementation in 1979 it was also known as the "Redirection" (Studt 1981).

45. In chapter six we will examine in more detail some of the new practices introduced by the New Model; here we will focus mainly on its overall approach.

promised to develop specific programming options to meet most situations.

Classification, in turn, supported a third fundamental component, functional specialization. The clinical model placed great emphasis on the parole agent as an individual relating to the parolee as individual. From the perspective of the New Model designers, this created an army of generalists with an inadequate capacity to bring the best technologies available to bear on the specific cases that needed them the most. Functional specialization was defined by breaking parole work down into component functions: managing cases, assessing and reassessing risks and needs, developing and updating action plans, applying or securing controls, providing or securing services, and preparing for status change.[46]

Organizationally, the most ambitious aspect of this classification scheme was its attempt to break up the "case" as the central unit of parole management and thinking. Traditionally workload was linked to caseload. Parole agents were credited for the number of parolees on their caseload, and although they might be called to account for a widely publicized incident by a parolee on their caseload, there was no attempt to monitor the content of activity. Workforce discipline under the clinical model was pursued by setting minimum contacts which required the agent to meet with the parolee a fixed number of times, regardless of the justification or result.[47] Under the New Model, results, in the form of specified "actions," would be tracked rather than contacts per se. Action was not to be judged solely by recidivism, but by a range of considerations which the report of January 1979 left for future determination.

The final version of the New Model left it up to local districts to decide how to implement functional specialization. Units were expected to assign the majority of their agents to either a control or service caseload, but a wide variety of possible arrangements were considered. The published report included several exemplary ones.

The primary arrangement sketched was labeled the "Integrated Unit." Each parole unit would consist of several control and several service agents, one who could take both kinds of cases, one minimum supervision agent, and one agent to do risks and needs assessments and coordinate action plans. Each unit remained under the control of a single supervisor who coordinated the clerical support for the unit and answered directly to the district administrator.

More radical plans included the "Team Supervision" plan which would replace supervisors altogether with "team leaders" who would rotate and which

46. Most of the titles speak for themselves. The Orwellian sounding "preparing for status change" involved the violation process mandated by *Morrissey* and its progeny.

47. In the minds of many veterans such investigations were bound to find some way to pin the blame on the agent, so it didn't really matter how careful you had been.

would allow cases to be assigned flexibly to any number of agents, and the "District Supervision" plan, under which supervisors would change into "function supervisors" who would take responsibility for all the specialists in the district for that function (control specialists, for example).

As the plan was implemented, the less radical modes dominated, but the very fact that radical changes in the distribution of power and responsibility were considered suggests that the New Model intended to work a fundamental shift in parole. A parole system built around the parolee was being replaced by one which worked from the organization itself, conceived as system.

The New Model drew its innovations from multiple sources. One source was an analysis of the agency's current practice undertaken on commission by two operations research analysts, John Keller and Frank Trinkl, systems engineers schooled in Robert McNamara's Defense Department. Following a systems theory approach they undertook a survey of all phases of the Parole Division's work. Examining each of the Division's functions as a series of operations, they recommended redesigns to make those operations flow effectively as a system. The approach was quite different from the traditional correctional focus on the offender (both as individual and collectively as a social system with distinct subgroups).[48]

The operations research perspective was far from uniformly appreciated by corrections, nor were its techniques fully learned. Its fundamental contribution was, rather, to create an institutional capacity of focus on the level of the system. Under the New Model the system—its inputs, its resources, its outputs—defines the quality of the work product, not the social objectives. It offered a way to rebuild parole's confidence even in the absence of a clear social mission because the system could be improved on its own terms by making its components run better, just as airplane production, bombing missions, or airline reservations could be.

The nationwide debate over sentencing reform was also an important stream of influence. Since the 1970s there had been increasing interest in decision-making guidelines that would generate specific outcomes with little or no discretion in the sentencer (Bohnstedt 1979). Two widely discussed efforts which appear to have influenced the New Model's adoption of a classification matrix were the parole guidelines adopted by the United States Parole Commission and the sentencing grid created by the Minnesota Sentencing Commission. California adopted Wisconsin's risks and needs model (Baird 1981). Different factors were combined in each matrix, but they all pointed to the essential political felicity of the matrix grid as an architecture of power. By

---

48. In this regard the New Model anticipated the larger paradigm shift in correctional thinking from the criminality of the offender to the generic needs of the system itself. For a positive view of this shift see DiIulio (1987); for a more negative view see Feeley and Simon (1992).

enabling hitherto unarticulated substantive choices about punishment to be made by a simple and transparent process, the matrix reduced the political costs of exercising power immensely.

The sense of crisis in the agency, generated by discussion of abolishing parole, doubtless aided the promoters of the New Model in creating conditions conducive to a wholesale remodeling of the Division, and encouraged its initial acceptance by the staff. The New Model envisioned a radical reorganization of work through its emphasis on functional specialization and regular case reviews. Although its promoters believed that, in the end, higher productivity would be achieved with no real growth in workload, parole agents, like workers in all fields, tended to doubt such reassurances. In this case, all parties agreed the transition period would be difficult for the staff.

The adoption of the determinate sentence law weakened immeasurably the strength of resistance that might otherwise have arisen. The proximity of institutional demise reduced the strong resistance any organization generates to placing its competence in question by admitting the need for a ground-up change in operations. They had nothing left to lose in reexamining basic assumptions. With the parole supervision term reduced to a maximum, in normal cases, of twelve months, it appeared likely that staff cutbacks would eventually be forthcoming, although initially there would be a bulge of new cases released as indeterminate sentences were reset and released under the new formula (Studt 1981, 28–34). For those confident of retaining their job, the prospects of working in an organization with little growth (and thus opportunity for promotion) and little apparent stability were demoralizing at best. Some did not waste any time in looking for new careers.

The New Model promised to enhance the accountability and rationality of parole actions just when these were being publicly questioned. The combination of objective classification, minimum specifications, and written reporting requirements was seen as ensuring that parole actions would be measured, consistent, and proximate to the rational justifications for action.[49] Moreover, they promised to function as an automatic auditing device to make sure that the agency did not promise what it could not perform or deliver less than it promised. To its critics this constituted a retreat from the professionalization of parole agents; it treated them as assembly-line producers rather than experts:

> It had to do with a pervasive sense of mistrust. We can't trust the workers to get the job done so we set up minimum specs but don't provide them with any guidelines about what to do. I think an agent ought to have a reason for making contacts other than fulfilling his quota.

49. The DSL offered a comparable design to make the structure and path of decision making in the criminal courts more visible. Despite the fact that the DSL did not apply legally to parole, the architects of the New Model undoubtedly appreciated its lessons in political design.

Elliot Studt, a retired professor of social work at the University of California at Los Angeles and a long-time scholar of parole in California (as well as teacher of some of its managers), was one of its earliest and strongest critics (Studt 1981). Although she appreciated the political crisis that faced the Division, Studt saw the New Model as a faulty lifeline. A program that promised to objectify the control values of parole, at the cost of undermining the strategies from which control emerged, was on a path that went nowhere. To Studt, the essentials of parole remained the special role of the agent in the life of the individual parolee, and the power of community reintegration as a path of control. She speculated that in the end, the lack of real control combined with the emphasis on visibility might reduce, rather than support, parole's case for organizational existence.

During subsequent years the implementation of the New Model has been intermittent and inconsistent. Caseloads continue to be organized by risks and needs scores (a subject explored more fully in chapter six), but from the very start, units resisted the idea of devoting most of their resources to the specialized units and instead placed most parolees in a mixed "control/service" caseload, effectively reinstating the very generality which the New Model attacked.

Planning and auditing remain important institutional norms, but in the business of managing the incredible flow of cases (four times the number it was in 1979), they are ignored with the same impunity to deviation that came to surround pre-release planning in the mid-1960s (Takagi 1967). Those elements of the New Model that emphasized responsibility for the effectiveness of specific practices have remained static, or withered.

The linkage of workload to the six functions has never been developed fully. Certain functions, like jail interviews and revocations, are handled by specialists, but the basic accounting of workload remains case rather than function dependent. Little monitoring or review takes place. In the eyes of one of the New Model's architects, this is a result of predictable political shifts in administration.

> As resources and directors change what we have is a mixed system. A little New Model, a little Old Model, in short, a bastardized system. We keep some of the clichés and some of the rhetoric and some of the principles, but the system as a whole does not really have a complete program. It would be my recommendation to either use the New Model or scrap it. Either do it or don't.

The New Model saw the logic of system at the center where the subject of punishment had once resided. As an ideology, the New Model, like the determinate sentence law, articulated a vision of how to bring the power to punish in line with the norms of rationality that increasingly characterized other functions of modern government. As practice, the New Model's incompleteness suggests that the nature of parole work, the populations with which it deals, and the normative tasks it pursues make it particularly difficult to rationalize as a system.[50]

Conclusion

There is a widespread sense, both inside and outside of corrections, that the legal reforms of the 1970s stripped correctional professionals of the power to control the penal apparatus (DiIulio 1987). It is important, however, to distinguish between power and the conditions under which it can be exercised. None of these reforms were intended to alter the substantive exercise of power over parolees or its objectives. Yet to varying degrees, and in their interactions, these legal reforms carved out a new political space for the exercise of the power to punish in parole that includes the following general imperatives.

1. *Uniformity.* The application of power should be regular and consistent among individuals with similar legal and organizational status, regardless of distinctions among individuals that are rooted in the social, economic, or moral life of the community.

2. *Visibility.* The rationale for, as well as information supporting the exercise of power, must be consistently visible at all levels.

3. *Technocratic Rationality.* Rather than administering justice, controlling crime, or rehabilitating offenders, the criminal justice system must achieve internal efficiency: reports completed on a timely basis, visits made, drug tests taken, and the like.

We must evaluate the transformation of the parole model during the 1970s and 1980s in terms of these institutional vectors, rather than in the legal and theoretical terms—terms like justice, fairness, or rehabilitation—in which the debates around due process or determinate sentencing were originally framed. Since the adoption of the determinate sentence law, the Department of Corrections and its subdivision the Parole and Community Services Division (the Parole Division) have more control than ever to shape the distribution of the power to punish. Under the determinate sentence law, the prison population can be as directly affected through the flow of parole revocations as was ever the case in the past. Moreover, this revocation power is more firmly in the hands of the Parole Division. Yet it is a power that must be exercised in this very different political space than in the past. Significant changes have taken

50. It may also be that punishment is a distinctive power belonging to an earlier and quite different stage of the western state which resists rationalization (Simon 1988). The subject of punishment may not be as easily decentered as the subject of other civil powers such as those manifest in tort law (Simon 1987).

place both at the macro-level of organizational environment and at the micro-level of internal decision making.

On the macro-level, legal reform changed the economy of power by lowering the thresholds of visibility and raising the standards of rationality for parole actions. Had this taken place at a time of growing social wealth and public optimism, it might have been expected to lead to a more substantively rational system through a process of clarifying the different demands for public goods made on the prison and parole system and a rational balancing of resources and objectives. Instead, legal reforms took place at the very moment when changing social and economic conditions were undermining the system's capacity for innovation. In the face of both public pessimism about government programs and public fear of crime, the result has been heightened formal rationality with little pressure to reveal or refine the substantive purposes of the system.

Today, both the Parole Division and the Board of Prison Terms are placed in the ironic position of promising less than ever at a greater fiscal and political cost to the State. It is not surprising that all the involved agencies maneuver, not to give themselves more control, but to surrender as much control as possible to legal requirements, or simply to the inertial pressure of the case flow itself. While under the indeterminate sentence law there were incentives for both agencies to develop a plausible model for exercising power, today there is only the incentive to deny any ability to shape the power to punish.

On the micro-level, legal reform changed the "physics of power." Perhaps the single most important example of this is the unit supervisor's position. Once supervisors were situated at the pivotal intersection of the major lines of force in parole and the community. That gave them the ability to shape a parole program linked to the circumstances of their communities as they knew them. A statewide chief could have an impact on decision making, as Milton Burdman did during the 1960s when he ordered the supervisors to send fewer parolees back on revocation. Even then, Burdman could not rely on changes in official policies and rules or the regional administrative structure; he had to take his policy changes directly to the supervisors.

Today unit supervisors are severely constrained by procedures and isolated from the opportunity to shape them or give them substance. In the graphic, if polemical, words of one veteran administrator, a supervisor today is a "token collector in a toll booth." The power to maneuver and to shape a local parole policy has been moved upwards toward the central administration, which can set the parole agent manual's specifications, and downwards, to the agents, who through their union can influence both the legislature and the administration. Yet there is little incentive, and no organizational cover, for any party to take up this power.

Just as importantly, the ability of unit culture to transmit practical knowledge has been undermined by formalization of procedure mandated by each of the changes we have examined, a process furthered by the Department's affirmative action program in the 1970s. The program succeeded in advancing staff diversity, but by altering the pattern of promotions it also had unintended effects on continuity of leadership in the units and the role of experience.

In short, there is nobody in parole today whose job it is to imagine what parole is and could be. Increasingly the power to manage the system by defining the work is situated not in any organizational role, or community connection, but in the architecture of the system itself, and in the new organizational and machine technologies that keep it running.[51]

51. Wolf Heydebrand's view that technocratic rationalization in state apparatuses, like courts and corrections, goes beyond a Weberian shift from charismatic to bureaucratic domination is applicable to these developments (1979, 31).

CHAPTER FIVE

Parole and the Hardening of Urban Poverty, 1970–1990

From the 1880s to the 1950s, during America's industrial era parole operated largely through the mechanisms of private life: work, family, community. The parole administration relied on the cooperation of employers and local people with an interest in the parolee's behavior. At the same time the parole process was guided by a narrative emphasizing work and family responsibility which made it responsive to community concerns about the parolee. Although the power of the parole apparatus as a public bureaucracy was limited by its small staff, that power was magnified greatly by the numerous private networks through which it was conducted.

Today the economy of parole power is the reverse. A large apparatus attempts to focus its power on a population of parolees who are largely unconstrained by private networks of social control. While the objective power of the bureaucracy is great in terms of numbers of agents, financial resources, and legal authority, the crisis of urban economies and families makes it very difficult to conduct that power effectively over the surface of the parolee's life.

The normative and normalizing potential of community life is determined to a significant degree by structural economic conditions. All social life is "organized" in some sense (to that extent the term "social organization" is redundant), but the type and extent of organization are closely tied to economic structure. The growth of an industrial economy in the late nineteenth century and the first half of the twentieth century allowed for the disciplinary organization of social life, a change made manifest in declining rates of careless accidents and interpersonal violence (Lane 1979). This social discipline in turn made a strategy of suppressing crime by reinforcing the disciplinary logic of normal social practices through prisons and community supervision techniques like probation and parole.

Today the decline of the industrial economy and the failure of postindustrial economic activity to reach the inner city where so many clients of the penal system are based have produced a crisis in corrections of which the crisis in parole is one of the most visible and salient features.

The Underclass Controversy

The features of poverty in urban America and its causes have been the subject of considerable recent controversy. Some experts have suggested that increasing economic and geographic isolation of inner-city communities since the 1970s has created a profoundly new form of poverty in America. They describe the new formation of the poor as an "underclass," a population for which the primary means of social organization in the mainstream society are inaccessible (W. J. Wilson 1985, 1987, 1991; Auletta 1982; Gibbs 1988).[1]

The most comprehensive and powerful version of this argument has been offered by William Julius Wilson (1987, 1991) who suggests that the underclass is a creation of two profound changes in American social and economic life. First, the deindustrialization of American cities has placed the stability of traditional working-class life out of reach for the inner-city poor. Second, the opening up of housing opportunities for working- and middle-class minorities outside of the inner cities has led to the bifurcation by economic status of minority communities and the social isolation of the minority poor. The underclass is thus defined by both a shortage of direct employment opportunity and an absence of the normative structures indirectly providing attachment to the labor market.

Wilson argues that these developments have been especially significant for minorities, and African-Americans in particular. White urban poverty remains, but not in the intense geographical concentrations that Wilson sees at the center of the underclass phenomenon.

While the high level of unemployment is a critical feature of the contemporary underclass, other social variables are salient in providing the pessimistic aura surrounding that designation, including family disintegration, deteriorating schools,[2] high rates of teenage pregnancy, and health conditions com-

1. Some, including Gibbs, reject the term "underclass" because it appears to place the onus on the poor. For an interesting discussion of the semantic/political issues see DeParle (1991). While rejecting the notion that the urban poor are responsible for their predicament through cultural or individual defects, I choose to use the term to emphasize two relevant aspects of the present situation. First, the irrelevance of traditional class terms, Marxist and otherwise, for making sense of the social conditions of a population defined largely by its exclusion from, rather than its place in, the economic system. Second, the increasing tendency of the public and policy makers alike to view today's urban poor as a degraded and irremediable class is itself a highly salient feature of the current situation.

2. Marked not only by a high dropout rate but also by the failure of many students to obtain even basic literacy skills.

parable to many third-world nations (Anderson 1985). Wilson acknowledges the seriousness of these problems but argues that economic restructuring is the critical causal variable. Nonetheless the combination of these behavioral features, which Wilson calls "the tangle of urban pathologies" (1987, x), creates a dynamic process which makes improvement of any one of them difficult and escape from the totality of them practically impossible.

Not everyone agrees with Wilson's assessment of the situation. Christopher Jencks, in a recent analysis of economic and social trends, contended that contemporary urban poverty is not especially different from the situation of the lower classes described by sociologists and economists for the last several decades. Indeed, Jencks questions the widespread assumption that the lower class has grown in recent years. What Jencks does see as new, however, is that men at all income levels are working less (1991, 56).

Another perspective has been offered by conservative social critics such as Charles Murray (1984) and Lawrence Mead (1986). Murray (1984), whose views are often matched against Wilson's, agrees that the well-being of the urban poor has changed for the worst, but he offers a different explanation. What has collapsed are the family structures and social mores which once enforced attachment to the labor market. This process is largely a result of liberal governmental policies which have subsidized the lifestyles of those who are not attached to the labor market and increased social tolerance for unemployment, out-of-wedlock births, and criminal involvements.

Mead (1986) argues that joblessness is only partially a function of declining employment opportunities. Mead stresses the role of cultural changes (once again encouraged by government policy) that have left the urban poor less willing to accept low-paying, low-social-prestige jobs.

Determining the causes of this decline is central to defining policy initiatives capable of countering it, and we shall return to that question in the conclusion. It is not necessary for our purposes in this chapter to resolve this contentious dispute. Virtually all observers agree that joblessness is increasing and attachment to the labor market is declining, perhaps generally, but clearly among those populations referred to as making up the "underclass."

Whatever its causes, the declining power of the labor market to structure the lives of many in the communities of the urban poor has dire consequences for the criminal justice system and corrections in particular.[3] The very term "attachment to the labor market" usefully highlights the relationship between individual behavior and economic conditions. Wilson defines it in terms of the

3. It bears stressing here that a large portion of the urban poor is working more than ever, a result in part of a declining wage structure that forces large numbers of people to work more hours to maintain constant family income (Jencks 1991). What is critical is that the populations producing the proportionately largest flows into the prison system (and out on parole) are characterized by a drastically lower attachment to the labor force than at previous times in our history.

social links individuals have with the world of work including employment opportunities and networks of contacts that provide a flow of information about where and how to get jobs (1991, 472), and how to live within the social rhythms set by the labor market. Reinforcing the objective side of attachment was the central concern of the disciplinary model of parole, which sought quite directly to link released prisoners to disciplinary jobs. The clinical model targeted the subjective side of attachment, that is, the "adjustment" of the parolee to the normative demands of the community. But the labor market remained a major defining factor for normality. It is the absence of this gravitational pull that makes the task of securing parolees so difficult to conceive, let alone carry out.

The Pathological Tangle of Crime and Joblessness

The hardening of urban poverty over the last two decades has paralleled an unprecedented increase in the percentage of Americans in the criminal justice system.[4] The fact that the current "boomlet" of teenagers now moving through the United States age structure are experiencing a more constricting economic horizon today than those a generation ago, when crime seized our national attention, must be worrisome from any perspective. Criminological theories pointing to a relationship between detachment from the labor market and crime support even greater concern, given the unprecedented scale of unemployment for young minority males, most especially those trapped in urban poverty zones (Greenberg 1977, 213; Currie 1987).

In the African-American community this situation is truly staggering, with one of four young African-American men in custody of some sort on any one day during 1989 (Mauer 1990, 1). While national figures do not permit analysis of the distribution of this rate among economic classes, research using census data provides some evidence that the disintegrating labor force attachment of those with the least education is a causal factor. John Bound and Richard Freeman (1991, 22–23) estimate that 7.4 percent of eighteen- to twenty-nine-year-old African-American male high-school dropouts were in prison or jail in 1980, while 20.1 percent were in prison or jail in 1986. The figures today may be significantly higher.

For far too many of those not in custody life consists of forced idleness, deprivation, and exposure to criminal violence (conditions experienced by

4. While overall imprisonment rates have more than doubled since the early 1970s (Bureau of Justice Statistics 1989a, 582), rates for African-Americans have risen at a staggering pace. Consider that in 1991 fully 42.5 percent of the young African-American men in Washington, D.C., were under correctional custody on any given day, while in Baltimore during 1990, 56 percent of the city's African-American males between the ages of 18 and 35 were either under the control of the criminal justice system or wanted on warrants (Terry 1992a).

many *in* custody as well). The resulting sense of despair leaves many vulnerable to the attraction of drugs, unsafe sex, and involvement in criminal lifestyles.

In the same paper, Bound and Freeman (ibid.) argued that incarceration operates to worsen the labor market chances for inmates when they return to the community. They estimate that for young African-American male high-school dropouts incarceration lowered their chances of employment by 21 percent in 1983 and 17 percent in 1988, probation by 16 and 11 percent, respectively, in these two years.

This cycle of crime and joblessness profoundly challenges the capacity of corrections to influence the behavior of offenders released to the community. Without the labor market community supervision has little framework of social discipline to which it can enforce adherence. Not only is there no legal power to return to prison parolees who refuse to work (as there was at least nominally in California until 1977), but more importantly the demand has little credibility when many in the community, criminal and not, are unemployed. Therapeutic techniques, which provided an alternative to work discipline in the 1960s, are less available because of public funding cutbacks at all levels, and less salient in a social world that offers little hope for even the "well-adjusted" person to achieve the objective features of normal life.

Over twenty-five years ago Lee Rainwater pointed out that the maintenance of entry-level work opportunities was the crucial factor in taking advantage of the predictable pattern of "burnout" that criminals often face as they move into their twenties and thirties (1966, 120–22). Rainwater argued (1967) that while many juvenile delinquents choose crime over low-wage jobs in order to fulfill status expectations inculcated by the larger society, they eventually find that a lifestyle of work and moderate means is both acceptable and supportable within the value system of the larger society, and, most importantly, that it is a real option for those exhausted by the high-stress street life of the hustler or criminal.

Looking at the African-American youth population in particular, Troy Duster (1987, 303) has argued that hardening of unemployment is locking a whole portion of the population out of the labor market and into continuing contact with the criminal justice system. This view has been supported by the grim statistics cited above. Parolees enter even a healthy labor market at a considerable disadvantage. It is obvious that where a quarter to half the adult men in a community are unemployed, those fresh out of prison are up against tremendous odds unless they have a special skill or inside track.

At its deepest levels, the emergence of an underclass through the hardening of urban poverty in America has done more than make the parole task incrementally more difficult, it has made the task conceptually less coherent. The basic idea of normalization, that the efforts of the correctional system can result in the "reintegration" of an offender into the community, has flipped around. Parole staff continue to believe in this mission (perhaps because it is so fundamental to the very idea of parole), but their practice is increasingly oriented to the opposite of reintegration, to preventing released offenders from returning to the tangle of urban pathologies that characterize the communities to which they return.

The supervision of inner-city parolees takes place in an environment where the web of demands placed on individual parolees by institutions of private social control (e.g., work and family) is far less comprehensive than in the past,[5] leaving a far larger share of control to the coercion that the state is able to direct at them. This chapter draws on the experiences of a sample of California parolees in conjunction with other recent studies of urban conditions to document this growing crisis in the social base of corrections. In the next chapter we will look more closely at the efforts of the parole organization to develop techniques capable of handling this new situation.

The Poverty of Parolees

Not all parolees come from or are returned to the inner cities, and not all of those that do meet the profile of the underclass. California maintains parole units in virtually every part of the state and sends agents into rural areas (where poverty is great, but far different than its urban forms) and to the most affluent suburban communities in the state (to which white collar criminals or wealthy drug dealers return upon their release from prison). Yet because the inner city and the conditions of the underclass concentrated there present the most serious obstacles faced by parole, and provide the initial experiences for virtually all agents,[6] this chapter will concentrate almost exclusively on that setting. Whatever form parole takes today, and will take tomorrow, must somehow cope with the "tangle of urban pathologies" that exists in the inner cities of California.

The urban poor have always been the major source of admissions to the prison system, and thus to postprison sanctions like parole. Whether that is more true today than a generation ago is difficult to determine from official

5. The ethnography of poverty has shown that the sociological concept of social disorganization is inappropriate (Suttles 1968; Stack 1974). What is really meant is that the forms of social organization that predominate among the poor are either disregarded, or regarded as illegitimate, by the more privileged sectors of society. Even in today's conditions of hardened urban poverty new and opportunistic forms of social organization, like drug gangs, are present (Williams 1989). Nonetheless, the disjunction between social organization in the underclass and that in the rest of society is of the greatest consequence for the operation of governmental agencies charged with social control.

6. Virtually all parole agents spend the beginning of their careers in inner-city units. When they obtain seniority they can, and often do, seek transfers to units which are farther from the center, and closer to their own residences, and which provide less stressful working conditions.

data sources. What is clear, however, is that the conditions of social life for the urban poor have deteriorated, and that this deterioration has profoundly affected the ability of the parole organization to maintain effective controls on those placed in its custody.

The Setting

The central cities of California are, in the public imagination, far from the utter disaster areas that have come to characterize northeastern locations like New Haven or Newark, or those in the Midwest like Detroit. Their populations continued to grow in the 1970s at a time when most central cities were shrinking. Their industrial base kept expanding as well, although sluggishly. To the visitor these cities appear lively and inviting, having maintained shopping, good housing, and cultural facilities downtown. Yet the three examined here, Los Angeles, San Francisco, and Oakland, all contain large areas of concentrated poverty.[7]

In Los Angeles the poorest neighborhoods spread out southwest and southeast of downtown—the areas highlighted in the civil disorders that broke out in May 1992. To the southeast the communities are predominantly African-American, while to the southwest they are predominantly Hispanic. As the civil disorders in "South Central" Los Angeles demonstrated, these communities overlap to a large extent.[8] In the midst of Los Angeles's powerful economy these areas show little vitality. Ironically this area was once the center of one of the largest industrial complexes on the West Coast (Davis 1992, 61), producing cars, steel, and oil machinery, a concentration of unionized blue-collar workers that typified the social base for disciplinary corrections. The area remained economically strong during the 1970s at a time when African-Americans and Hispanics became the predominant population. During the 1980s, however, the central areas of Los Angeles lost an aggregate of some 200,000 manufacturing jobs, mostly in the South Central area (Mydans 1992, 20).

Today few industrialized production shops or large retail outfits are in evidence. The business streets are composed of small restaurants, wig shops, and liquor stores. Those large institutions that have been maintained in the

7. William Julius Wilson has argued that his analysis of the underclass has particular relevance to the conditions in the Midwest and Northeast (1991, 456). While the California economy has been stronger (at least before the most recent recession) a pattern of concentrating poverty such as that described by Wilson has been evident there as well (Davis 1992).

8. The category "Hispanic" used in this chapter and in the tables masks tremendous variation among different groups, including those who are of Mexican ancestry but long settlement in southern California, those who have migrated quite recently from Mexico, as well as Salvadorans and Guatemalans who fled war and state terrorism in their own lands during the 1980s (Davis 1990, chapter 6). Those that live in South Central are among the most recent and most impoverished arrivals.

poverty area, such as the University of Southern California, are designed to maximize security and minimize interaction with the impoverished residents. There are some jobs here. Many of the old manufacturing sites have been taken over by low-tech production jobs (Davis 1992, 65). But these jobs are the antithesis of the old high-wage, high-organization jobs that existed here in the industrial era. Moreover, the employment opportunities they offer are overwhelmed by a huge pool of labor, much of it illegal immigrant labor, willing to take work in "sweatshop" conditions.

The poorest areas of Oakland occupy a concentric ring around the central business district stretching in three directions. To the west, the poverty area reaches almost to San Francisco Bay, but it is stopped by the freeway (part of which was destroyed in the earthquake of 17 October 1989) and a narrow band of warehouses and businesses. To the north, it reaches about halfway to the Berkeley border. To the south, it stretches far toward the airport and Coliseum complexes, broken up along the west by the port of Oakland and the warehousing and manufacturing districts around it. To the east, its spread is cut off by a well-maintained apartment district around Lake Merritt, and then by the affluent Oakland hills. Although there are poor Hispanics in Oakland, most of the poor community consists of African-Americans. The parole units I studied are located in an office building in the midst of a bustling shopping area which borders on the Oakland hills. The two units that are based there do not divide the area up geographically but are jointly responsible for the whole city except for the far south side which is covered by a unit located out by the airport.

San Francisco is often thought of as a city without slums, and many of its poorer quarters have given in to the steady pressure of real estate prices. To the west of downtown, the old Western-Addition neighborhood retains a core of lower-income housing with a predominantly African-American population based in several older housing projects and a shrinking collection of rundown private apartments. To the south is the Mission District, a large area that is predominantly Hispanic, but increasingly interspersed with young affluent whites.

To the far south and east is the Hunter's Point neighborhood, a predominantly African-American area of severe poverty. Its housing stock, built for the Navy's shipbuilding work force during the Second World War, appears to hold little attraction for gentrifiers, although change may eventually come in the form of wholesale redevelopment. The streets are strikingly busy, although shops and businesses are not especially abundant.

These settings are an important workplace for California parole agents. Unlike many probation officers in the large cities whose caseloads far exceed any realistic expectation of community visits, California parole officers are expected as a matter of administrative regulation to see their parolees regularly outside of the office, and if possible without prior warning. That doesn't mean it happens all the time. During the time I observed in the Parole Division urban agents found it difficult to actually get out of the office due to the rapid growth of the parole population which left many agents with abnormally large loads and consequent paperwork. While it remains integral to the official account of parole, fieldwork inevitably takes place in competition against other tasks with stricter deadlines that demand and receive priority (like revocation hearings).

When the agent does get into the community, actually making contact with a parolee is often very difficult. Crowded living conditions provide few incentives for parolees to stay home where they can be easily located. Since most of them, most of the time, are not regularly employed, they cannot be located in fixed work locations.[9] This means that even the parolee who is staying absolutely "clean," as the agents like to say, can be hard to find.

While physical contact is eventually made with most parolees who have not willfully evaded parole (and a shockingly high number do), it is rarely sufficient to establish any credible claim to ensuring the noncriminality of parolees. The unemployment and underemployment of the inner-city parolee creates the most difficult problems of judgment for the agents. All agents agree that a parolee who does not have a job is at greater risk of reinvolvement in crime, and thus in need of tighter supervision. Yet in the absence of the constraining and regulating environment that work provides, it is difficult to "tighten" supervision because there is nothing to bind the parolee to accept the agent and the parole process itself. This problem becomes clearer when we move from description to an analysis of the income and domestic situation of a sample of inner-city parolees.

Work and Income

It might be expected that all released prisoners would experience greater levels of poverty than other citizens for a variety of reasons. They are disproportionately more likely to be unskilled and uneducated, they are disproportionately more likely to have had a history of poor employment, and the very fact of a prison record might be expected to have a discouraging effect on their employment prospects. The extremely bad economic situation of inner-city parolees, however, is made manifest when they are compared to parolees released from prison at the same time, but to communities outside the inner city, communities not characterized by the "tangle of urban pathologies" described by William Julius Wilson and others.

In table 5.1 are contrasted the sources of income for parolees who live in

9. Those that do stay employed often shift around between various day jobs.

Table 5.1   Income Sources of Outer- and Inner-City Parolees (in percent)

Community Type	Work	Welfare	None	Total
Outer	68.2	6.8	25.0	100.0
Inner	38.5	18.1	43.4	100.0
Total sample	43.4	16.2	40.4	100.0

Notes: Income source data were missing on nine inner-city and one outer-city parolee. Probability measurements for all tables in the text are based on the chi-square test.

$N = 265$ $P < .01$

inner-city poverty areas with those for parolees who live in communities at the periphery or inner suburban rings of Los Angeles and the Bay Area. These latter communities are mainly traditional blue-collar neighborhoods characterized in general by less unemployment, fewer welfare recipients, and a greater proportion of whites than is found in inner-city communities. [10]

From table 5.1 we see that parolees residing in the "outer" city were almost twice as likely to be employed during their free time in the community, a result significant at the 99 percent confidence level. Almost three-quarters of these outer-city parolees had some known source of income, while almost half of the inner-city parolees had no known source. [11]

As shown in tables 5.2 and 5.3, differences between outer- and inner-city communities interact with important racial differences in economic life. [12] White and Hispanic parolees in the outer-city communities are more likely to be employed than their counterparts in inner-city communities.

10. Outer city is an admittedly unattractive neologism for the non-inner city. Recent research on the way Chicago employers viewed prospective employees demonstrated broad use of spatial designations (inner city vs. suburbs) which were both independent and interactive with notions of race and class (Kirschenman and Neckerman 1991).

11. Income source was coded in a way that I now believe overstates the extent of employment. Work here means any kind of paid work, whether full-time, part-time, or irregular day work. A person was categorized as having a work or welfare income source if they received income from that source for at least 51 percent of the time they were under supervision in the community (if they worked part of the time and received welfare part of the time, they were coded for the more prevalent source). That means a parolee who was released in October 1988, found a part-time job in November, absconded (disappeared) in December, and was rearrested in September 1989 would be listed in table 5.1 as receiving income from work. While this is an extreme profile, many of the parolees absconded for some part of the year studied, and most spent at least some time back in prison on revocations. Many of those listed as receiving work or welfare income were actually struggling with no income for much of their time. On the other hand, many of those listed as receiving income from no source may have spent some time working or on welfare. In addition they may well have received income in the form of loans and gifts from family and friends.

12. Recent research by Joleen Kirschenman and Kathryn M. Neckerman on the way Chicago employers view their work force documents that spatial designations like "inner city" provide a critical marker for many disfavored worker characteristics. They found that spatial mappings overlap with but remain independent of racial meanings (1991, 217).

Table 5.2   Outer-City Parolees with Income from
Work by Race (in percent)

	Income from Work?		
Race	No	Yes	Total
African-American	63.6	36.4	100.0
Hispanic	32.3	67.7	100.0
White	6.3	93.7	100.0
Total sample	32.3	67.7	100.0

Note: Three Asian parolees were excluded.
$N = 42$ $P < .01$

For Hispanics the difference between outer and inner city is marginal,
while for whites it is quite dramatic. For African-American parolees the employment situation is uniformly dismal in both communit es. Only approximately one-third of African-American parolees in either type of community
were employed for more than half the time they were free in the community
during the year studied.

The fact that African-American parolees in this sample were unlikely to
obtain income from employment, reflected in tables 5.2 and 5.3, is partly explained by the fact that they are overall much more likely to be based in the
inner-city communities caught in Wilson's "tangle of urban pathologies" and
cut off from economic opportunities. The fact that even those African-
American parolees in the sample who lived in outer-city communities experienced relatively low rates of employment may simply be an artifact of the small
sample size, but it may also indicate the existence of racial prejudice in employment.

Table 5.3   Inner-City Parolees with Income from
Work by Race (in percent)

	Income from Work?		
Race	No	Yes	Total
African-American	69.8	30.2	100.0
Hispanic	44.4	55.6	100.0
White	68.6	31.4	100.0
Total sample	63.0	37.0	100.0

Note: Income data were missing for nine inner-
city parolees. Five Asian and Native Americans
were also excluded.
$N = 216$ $P < .01$

This may be wrapped in a contemporary form which emphasizes security concerns more than traditional racial animus. Suburban employers may assume an African-American applicant has "inner-city" problems regardless of his actual residence (Kirschenman and Neckerman 1991, 217). (Obviously the fact of a prison term, if it comes out, may harden that assumption.) It may also reflect the inadequacy of the simple dichotomy of outer and inner city. The areas designated outer city may well include pockets of hardened poverty, disproportionately African-American in composition, that have escaped the inner-city location but not the social circumstances.

The problems of African-Americans in the labor market are not, however, a recent phenomenon. Historically they were excluded from whole industries and even classes of employment (Lane 1986). Although many job categories opened up to African-Americans after the Second World War, immigration from the rural South and other factors operated to generate higher unemployment and lower labor force participation rates for African-Americans nationally and in California. As seen in table 5.4 this pattern has been evident in California cities since the 1940s.

In 1980 the ratio of African-American to white unemployment was 2:1 (Wilson 1985, table 5.4). Even when education and central-city location are controlled, African-Americans are still more than twice as likely as whites to be unemployed (Kasarda 1985, table 8).

The problem of racial disproportion in joblessness and unemployment is particularly critical for corrections because the percentage of African-Americans in the California penal population has been growing since the mid-1960s. In the 1950s African-Americans made up less than 10 percent of

Table 5.4   Percent Adult Male Population Unemployed by Race, 1940–1980

Race	1940	1950	1960	1970	1980
Los Angeles					
White	12.0	6.9	5.2	5.4	5.2
Non-white	**18.3**	12.0	9.4	**10.2**	**11.7**
Hispanic	NA	NA	NA	6.6	7.8
San Francisco–Oakland					
White	9.8	6.8	3.4	4.9	4.9
Non-white	**12.0**	16.5	11.3	**11.1**	13.4
Hispanic	NA	NA	NA	6.3	8.5

Note: Bold numerals represent number for African-Americans exclusive of other non-whites; in 1950 and 1960 this figure includes Asians and other non-whites. White includes Hispanics until 1970, then Asians and other non-white, non-Hispanic groups in 1970. Figures are for SMSAs except for 1940. Figures are from *Sixteenth Census of the United States, 1940*, Population, vol. 3, The Labor Force, part 2 (California), table 4; and from *Census of Population: 1950*, vol. 2., part 5, table 66; *1960*, vol. 1., part 6, table 73; *1970*, vol. 1., part 6, table 164; *1980*, vol. 1., Chap. D, part 6, table 213.

the prison population; in 1986 they made up 32 percent (ccmbined, African-Americans and Hispanics made up over 60 percent of the prison population) (California Department of Corrections, Data Analysis Unit 1988, 13).

The effects of hardening urban poverty on the inner-city parolees in our sample are manifest for all races, as shown in table 5.5. While inner-city Hispanics do significantly better than whites or African-Americans, 40 percent of Hispanic parolees had no employment for most of the time they were in the community. For African-Americans and whites more than 60 percent had no employment for most of the time they were in the community.

The situation is bad for inner-city parolees, but is it any worse than it was twenty, thirty, or forty years ago? Data on the employment of earlier cohorts of California parolees have not been systematically collected, but given the changes in the economies of the communities to which they returned, we may assume significant change for the worse. The situation of parolees is probably worse than that of other citizens in the same communities for the reasons suggested above.

California and the nation overall enjoyed a lower employment rate in the mid- and late 1980s than they had since the Vietnam War boom. The overall unemployment rate does not, however, provide a good picture of employment opportunity for inner-city residents, let alone the former prisoners among them. The unemployment rate is a measure of those looking for work who cannot locate it. Labor economists have long pointed out that many more people are jobless or working less than they want to be than are counted as unemployed. Some are engaged in socially desirable activities for which they are generally rewarded and during which they are subject to many of the same social controls that work seems to provide. This is true of soldiers, students, and to some extent those engaged in personal care for family members. Putting unemployment and non-labor-force participation together, Christopher

Table 5.5   Income Sources for Inner-City Parolees by Race
(in percent)

	Income Source			
Race	Work	Welfare	None	Total
African-American	30.6	17.9	51.5	100.0
Hispanic	60.0	14.0	26.0	100.0
White	34.4	21.9	43.7	100.0
Total sample	38.5	18.1	43.4	100.0

Note: Income data were missing for nine inner-city parolees. Five Asian and Native American inner-city parolees also excluded.

$N = 216$ $P < .01$

Jencks (1991, 41–43) has shown that "joblessness" among men has been increasing (as a trend) since the late 1960s.[13]

The situation is also troubling when we look at the kinds of jobs that are available today. While the overall number of jobs offered in the economy may not have declined, the mix of jobs and the opportunity structure for them have also changed both overall and in their geographic dispersion. Virtually all observers agree that America lost manufacturing jobs during the 1970s and 1980s, while gaining jobs in both the high and low end of the service sector (Bluestone and Harrison 1982; Wilson 1987; Bound and Freeman 1991, 1).[14] The results have been particularly manifest in the older industrial regions of the Northeast and Midwest. In the absence of new economic developments these regions have experienced deindustrialization as a general economic decline. Yet even where strong service industry growth maintained a robust and growing economy, like California's in the 1980s, the loss of manufacturing jobs erodes the social base that corrections has historically depended on.[15]

This overall decline is particularly concentrated in large central cities that were the base of industrial growth for most of the nineteenth and twentieth centuries. Those manufacturing jobs that are staying in America are increasingly to be found in suburban locations. This creates an obvious problem for the inner-city poor which John Kasarda has described as the "spatial mismatch hypothesis."[16]

Recent employment growth has generally been in two types of employment: jobs, such as those in the electronics industry, requiring higher levels of education and skill (Kasarda 1985), and service sector jobs, such as fast-food preparer, calling for little skill but providing poor wages and benefits. The

13. As Jencks shows, the causes of joblessness are more complicated, as is the relationship between poverty and joblessness. His analysis is subtle and fascinating. For the argument here, however, the level of joblessness, measured both by the labor market participation rate and the unemployment rate, is sufficient proxy for the cultural judgment that, with sufficient state help, the labor market can both absorb and control criminal offenders.

14. The new service sector jobs created in the 1980s are often highly disciplinary at both the low and high ends (Zuboff 1988).

15. California cities continued to gain entry-level manufacturing jobs between 1970 and 1985 even while urban areas in much of the rest of the country were losing them (although as in cities in other states, higher education threshold jobs grew faster) (Kasarda 1988, table 10). The additional slack that this gives the urban economy may have been more than made up for by the large immigration of people to California during that period (Kasarda 1988).

16. There is in fact a considerable amount of controversy among labor economists as to whether the hypothesis is correct or important (Holzer 1991). It is not clear how mobile the poor are within metropolitan areas or how neutral suburban employers are to where their labor supply comes from. Parolees have a particularly hard time since their parole conditions generally require an official approval of the Board of Prison Terms before they can move to a different county.

former category are off-limits to most parolees (and of course many other inner-city residents) who lack adequate education. This has been called the "skill mismatch" by some economists who argue that it has a direct relationship with the spiraling joblessness among young African-American males, especially those who fail to complete high school.

Economic effects, like earthquakes, are profoundly influenced by the micro-level. Two people equally distant from the epicenter of the 1989 Bay Area quake had starkly different chances of survival if one was lying in the grass in Golden Gate Park and another was on the lower ceck of the Cypress Avenue freeway structure. Aggregate statistics are not useless, however, because they tell us something about the frequencies of different circumstances.

Parolees in the inner-city areas I studied are on the losing side of all the structural mismatches traced by social scientists. Indeec, their legal status includes restrictions on their movement across county lines which may limit them from pursuing suburban employment opportunities even if they are so inclined.[17] Their skills are generally minimal and unlikely to have been improved by prison.

The Welfare Alternative

Some of the slack in both support and control created by joblessness may be taken up by public assistance, or as it is popularly called, "welfare." Eighteen percent of the inner-city parolees in my sample obtained income from welfare during a majority of their time under supervision in the community. Welfare recipients in the sample were typically older than average, and a disproportionate percentage of them were female. This reflects, to some extent, the variation in benefits available for different segments of the population, as well as variation in those who seek welfare income.

Parolees are for the most part able-bodied young adult males and thus belong to a group which is among the least protected by public assistance programs. Unemployment payments, the type of public assistance most likely to be utilized by males in the general population, are typically available for a limited time following displacement from a job covered by unemployment insurance laws. They are not available to parolees who have been unemployed since their release from prison, or who were engaged in various sorts of less-organized labor including temporary "day labor" jobs and jobs in which the laborer is treated as a subcontractor. In such jobs employers often do not pay

17. Transfers are not impossible but are difficult to get and practically impossible without a solid advance offer of better work or housing than the parolee has in the county he is originally assigned to.

into the state's unemployment insurance fund.[18]

A second important source of public assistance, available for both sexes in California and elsewhere, comes from two national Social Security Administration programs for the mentally and physically disabled: Disability Insurance (DI) and Supplemental Security Income (SSI). Although both programs provide income assistance for those whose mental or physical disabilities prevent them from entering the labor market, they differ in their target population. DI is directed primarily at the working population and the survivors of workers. SSI is aimed at people with very little income or history of earnings (McCoy and Weems 1988, 17).

Few parolees are eligible for DI for the same reason that they do not receive unemployment insurance payments: they typically have little or no history of regular employment. Prison inmates who suffer from severe mental or physical disabilities may be eligible for SSI. For the 5 to 15 percent of inner-city parolees in the sample who are mentally ill, SSI represents the best hope for a stable and sufficient income source. Many emerge from prison already eligible for SSI because of a long history of mental illness before imprisonment. But eligibility is a bureaucratic concept which can be difficult to vindicate. The application process is a long one, often lasting months or even years. During the interim period mentally ill parolees must survive on other sources of income. Parole agents who expect a parolee to be approved by SSI often allow a small stream of cash assistance as a loan to be paid back once the benefits start coming.

The benefits themselves are quite high compared with alternative forms of assistance. Receiving around $600 a month, an SSI beneficiary in Oakland, San Francisco, or Los Angeles can typically afford a room in a single room occupancy (SRO) hotel and still pay for basic food and clothing needs. Once a person is on SSI, the state agency which administers the funds demands little in the way of interaction. This is beneficial for a population of people with a limited capacity to cope with bureaucratic norms like appointments, deadlines, and forms. Some SSI recipients have a sponsor who cosigns the check for them. This can be a parole agent in the case of a parolee. But this kind of structure is not mandatory, nor is it available to many parolees who simply do not have anybody intervening in their lives except for the parole staff.

The public assistance program most widely available to the typical male parolee is General Assistance (GA) provided by local governments in Califor-

18. Although most parolees were engaged in some form of work inside the prison, prison work is not covered by unemployment insurance in California or any other state. Cash assistance modeled on unemployment insurance has been used experimentally with parolees (Berk, Lenihan, and Rossi 1980, 766–86).

nia.[19] GA is available to almost anyone who can show that he or she is indigent. Benefit levels and conditions for GA are set locally. In Oakland, for example, it pays approximately $365 a month for single men or women. Some cities require drug testing and treatment, job search skill training, or community service work. If grantees fail to show up for training or work assignments they will be canceled from the program. Cancellations tend to be strictly enforced and are all too frequent among a population with shifting addresses and poor bureaucratic interaction skills.

Although GA is available to most parolees with no other source of income, few take it. For some the requirements for contact are effective disincentives. For many more the social status of a welfare recipient is itself a disincentive. These requirements, combined with the low view of welfare income held by many young indigent parolees, have proved too high a barrier for many. Young men in particular are reluctant to pursue GA benefits. Around 14 percent of parolees age nineteen to twenty-nine in the sample received it, while almost half had no source of income at all. Many look on it as shameful and incompatible with an image of being a "man" in their community. The low benefits, which do not suffice in most instances to pay for an apartment and food, are simply not worth the cost in self-esteem.

Women in the sample are more likely to receive welfare than men. Nearly a third of all women parolees in the inner city received welfare benefits, while only around a tenth of the men did. Although information was not collected on the types of welfare received for the sample, Aid to Families with Dependent Children (AFDC), a combined state and federal program aimed at children and their primary caretakers, is probably a most significant source.

Male parolees rarely if ever receive AFDC directly. Although the law permits males who live with and care for their children to receive AFDC, few male parolees qualify (although a large portion have fathered children). AFDC may, nonetheless, play a significant but invisible role in supplementing the income of many male parolees. Although the male parolee doesn't receive benefits directly, females who are part of the male parolee's support network—girlfriends, sisters, mothers—often do (Stack 1974). The steady decline in real income from AFDC has undoubtedly diminished the ability of these support networks to sustain male parolees (McLanahan, Garfinkel, and Watson 1988, 108).

19. The future of general assistance in the 1990s is uncertain. Unlike AFDC which is paid for by both state and federal governments, GA is generally funded by state or sometimes county governments. Since these levels of government are going through profound revenue crises, funding for GA is in jeopardy. Including Michigan, four states have completely eliminated GA benefits in recent years (Arkansas, Louisiana, Oklahoma), and four others have substantially cut or restricted benefits (deCourcy Hinds 1991).

Domestic Situation

Given the poor employment situation and the meager forms of public assistance available to inner-city parolees, a crucial role is played by the existence of a personal support network composed of the family and friends of the returning prisoner. This network, created during his life in the community (Stack 1974), is a crucial (if difficult to analyze) variable in survival. If it can absorb the parolee and meet his material needs, he will stand a far greater chance of avoiding or delaying reconfinement. In contrast, the parolee who comes out with no personal support network faces a difficult passage through shelters and weekly hotel rooms, environments that may compare disfavorably with prison itself.

A place to live is the most important resource that a parolee's personal support network can provide in helping him get through parole. Parole agents want to know, more than any other general fact, where parolees live. Without such knowledge the agent cannot maintain even a pretense of control. Parolees who cannot locate a permanent home and move frequently among relatives and friends find themselves under greater scrutiny and with a smaller margin of toleration for violations (see chapter seven). At the same time, a place to live is often easier for a family to provide out of even a meager resource base than cash loans or gifts. Tracking with whom parolees live while in the community provides some rough indications of the kind of support networks available and their relative strengths.

A high percentage of all parolees live with their relatives, predominantly their parents. Parents are providers of last resort, the people least likely to reject a parolee with no other options. From the perspective of parole agents such living circumstances, while better than homelessness or emergency shelter, do not provide much confidence that the parolee can actually be located at the reported home address. Parents may permit a parolee to stay there because they cannot refuse, while in actuality the home is already overcrowded with other children or grandchildren. In many cases a parolee who reports that he is living with his parents or siblings only maintains an irregular connection to that address.

Racial differences which are statistically significant at almost the 95 percent confidence level are disclosed in table 5.6. Whites and Hispanics were more likely than African-Americans to live with a significant other. Such living situations are generally treated with more confidence by parole agents because they assume that the fact of a relationship will increase the likelihood that the parolee will maintain an active involvement with the household.

The data, as coded in table 5.7, cannot fully reveal the economic diversity of living situations. Those who can afford their own apartment and those who

Table 5.6   Domestic Situation of Inner-City Parolees by Race (in percent)

| | Lives With Whom? | | | |
Race	Lives Alone	Lives with S.O.	Lives with Kin	Total
African-American	17.3	17.3	65.4	100.0
Hispanic	11.8	27.4	60.8	100.0
White	32.0	28.0	40.0	100.0
Total sample	17.7	21.6	60.7	100.0

Note: S.O. = Significant Other. Domestic situation data were missing for forty cases. Four Asian and Native Americans parolees were also excluded.
$N = 186$ $P < .01$

Table 5.7   Domestic Situation of Inner-City Parolees by Income Source (in percent)

| | Lives With Whom? | | | |
Income Source	Lives Alone	Lives with S.O.	Lives with Kin	Total
Work	10.7	34.5	54.8	100.0
Welfare	23.7	13.2	63.1	100.0
None	22.6	12.9	64.5	100.0
Total sample	17.4	22.8	59.8	100.0

Note: S.O. = Significant Other. Income source and/or domestic situation data were missing for forty-six cases.
$N = 184$ $P < .01$

are in a weekly hotel room paid for by public assistance equally tend to live alone, although their living situations differ greatly. Those with income from work live with kin for the most part, as do those with no known source of income at all. The most significant association may be between work and living with a significant other. As Wilson (1987) has argued, there is a strong connection between employment and the marriage rate. Even living together outside of marriage takes financial resources. Parole agents are also likely to put much more confidence in a parolee living with a spouse or consistent significant other on the grounds that such commitments indicate a strong incentive on the part of both partners to avoid a return to prison for the parolee.

Work and the Behavior of Parolees

Troy Duster, Elliot Currie, and others have argued persuasively that the absence of employment generates powerful incentives to remain in a criminal career. The sample analyzed here is too small to permit an adequate analysis of causation, but it points in the direction they predicted.

Table 5.8   Drug Sale Violations of Inner-City
Parolees by Income Source (in percent)

Income Source	Drug Sale Offense?		
	No	Yes	Total
Work	90.6	9.4	100.0
Welfare	87.5	12.5	100.0
None	74.0	26.0	100.0
Total sample	83.5	17.5	100.0

Note: Data on income source were missing in
nine cases.
$N = 221$ $P < .01$

Acquisitive Crime

In the sample of parolees examined here the absence of work was strongly
related to involvement in drug sales, a criminal industry that has grown significantly in the inner city during the 1980s. In table 5.8 we see that fewer than
10 percent of those who received income from work engaged in drug sales,
while more than 25 percent of those with no income engaged in drug sale activity, differences significant at the 95 percent confidence level. Welfare recipients, disproportionately older and female, seem to avoid drug sales
(although, as seen below, they engage in considerable drug use).[20]

Drug Use

Table 5.9 suggests that work may provide not only an alternative source of
income, but a pattern of life that is less conducive to drug use.

In the analysis of drug sales in table 5.8, parolees with welfare income
looked more like those with work income than like those with none. In table
5.9 the opposite is the case. Welfare recipients use drugs in slightly higher
proportions (or at least are discovered using drugs more) than those with no
income. Table 5.9 suggests that while the provision of regular income (for example, through welfare) may remove incentives for involvement in drug sales,
income alone does little to discourage drug use. At best it may mitigate the
need to pursue predatory crime or drug sales as a means of supporting a modest habit.

Whether work provides a structure of expectations and constraints that dis-
courages drug use, or whether those without drug use habits are more likely to

20. Interestingly, the negative association between work and crime in this sample is not apparent in
property crimes.

Table 5.9   Drug Use Violations of Inner-City
Parolees (in percent)

Income Source	Drug Use Offense?		
	No	Yes	Total
Work	62.3	37.7	100.0
Welfare	42.5	57.5	100.0
None	43.7	56.3	100.0
Total sample	50.7	49.3	100.0

Note: Data on income source were missing for
nine cases.
$N = 221$ $P < .05$

get work, is not determinable from these data. Fieldwork suggests that both effects are likely to be involved. A person who wants to keep a full-time job must strive to eliminate, or at least regulate, a drug use habit that encourages absenteeism and low productivity. Most agents believe that a parolee who is using drugs will inevitably lose his job. An employed parolee who begins to turn in positive drug tests for cocaine or heroin will be pressured to enter a drug treatment program.

Employment and Violations

These data for the most part only tell us that joblessness and violation behavior run together, not whether work is a causal force.[21] It may well be that those who can resist drug use, avoid violations, and manage the demands of supervision, those good at resisting the temptations of crime, are the same people with the personal organization resources to get a job. It may also be that when the labor market is slack the least resourceful are likely to get by through hustling activities, borrowing and panhandling, as well as small-time thievery and drug dealing (if not through felony crimes).

Yet it is a mistake of many economic analyses to focus exclusively on work as a source of income. As Berk, Lenihan, and Rossi argue:

> The sociological perspective on employment provides a number of additional dimensions. First, being employed at any job is a valued status.
> . . . Second, employment on the usual legitimate job implies being placed in contact with fellow workers, providing an interpersonal environment that may lead to new social circles, exposure to different values concerning the legitimacy of illegal activities, and so on. (1980, 772)

21. See the discussion of causal attribution problems in studies of employment and recidivism in Berk, Rossi, and Lenihan (1980). In their study of Georgia and Texas parolees they found a significant negative effect of employment on arrest for both property and violence offenses (781–83).

In addition to values, work surely supplies a measure of social control. The simple fact of having to show up at a certain place, at a certain time every day, and maintain a level of performance over several hours has a powerful influence on conduct even in time spent outside of work. A pervasive problem of inner-city parolees is having little to do. Even for those with no intention of reinvolvement with crime, the simple fact of congregating with peers on the streets and public parts of housing projects increases their chances of encountering law enforcement and risking arrests.

Boredom and despair (which we have every reason to believe is a potent criminogenic combination) among inner-city parolees came through clearly in my field observations. For many of them the business of everyday life is characterized paradoxically by few demands and great pressures. In the absence of a job the day may be spent in the home (assuming one has one) or on the street. The parolee faces pressure not to "hang around" the dwelling, which is typically the home of the parolee's parents or relatives and may well be overcrowded. The parolee faces pressure from parole officer and police to avoid practices which predominate on the street (drug use, sales, or even congregating in groups on the thoroughfares).[22]

Criminogenic effects do not come through clearly in the quantitative analysis of the sample of inner-city parolees presented here. This may be due to the small sample size, the imprecision of the code definitions, and the overall complexity of capturing causation in a phenomenon as overdetermined as crime among paroled felons. Some trends, nevertheless, are suggestive.

Parolees with work were far less likely to sell drugs and less likely to use them. The fact that those with work were detected using drugs less frequently than those with welfare suggests the disciplinary function of work selects for or encourages more controlled personal behavior.

In violation behavior, welfare recipients occupied a midpoint between those with work and those with no income source at all. Few welfare recipients are engaged in drug sales or property crimes, although many of them use drugs. In part this reflects the larger proportion of women and older people among parolees receiving welfare. (These populations have often been shown to be less active in crime.) It also suggests that the provision of a small income encourages a kind of benign withdrawal. In fieldwork I observed many parolees who get by on welfare by living alone in small hotel rooms and remain-

22. Parole agents in all three study cities were annoyed by the frequency with which their parolees were arrested by police under a variety of offense codes for activity which amounted to being out in the streets near areas of frequent drug sales. Although such arrests would generally be thrown out by a district attorney, the parole agent must at least file a report for an arrest, and may well feel compelled to seek a revocation rather than appear to be ignoring criminal behavior. During the study period the Los Angeles Police Department was conducting "sweeps" of busy streets downtown and in South Central which netted scores of parolees (Davis 1990, 276–77).

ing aloof from most of the activities going on in their community (criminal and otherwise) except to purchase drugs for use alone at home. These welfare parolees get by at the margins of their community seeking satisfaction from drugs while posing little threat to others.[23]

The Consequences for Parole Supervision of the Hardening of Urban Poverty

The statistical profile above only provides a partial picture of the problems faced by parolees in the inner city. The lack of income speaks for itself (although, for the reasons stated above, it is understated at best). The descriptions of residential situations do not adequately describe the large numbers who are marginally sheltered. In all three cities substantial numbers of parolees lived in a constant shuffle, starting off with a family member or friend, but quickly moving to series of public assistance hotel rooms as they burned through the resources their supporters could provide.

The Capacity of the Community to Absorb Released Prisoners

Over the last generation sociologists have taught us that it is a mistake to move from the absence of conventional life structures typical of the middle class, for example, employment and marriage, to the assumption that social life in the community of the poor is lacking in social organization. Often outsiders, such as this author, miss the subtle but potent forms of social organization in impoverished neighborhoods. Sociologist Gerald Suttles, who spent several years living on Chicago's Near West Side, pointed out that the disorganized slum that outsiders saw as they drove through the neighborhood had little resemblance to the community as seen by insiders:

> Seen from the inside, however, the Addams area is intricately organized according to its own standards and the residents are fairly insistent on their demands. These demands require discipline and self restraint in the same way as do the moral dictates of the wider community. Conventional norms are not rejected but differently emphasized or suspended for established reasons. (1968, 3)

Likewise the absence of employment does not mean the absence of organized systems for exchanging goods and services. Carol Stack's ethnography of ghetto life in the early 1970s provides a detailed analysis of such a non-

23. It is likely that those parolees who seek welfare are those less inclined toward aggressive and illegal behavior. On the other hand, the study of Berk, Lenihan, and Rossi (1980), designed to identify causal influences of small income support payments on a random sample of parolees, showed a negative effect of unemployment payments on arrests for property and nonproperty crimes, suggesting some causal role.

employment-based economy and society. The community of urban poor people Stack lived among and studied managed to survive because of their "kin," the networks of family and close friends who exchanged assistance and materials back and forth in a "gift" cycle that maximized the meager resources of the community.

Stack (1974) argued that kin networks provide security and stability for poor people complete with their own rules of conduct, rights and duties, and modes of conflict resolution. Ironically the security of the kin may provide powerful disincentives for pursuing conventional paths to security through employment and marriage:

> Those who attempt social mobility must carefully evaluate their job security, even if it is at the poverty level before they risk removing themselves from the collective help of kinsmen. The collective expectations and obligations created by cooperative networks of poverty stricken kinsmen . . . result in a stability within the kin group, and the success of these networks of kinsmen depends upon this stability. (1974, 24)

> Forms of social control both within the kin network and in the larger society work against successful marriages. . . . In fact, couples rarely chance marriage unless a man has a job. . . . Women come to realize that welfare benefits and the ties within kin networks provide greater security for them and their children. (113)

The kin networks Stack studied mainly involved women and children, but they also helped sustain men who as adults continued to draw support from their childhood kin network and from new ones joined by relationships with women.

It is possible to imagine a correctional regime that tries to ground itself in these less formal institutions of poor community life. Suspending the disciplinary norms of the work world, which corrections has traditionally sought to reproduce, a regime of supervision might act as a mobilizer and stabilizer for those parolees who have networks of kin or the possibility of neighborhood support, a subsidizer of their costs, and an enforcer of informal arrangements.

In the late 1960s a number of Los Angeles parole units (involved in the Civil Addict program described in chapter three) moved toward this model. They set up storefront offices along with caseworkers from other social service agencies and tried to work with the community more on its own terms rather than imposing standards of normality on the poor. Such innovations met resistance from many who felt that they were incompatible with the goals of control and law enforcement. They withered with the general decline in community-based social service programs during the 1970s. Their applicability as a model for parole today is limited by a significant decline in the social service resources directed at the urban poor, which has severely limited the absorptive capacity of the kind of support networks that Stack described.

The growing inability of inner-city communities to sustain their most marginal members (young men) is manifest in the growth of the now all-too-familiar phenomenon of homelessness.[24] Peter Rossi (1989) points out that the population of homeless (variably estimated at 350,000 to 3.5 million) can be usefully compared with the much larger population (17 million) of extremely poor (defined as incomes at one-half the poverty level or less). Like the typical homeless person, the extremely poor tend to be unemployed and unmarried. They differ in being younger, having been without regular employment for less time, and having fewer disabilities (1989, 28). The real social mystery, Rossi points out, is not the large numbers of homeless, but the ability of so many of the extremely poor to manage to remain domiciled.

Rossi's answer is that many of the extreme poor are simply at an earlier point on the same time line as the homeless. They have fallen out of the labor market more recently (for reasons that Rossi does not adequately address, but see Kasarda 1985), and they are being kept from the extremely destructive effects of homelessness by the provision of help from what Rossi calls "private temporary support systems," which closely parallel Stack's description of kin (1989, 37).

Yet the capacity of private support networks to sustain people without employment is not endless. A crucial parameter is the flow of income into the community, primarily through welfare. Rossi concludes that a major source of increased homelessness in the 1980s is the dramatic decrease in real income from welfare since the early 1970s.[25] Those receiving public support have suffered a loss in purchasing power of almost 40 percent since 1968 as a result of stagnation in the benefit levels and the severe inflation of the 1970s (1989, 40). The decline in welfare income directly stunts the capacity of the poor to absorb and sustain those without resources. The homeless are those who have worn out the resources that can be mobilized by their personal support network.

Rossi's analysis is helpful for understanding the ecological reality of parole. Prisoners emerging into parole in the 1980s reentered communities with catastrophically low employment opportunities, and no substantial government or private efforts at community reorganization. Whatever remained in the way of opportunities and programs, they were not obtained by those marked as state

24. It may be a mark of industrial societies that they make young men extremely valuable. In pre- and postindustrial societies they seem to compose the most marginal and dangerous class.

25. Rossi suggests that there is no reason to doubt the persistence of support networks among the poor in the 1980s. He points to attitude research which documents high identification with norms of family mutual aid among the poor which are comparable to other classes. The essence of his argument is to suggest that the reduction in the wealth of the poor has directly sapped the endurance of private support.

prisoners, certainly not if the sample of inner-city parolees analyzed above is accurate.

It is not surprising that like other males they found that access to private (primarily family-based) support networks was crucial to their effort to avoid drifting into homelessness or predatory criminal activity.[26] The rapid rate of return to prisons reflects in part the fact that parolees, once having exhausted or burned out the support of their kin, turn to crime or simply become too marginal for parole agents to risk letting them remain in the community in the face of danger signals like drug use.

Just as the streets collect large numbers of impoverished people who can no longer be sustained by private support networks, the prisons are collecting many who have been released on parole to communities with fewer and fewer resources to sustain them. Indeed, one suspects that parolees as a population are already skewed with respect to those characteristics most likely to facilitate burning through support networks, including behavior problems, aggressiveness, mental illness, drug abuse, or alcoholism, as well as crime.[27]

Unlike the average extremely poor adult moving toward homelessness, the returning prisoner probably starts with a lesser threshold of tolerance. There is a good likelihood that the offender has already burned through some of that good will prior to conviction and incarceration. The drug abuse, property crime, or violence that led to arrest and state prison may well have had repercussions at home prior to becoming legally visible.

Furthermore, prison is unlikely to enhance the civility of the inmate. Indeed, the social skills necessary to minimize conflict within a small group setting at best atrophy and more likely are altogether replaced with skills in aggressiveness and alienation. The felon who one day is controlled in a secured setting costing thousands of dollars is, all too often, the day following his release lodged in a household of little means.

Work and Parole Supervision

If the community provides a poorer conductive surface for the exercise of parole power now than in past due to the decline in economic resources, changes in law and policy discussed in chapter four have also helped to uncouple pa-

26. My point is not that the homeless are a criminal population, but that many in the parole population find themselves subject to the same circumstances that have left thousands of presumably law-abiding young people living on the streets. For those who have made the necessary moral adjustments and acquired the capacity to engage in predatory crime, it seems likely that crime might replace homelessness to some extent.

27. Insofar as all these factors correlate to economic conditions, the overall decline in employment and income growth experienced since the early 1970s probably would have pushed more people into homelessness through an overwhelming of the social control resources among the poor even if government support payments had maintained the economic capital.

role supervision from the networks of private social control in the community. Until the 1960s bona fide employment was a legal requirement for California prison inmates to be released on parole. After a parolee received a favorable vote to release from the Adult Agency (that is, after a specific parole date was set), actual release was contingent on the confirmation of employment in the community. The parole staff carried out the confirmation process by interviewing employers who had pledged to provide a job as arranged by the parolee or his family. Where the parolee was unable to come up with a job offer, the parole staff was supposed to attempt to place the parolee, and where they could not, parole release was forestalled.

The system had many holes in it. The fact that an employer confirmed intent to hire a parolee provided no real guarantee that the job would last any length of time, if it existed at all. Interviews with veterans of the 1950s and 1960s suggest that there was plenty of winking at alleged jobs put forward which might or might not really exist. For those without any network of support there were positions with social service organizations like the Salvation Army which paid only room and board.

Parole agents retained power to seek the revocation of parole where an already released parolee lost his job, but it is safe to assume that enforcement on the return end was less strict than in the initial release decision. The parole staff had incentives to avoid the appearance of many failures and probably rarely sought return unless the unemployed parolee appeared to be failing in other respects.

It is clear from the historical record that the steady employment condition of parole operated to impede the release and speed the reimprisonment of at least some of those with the most marginal economic links to the community. During the Depression when jobs became hard to find and family resources were strained, prisoners in many states were held beyond their parole date for lack of a position.

In 1960 thirty states required a prisoner to have a job offer in order to be released, and most of the other eighteen exercised discretion to hold many without jobs (Clevenger and Stanton 1960, 159). The work requirement for release became a far slacker constraint in many states including California in the course of the 1960s and 1970s. California parole agents still had to devote a significant portion of their time to "pre-release" work and go through deliberate dissembling to meet the formal rules of the organization, but the expectation that the steady work requirement could be seriously enforced on either the release or revocation end had waned.

Finally in 1977 the adoption of the determinate sentence law eliminated discretionary parole release in California and with it the work requirement.

Under current rules it is neither necessary nor legal for the Department of Corrections to refuse to release a prisoner at the end of his term less good-time credits on the grounds that he does not have a job.[28] During their statutorily set parole supervision term parolees cannot be sent back on the grounds that they are unemployed or refuse to look for work.

This has had several important consequences for the task of managing the parole population in the community. The most obvious is that the system cannot keep in prison those with no support. More important is the utility of employment requirements in putting pressure on parolees or their private networks to mobilize resources in the community for their support. The old law pressured the parolee to mobilize his supporters in the community to find employment, or a credible offer of such. Now the parolee comes out with no requirements, and once in the community the parolee faces no legal obligation to accept employment that he does not want or even to enter the labor market.

Perhaps the most important organizational consequence is that parole staff are not required to spend time attempting to mobilize economic and social support for the parolee in the community. Under the indeterminate sentence law the release program task was considered burdensome. Agents sometimes resorted to verifying jobs that they knew were unlikely to be very solid. Still, they had institutional pressure to develop as many ties as possible in the community, among service agencies, and with employers. In this endeavor they were supported by supervisors who devoted much time to building connections with local employers to develop job pools. The best of them always had a ready supply of available, if lowly, jobs.

Today the pressure to complete mandatory items like board reports is not counterbalanced by pressure to locate employment opportunities.[29] In its absence parole staff are less likely to get engaged early on with the parolee's family or other members of his community. The influence of this microcommunity over parole decision making is thereby diminished, leaving the community with less access to penal power and parole supervision more isolated.

28. This reflects the current interpretation of these rules by the Department's own counsel. The language of the statutes themselves leaves a good deal of room for maneuver, and future reinterpretations by the Department could conceivably find authority to reimprison for unwillingness to work or look for work without drafting new statutory language. It is also possible for the law to be changed. Imprisonment for failure to work obviously raises constitutional questions. Formally, forty jurisdictions required maintenance of employment as a condition of parole (Rhine, Smith, and Jackson 1991, 106), but these are not enforced.

29. Individual supervisors can and do make their own rules about employment efforts. Such local norms can have specific effects but cannot compete with those demands that are centrally monitored like the timeliness of report preparation. Agents are encouraged to drum up jobs, but it is not a task that defines their own job success or failure in the way meeting revocations report deadlines and certain other organizational tasks does.

Conclusion: Surveillance in No-Man's-Land

The ethnographic work on poor urban communities in the 1960s was written in part as a rebuttal to extremely pessimistic evaluations of the social life of the urban poor like those associated with the Moynihan Report (Rainwater and Yancey 1967). They remain relevant in preventing us from assuming that beyond the major institutions of work and marriage there lies only chaos and crime. But the evidence of a dramatic decline in the economies of the inner-city poor suggests that the worst fears of the urban pathologists of the 1960s have materialized.

One conclusion to be drawn is that the control capacity of the informal institutions Suttles and Stack described has diminished radically. Stack (1974) contended that gift exchange among the kin expanded many times over the sustenance provided by the impoverished cash economy, but she did not hold out that kin networks could make soup out of stones. No one should be surprised after reading Stack's study that cuts in welfare rates are followed by significant increases in crime control costs.

Suttles viewed the rich symbolic coding of territory in the slum as a resource for social order, but he also recognized the potential of encroaching changes in urban economics and morphology to wipe this out. One result, already visible to Suttles in the late 1960s, was the eerie "no-man's-lands" which urban renewal had left on the edges of the Chicago "slum" he studied:

> All of them are sections where people do not live permanently and over which no one exercises a personal surveillance. Given local ideas about who an area can "belong to" this creates a kind of social vacuum where the usual guarantees of social order and control are lacking. (1968, 35)

"No-man's-land" is only a metaphor for the crisis generated in a community by the withdrawal of mainstream organizing forces from social life.[30] While labor is far from the only significant organizing force, the nature of modern society makes virtually all other forms heavily dependent on work. Social scientists studying the Austrian village of Marienthal, a community where employment was virtually wiped out in the depression of the 1930s, concluded that unemployment altered the experience of time, reduced social contacts, reduced participation in collective purposes, and ultimately undermined the very sense of identity in those affected (Jahoda, Lazarsfeld, and Ziesel [1933] 1972).

The decline of employment does not necessarily wipe out family life, but even where family relations are strong they may not be able to provide the full range of organization required for self-regulation:

---

30. Paul Fussell traces this metaphor back to the First World War where it was used to describe the tortured strips of land between hostile trenches (1975, 189–90).

One reason why family relations cannot replace the need for wider contacts such as employment provides lies in the different nature of these
two types of human relations: family relations are as a rule much more
emotionally charged than relations with others in employment. For better or worse, family relations enrich or impoverish emotional life; the
emotionally calmer climate of relations with colleagues provides more
information, more opportunity for judgment and rational appraisal of
other human beings with their various foibles, opinions and ways of life.
(Jahoda 1982, 25–26)

The rich social contexts described by Suttles and Stack were alternatives to
participation in the wage labor economy that provided their own forms of social organization. Work in a more cultural sense may involve the full range of
activities through which social life is reproduced. Yet in our particular society
there is little space for elaboration of ways of life not linked to the labor
market:

To blame the unemployed for their inability to use their time [in] a more
satisfactory way is pointless; it would amount to asking that they single-
handedly overthrow the compelling social norms under which we all live
and which provide a supportive frame within which individuals shape
their individual lives. (Jahoda 1982, 23)

The work of Suttles and Stack suggests that the potential for the construction
of normative structures of everyday life in communities is great outside the
labor market, but dependent in the end on some source of economic support.
Whatever cultural forms might have resulted from the expansion of the welfare
system during the 1970s, the actual course of events evidenced the great reluctance of U.S. society to sanction an alternative form of social organization
to the labor market. The result in the 1990s as the labor market contracts
within the underclass is a vacuum of social control resources.[31]

The tactical difficulties of this situation for the parole staff can be best expressed in a model of time. Think of a weekly planning calendar that might be
kept by a parole officer. Large areas are highlighted representing times when
he can expect to be at work, taking responsibility for children, and the like.
Imagine also that he notes down with an asterisk all the times during the week
when he checks in with organizations that keep track of his transactions, at

31. The social and psychological effects on those trapped in circumstances of hardening poverty are
also of great concern. This study has tended to focus on the question of control. This often implies a
kind of indifference to human beings and their suffering for which I apologize. My aim has been to
document that even from the most instrumental point of view the social and economic conditions of the
poor in the United States are intolerable. A powerful portrait of support networks struggling to survive
in the deprived soil of today's inner-city community is to be found in a recent series in the *New Yorker*
magazine by author William Finnegan (1990). Finnegan's subjects, based in the slums of New Haven,
provide a useful 1990s contrast to the networks studied by Stack and the social order studied by
Suttles.

least once every weekday when he comes to work, stops at an automatic teller machine, uses his credit card, and maybe on the weekend if he makes a doctor appointment, attends a training workshop, or the like. Looking back on the week it is full of highlighting and asterisks. Now imagine the weekly planner of one of his parolees. There is little or no highlighting on the page at all. There may be one or two asterisks, a visit to the parole office, the parole outpatient clinic, or possibly a need to stand in line for a public assistance hotel room.

When you put the two calendars together the difficulty of supervision is clear. The parole agent has narrow openings in which to attempt to contact a parolee with virtually no compulsion to be any place in particular.

The strategy of contemporary parole is shaped by the problem of how to amplify the limited opportunities for direct contact through the creation of monitoring mechanisms that do not depend on the parolee's social world. In the following chapter we will turn to an exploration of contemporary efforts.

CHAPTER SIX

New Technologies of Control, 1970–1990

Parole supervision during the 1970s and 1980s was faced with the collapse of the social and economic conditions that had made it a plausible control strategy in the past. It was also challenged by a set of political and legal demands on the way parole power should be exercised. While social and economic changes made parole a harder job, legal and political changes made it more visible, less flexible, and more vulnerable. To a greater or lesser degree both sides of this pincer were being felt in jurisdictions across the country. These affected not so much the stated objectives of parole (which have changed only subtly throughout its history), but the coherence of the enterprise and the means for accomplishing these objectives.

The major response in California parole from the late 1970s has been to fashion a new control model around risk management. The risk model seeks to rationalize operations "technocratically," that is, on the basis of internal performance parameters rather than social or professional norms (Heydebrand and Seron 1990). This strategy calls for the development of technologies that can bolster the system's ability to create and then evaluate objective indicators of performance for both parolees and parole agents.

In the late 1960s the clinical model continued to provide the most salient narrative for corrections and parole supervision in particular, but it was also a period when a number of new practice technologies were being advanced while some old ones were being recast. In this chapter we will examine three: classification, offender-based data systems, and drug testing.[1] All three tech-

---

1. Each one has significant roots in the clinical era of parole discussed in chapter three. Then as now, parole looked for ways to address the erosion of its base in the community. It introduced new techniques that would permit it to rely more on its own bureaucratic resources and less on the commu-

nologies have quite distinct genealogies; they originated in different fields and were applied to criminal justice for different purposes. Each piece offered prospects for serving the clinical model, but as parole began to chart a course through a rapidly changing legal and political environmen: in the 1970s they began to form the outline of an altogether new ensemble.

Prediction and Classification

Classification had been a perennial topic in corrections for most of the century. It could fit perfectly well with the claims of individualized knowledge promoted in the Progressive Era and then after the Second World War. Good classification could be seen as the product of expert-judgment-particularized case knowledge. After all, that is what parole boards were supposed to do based on their expertise and the knowledge collected through investigation of the offender's life and his prison record. It could also be based on statistical analysis based on relatively few facts known about many individuals so that a mere clerical worker equipped with the right tables and information could make judgments. This basic ambiguity made classification a critical site for change in the correctional model.

Computerized Data Bases

Another technology which emerged during the 1970s was the automation of criminal justice information through computers (Gordon 1991). The 1967 report of the President's Commission on Law Enforcement and Administration of Justice strongly recommended offender-based data systems for use in tracking offenders in the system and storing information about them. Data systems were initially described as serving the clinical goal of supporting individualized decision making. Yet they also offered an ability to circumvent the pretenses of "expertise" through their possible use in the actuarial prediction systems mentioned above.

Drug Testing

Drugs and drug testing were central to the clinical model. Their applicability had improved considerably by the late 1960s through the development of efficient and less costly urine test methods which permitted easier detection of opiates as well as other drugs. The importance of this development was under-

---

nity for control or interpretive validity. If, as this chapter will attempt to show these techniques have changed considerably from their usage in the clinical era, it is due in part to how much wider the gap between parole and the community has become.

cut by the general decline in the perceived seriousness of the drug problem during the 1970s. After 1975 the Parole Division began experiments using the Enzyme Multiplying Immunossay Technique (EMIT), an inexpensive and reliable urine test for drug use.

Drugs returned to a central place in the discussion of crime and correctional strategy during the 1980s. Drug testing has become the major surveillance activity of many community supervision agents whether in probation or parole. However, contemporary testing has separated itself from the apparatus of treatment to become perhaps the most significant method of surveillance and control used in contemporary parole.

There was no overarching scheme that lent to any of these technologies a special priority for parole in the 1970s and 1980s. Like much in organizational life, their appearance was highly contingent, if not fortuitous (Cohen, March, and Olsen 1976, 26). With this in mind we must reexamine the development of new technologies in contemporary parole without assuming that the functional fit between successful technologies and the needs they fill provides an adequate account of their deployment.

The emergence of these technologies has been driven less by their ability to solve specific problems in the parole mission and more by their ability to fit well the new ideological and organizational environment left by the breakdown of the clinical model. Qualities like discretion, individualized decision making, and personal relationships between parole agents and parolees which had been absolutely central to the clinical model were becoming dangerous in the 1970s, and on their way out by the 1980s. Technologies that offered to limit the ability of any individuals as individuals to make decisions about other individuals looked good, as did those that provided information in ways that made it easy to objectify, transmit, and defend.

Prediction and Classification

From the start parole release involved a judgment that a particular inmate was likely to live lawfully if released. This inevitably required a prediction of future conduct, whether couched in terms of selecting unfortunates from among "natural criminal types," or as a process of predicting whether rehabilitation had been accomplished.

Genealogy of Prediction Techniques

From early on some of the leading academic experts on crime, including Ernest Burgess ([1928] 1974) of the University of Chicago and Sam Bass Warner of the University of Oregon, argued that this kind of clinical prediction could be usefully supplemented by the development of classification systems based on actuarial tables documenting the actual parole outcomes of previously released inmates in correlation with specific features of the offender.

The highly influential Burgess method consisted of identifying variables which correlated with parole outcome. The variables were then used additively to construct a predictive index for use in evaluating the likely performance of new candidates for parole. By contemporary standards the Burgess method was crudely mechanical. The salient variables were simply added to produce a score, rather than weighted as they are today using techniques of multiple regression analysis.[2] At the same time the Burgess tables attracted wide attention because of their ability to reduce the murky business of predicting criminality to the identification of specific factors, and because they held out the promise of continuing validation.[3]

During the 1930s and 1940s, actuarial prediction methods were further pursued by scholars such as Sheldon and Eleanor Glueck (1930), George Vold (1931), and Walter Argow (1935), but they did not attract much interest from parole boards. Following the Second World War, interest in actuarial prediction began to rise rapidly. One important influence was the prestige that systemic quantitative analyses gained in military use during the war. After the war military planners like Robert McNamara went back to the business world to advance the cause of administrative rationalization through the application of quantitative data and engineering principles to the corporate world.

One aspect of this military experience, the systematic effort to analyze the predictors of battlefield breakdown in soldiers, had obvious relevance to the management of deviance in the civilian sector. Psychologists and criminologists began to question whether parole boards or other decision makers could ever do better making predictions based on their assessment of an individual case than if decisions were made by classifying prisoners according to their actuarially estimated likelihood of success (Meehl 1954).

Despite the increasing prestige and sophistication of prediction instruments, they were not widely adopted until the 1970s. One problem was their quality. Prediction instruments of even the most sophisticated sort generally failed to do much better than the earliest methods in predicting outcomes (Bohnstedt 1979, 23). Furthermore, classification instruments predicted recidivism, but few parole boards were willing to make parole decisions simply on that basis. Whether officially recognized or not, retributive concerns made the seriousness of the crime and the prisoner's prior record important (Rothman 1980, 173).

2. This is true today in social science work but not necessarily the corrections use of predictive classification instruments.

3. Burgess's method was later validated by Clark Tibbits (1931). In later years it was criticized for its simple additive scoring system, but it remained a model for parole prediction through the 1970s and has influenced later models (Bohnstedt 1979).

As of 1961 only two parole boards in the nation used statistical prediction methods as an official part of the process (Bohnstedt 1979). Illinois adopted the Burgess method at the time of its invention, creating the position of a state prison actuary charged with collecting and compiling data on parole experience. Even in Illinois, however, the board remained free to make their release decision based on their own assessment of various information, informed by, but not controlled by, the actuarial tables.

During the 1950s and 1960s the technology of prediction changed dramatically with the application of multiple regression and other multivariate analysis methods then being diffused within the social sciences. Instead of simple additive scores, these new techniques weighted variables according to their contribution to the model's predictive efficiency.

The California Department of Corrections was at the forefront of corrections in the United States in applying the new multivariate methods (Bohnstedt 1979, 22). The first "Base/Expectancy Score" developed by the Department combined four elements: the number of prior commitments, offense type, the race of the inmate, and the number of escapes. The aggregate score was then used to classify prisoners according to their relative risk of failing on parole. High scores identified those with the best chance of succeeding. New formulas were developed periodically based on a larger data base of parole outcomes. Factors were added or dropped based on their performance on new data bases, or, in the case of race, because of the potential for political controversy.

The California Adult Authority, which had the legal mandate to make the release decision, never utilized the base expectancy score in determining parole releases,[4] but once on release the Parole Division used the base expectancy score to assign parolees to experimental caseloads and later during the mid-1960s to place higher-risk parolees in special work units with lower caseloads (and thus more time for each parolee).[5]

Classification and the Politics of Discretion

The appeal of statistical prediction methods was heightened when, in the 1970s, they were combined into matrices that also took offense seriousness into account, most notably in the United States Parole Commission's "Salient Factor" score system. By the end of the 1970s at least fifteen jurisdictions had

4. Other parole agencies, including the United States Parole Commission, did adopt some form of statistical risk prediction. Today, most parole release systems utilize prediction scoring as at least an advisory element.

5. Statistical risk prediction has also been used in determining the appropriate security level for incoming California inmates which, in turn, determines which facility they will be kept at. The classification system has greatly aided the Department in increasing utilization of medium and minimum security facilities, and in reducing the administrative complexity of determining appropriate facility placements.

adopted some form of actuarial prediction combined with offense severity (Bo-hnstedt 1979, 27).

The genius of the matrix solution was that it allowed the integration of several values in decision making while continuing to present the appearance of an almost mechanical simplicity. The growth in the popularity of actuarial prediction in the 1970s, however, was not driven by science so much as by politics. With public anxiety about criminal violence rising and confidence in criminal justice professionals plummeting, the need to find new grounds of credibility was clear. Risk prediction instruments, already several decades old, suddenly were seen in a new light. The old debate about whether or not the instruments could be shown to be more efficient in predicting risk than individual experts was quickly forgotten in the haste to replace the increasingly politically expensive discretion of parole boards and other decision makers with some kind of plausible alternative. Indeed, even simple Burgess-type instruments were adopted because, despite their methodological lack of sophistication, they provided a clear way to structure discretion (Bohnstedt 1979, 25).

The high cost of discretion was fully brought home to California corrections through the adoption, in 1977, of the determinate sentence law which called for uniformity of punishment and rejected the consideration of rehabilitation in determining prison terms. The Adult Authority did not survive that enlightenment. The law did not apply to parole directly, but parole leaders understood its implications for how power should not be exercised. The Parole Division responded by adopting the "New Model" in 1979, calling for the utilization of an actuarially based risks and needs classification system pioneered by Wisconsin for use in setting parole supervision levels.[6]

Prediction and Classification in the New Model

The Wisconsin model was developed from 1975 through 1977 under a development grant from the federal government's Law Enforcement Assistance Agency (Baird 1981, 36). Like earlier models, the Wisconsin model involved rating potential releasees against factors identified through actuarial analysis of past outcomes. In determining a risk score for each releasee, a correctional agent using the model must score the offender's record with a number score between zero and ten with ten the most severe in each of four risk categories: commitment offense, prior record, crime-related patterns such as drug abuse, psychological problems, etc., and prior pattern of response to custody and supervision. The raw scores are then multiplied by weighting factors derived from the application of multiple regression analysis to the outcome records of

6. Actuarial methods were also turned to for setting prison custody levels starting in 1980.

an earlier sample of parolees. A similar process is applied to the determination of a needs score designed to predict how much help a parolee is likely to need.[7]

In retrospect it is not difficult to see why the Wisconsin classification system, and like instruments, seemed perfectly suited to the kinds of political and legal demands facing parole in the 1970s when California began using it to classify inmates set for parole release to supervision. The style and texture of statistical prediction helped address concerns about uniformity. It ran on discrete information which allows compliance with demands to make explicit the basis of sanctioning decisions. It promised to yield results independent of the individuals who made the decisions, eliminating doubts about the capriciousness of the system. It appeared to disclose the full set of assumptions and objectives that are applied to information, permitting real review of a decision's rationality.

In practice, however, the risks and needs score was a constructive compromise that lent the aura of statistical prediction to the process without really taking away any power from the local case-by-case system or even accurately mirroring past experience. Its inventors assumed (or, more charitably, hoped) that the application of the scoring system would be carried out in a standardized manner and refined through the accumulation of a larger statistical data base. Neither was ever done systematically in California. Even its critics point out that after its initial adoption the classification scheme never really received an adequate implementation:

> The specialization mode [of the New Model] was a pseudo-scientific machinery to make paroles look more legitimate. . . . The only problem was that it was never improved or validated. It rapidly degenerated into a kind of check list. Completing the original document was considered burdensome, and it seemed to make no real difference anyway. When the expectation is that you are going to lock 'em up quick, what is the payoff in doing a careful individualized analysis?

To its supporters, the New Model in general and its risk prediction aspects in particular have been betrayed by the unwillingness of successive administrations to back up the form of scientific sophistication with the resources and attention necessary to sustain such sophistication.

> The New Model from a caseload standpoint starts with classification, but the system has deteriorated to nothing. Some people do the risks and needs very well so that one page summarizes the whole case. Other analyses just aren't worth a damn. Right now half are not even using it. No matter what the classification system is, it's no good if you don't validate

---

7. Over the last two decades most parole agencies have adopted some variant of the risks and needs scoring approach (Rhine, Smith, and Jackson 1991, 108).

it and we have never examined it. We haven't looked at second or third generation models.

The New Model had promised a way to appraise individual dangerousness that was simultaneously objective and standardized. In a report laying out the blueprints for the proposed reorganization of the Parole Division, classification was described as the critical steering device for supervision.

> The supervision provided for each adult offender should be based on the risks and needs posed by that offender as well as the levels of effectiveness of the various activities that can be undertaken by the offender and P&CSD to achieve case objectives. The depth, quality, and rapidity of services, controls, and case management activities that are undertaken should reflect those differences. (Parole and Community Services Division 1979, 7–8)

This formulation did one of the jobs that a successful model of parole must do: it provided a set of exemplary practices around which an account of control can be built. What it lacked were ways to actually link assessment and decision, such as programs that did show some specific connection to various classes as separated out by the risks and needs evaluation. Even more than the clinical model, the New Model set very high standards of visibility for its own project. Indeed, it made accountability and visibility of the power to punish one of the foundations of its claim to plausibility and legitimacy. This meant, however, that the Emperor had better have new clothes, and those clothes—the programs necessary to make action plans something concrete— never came. Yet while adopting validating appearance of actuarial risk prediction, contemporary parole has allowed classification to remain largely a matter of local judgment. Clear and Gallagher (1985) suggest that the most common approach in probation and parole agencies today is to use an instrument that has the appearance of statistical objectivity but that is in fact quite arbitrary. The risks and needs scoring, still in use, has no pretense to being statistically valid and provides at best a device for focusing the evaluation.

This does seem like a familiar story of reform, having its way with conscience once again (Rothman 1980). But seen against the background of premodernist strategies of community control, the imperative of local factors has its roots in more than administrative ease. Even before the clinical model parole had practiced a kind of crude individualization by requiring the prisoner to find local sponsors for a job. Despite the modernist claim to making this a scientific judgment, parole decision making during the clinical era remained quite ad hoc and open to local influences. The aspiration of the New Model to develop a full program of prestructured casework strategies which would be linked to a risks and needs assessment system remained unfulfilled. In the absence of such a program, the responsibility for developing responses to different sorts of threats remained at the local level.

For the moment most use of classification is fairly described as "management from disguised ignorance" (Clear and Gallagher 1985, 439). But risk prediction remains a potential source of rationalization for the future. In the view of one of its inventors, the New Model's development was constrained by competition from other procedures that drew more of the central administration's attention, most importantly revocation:

> What we have done is look at the revocation process because that is where the pressure and the resources have been. That part of parole has been separated out and works the way the total system should be worked on. The rest is basically paper.

As political pressure builds to find credible supervision strategies to keep parolees in the community longer, the technologies of prediction and classification will most certainly remain on center stage.

Offender-Based Data Systems

For over twenty years criminal justice planners have seen computer technology as the key to making other innovations mesh and transforming the criminal justice system into a bona fide "system." Drug testing, risk prediction, and specialized caseloads all offer the promise of a regime of control that is bureaucratic and internal, one that does not depend on the internal strength of community social control. The effectiveness of much of this new technology depends on the ability of correctional agencies to acquire, store, and retrieve information about its subjects.

One of the strongest recommendations of the 1967 President's Commission on Law Enforcement and Administration of Justice was for criminal justice at all levels to begin systematizing and linking their information on offenders through computerization.

> The importance of having complete and timely information about crimes and offenders available at the right place and the right time has been demonstrated throughout this chapter and, indeed, throughout this report. . . . Modern information technology now permits a massive assault on these problems at a level never before conceivable. . . . Criminal justice could benefit dramatically from computer-based information systems, and development of a network designed specifically for its operations could start immediately. (President's Commission 1967, 266)

Diana Gordon has recently examined the data bases of state criminal justice systems and concludes that they have developed so much that, in her view, they now pose a significant threat to civil liberties (1991, 56, 195). Since the early 1970s California has worked on developing such a system. The "Offender Based Information System" (OBIS) is an on-line information network that provides record and current status information on all individuals who are

arrested in California. It can be accessed and updated by police, court officials, and corrections.

Since 1979 when the New Model was introduced, California parole has
been premised on the collection and processing of such information. The report of January 1979 describing the program carried the following listing
of objectives for collecting information with which to evaluate parole's success.

> First, emphasis is placed on both criminality measures and on adjust-
> ment measures, since narrowly defined recidivism measures cannot
> fully capture the purposes of the parole system. Second, emphasis is
> also placed on summarizing the distribution of outcomes by focusing on
> the end intervals of these distributions, since these favorable and unfa-
> vorable intervals best convey essential information on accomplishment,
> or lack thereof. Third, measures reflect events relative to a specified
> time period; generally, information will be collected on a quarterly basis
> although a longer time period is relevant to certain measures. Fourth,
> summary measures should allow disaggregation to a relevant level of de-
> tail, levels of detail include forms and categories of supervision, specific
> criminal and delinquent activities, and organizational units as examples.
> (Parole and Community Services Division 1979, 83)

The auditing function mandated by the New Model has been realized in the
regular collection of statistics, broken down by unit, of violations, returns to
prison, jailed inmates, and decisions to release arrested parolees and/or continue them on parole. These measures permit the unit to be compared with
others along various outcomes, but it sheds little light into the decision-
making process itself. The official records related to a parolee, including risk
assessments, action plans, and field notes, are available for review at the district or regional level, but it remains impractical for the administration to examine large numbers of these.

The Parole Division's report noted that the

> entire problem of more efficient and responsive data collection and pro-
> cessing has been generally overlooked within the division for many
> years. Improvements to these processes will take much time and effort,
> and while they cannot be made all at once, efforts to systematize and
> automate data collection, processing, and presentation have high prior-
> ity and are already underway. (1979, 98)

A decade later the effort is only recently beginning to be realized. Budget
strains and logistical demands have made other priorities higher. The development of the statewide OBIS system has played only a marginal part in organizing parole supervision because the Division has not been computerized to
the point where each unit, let alone each parole officer, could easily access the

system. Parole administration requires far more parole-specific information than can efficiently be placed on OBIS.[8]

When computerization is complete it will create the conditions for a major transformation in parole operation by making it possible for the administration to monitor the flow of decisions and actions in the units. The major technologies of contemporary parole—drug testing, statistical classification, contact specifications—all operate to make the input into parole decisions more specifiable and trackable, but only if information can be accessed quickly and systematically by mid- and upper-level managers. The accumulation and regular review of these data should enhance tremendously the level of compliance with centrally defined standards if only through what one administrator already described as the "mindless mania to stay close to the mean in any category of performance."[9]

The provision of computers or terminals to agents could also dramatically alter agents' work patterns.[10] Report writing, currently done by hand and then retyped by clerical workers, eats away at the short time available for unit-level consideration of how to respond to violations.[11] Computers would also allow agents to review parole information rapidly in electronic form. A striking amount of current parole time is taken up with simply finding and moving bulky paper files. The expense and space of replicating paper files has led to tradeoffs that would be unnecessary from an electronic storage system. The parole agent's field book with the most recent notes about each parolee is traditionally taken along during agent home visits so that the agent can swiftly enter notes or check facts while in the field. On the other hand, with the arrest rate shooting up, it is essential for the office to be able to consult the most up-to-date notes about a parolee so that a decision can be made, if need be, on the spot (in the absence of the agent of record).

Not everyone in parole welcomes the slow but inevitable move toward computers. Some veterans see in the ubiquitous terminals a future parole which will have little room for either agents or parolees, and little tolerance for deviation from scripted outcomes:

8. In 1985 the Parole Division began development in earnest of an internal data base for use by parole which will hold much of the most important information for parole decisions. Installation of the system was only beginning during the period of this study.

9. That assumes that central administration actually seeks to create and implement specific standards, something which is far from clear, as will be suggested below.

10. Parole, like other state law enforcement agencies, looks more like a combination of high and low technology as portrayed in movies like *Brazil* or *Blade Runner* than the high-technology perfection of *2001*.

11. When especially hard pressed, some units have taken to sending handwritten reports to the Board.

We don't supervise people any more, we are supervised by the
computer. We do everything for the computer. It tells us when to get reports done and sets the priorities. Hell, if a client actually comes in we
get pissed off.

At the moment this remains an exaggeration. The computer system is far
from possessing the capacity to monitor the performance of agents. Yet the
comment reflects the potential for computers to intensify the emerging technocratic rationality of parole work. Veteran agents trained under the clinical
model will experience the contradictions between the professionalized agent
created by the clinical model and the role of the agent in the emerging risk
management model.

Drug Testing and Drug Use

After a hiatus of nearly a decade, the number of drug arrests in the United
States during the mid-1980s climbed to unprecedented levels fueled in large
measure by the spread of crack cocaine use and the heavy emphasis on arrests
to contain it (Currie 1993, 15). The effects on all organizations in the criminal
justice system have been staggering. Local jails, bloated with drug arrests,
have overwhelmed the existing infrastructure, and many are under court order
to hold fewer people. Trial courts are so clogged with drug cases that many
other kinds of charges are just dismissed. The proportion of the prison population composed of drug offenders has grown and now may be as high as 25 percent (Currie 1993, 151; Blumstein 1993, 5).

More drug offenders are being sent to prison through parole or probation
revocation procedures. For example, since 1987 California prosecutors have
been routinely pressing for revocations when individuals on probation are arrested on a drug charge (Feeley et al. 1988). Nearly a quarter of parole revocations in 1986 were for drug violations (California Department of Corrections
1988), and a large but unmeasured proportion of parolees sent back for failing
to adhere to their supervision requirements represent the direct consequences
of drug abuse among parolees.

Fed by growing political attention, research has begun to throw more light
on the role of drugs in crime. Since 1988 the National Institute of Justice has
tested urine samples from arrestees in major cities for drug use. Overall,
nearly half of all arrestees in the studied cities have tested positive for illegal
drugs, this reaching as high as 80 percent in some cities Bureau of Justice
Statistics 1989b, 459).

While no testing studies of comparable scope were carried out earlier, some
evidence suggests the growth of certain drugs, particularly cocaine, has been
quite sudden. In one analysis of a sample of New York City arrestees in 1984,
and at two observation points in 1986, cocaine use went up dramatically

among all offense groups. Whereas 38 percent of robbery arrestees in 1984 tested positive for cocaine, 92 percent of such arrestees in September and October 1986 tested positive (Wish 1987, 4). [12]

Crime has been a big political issue all through the 1980s, but only recently have drugs provided a definitive focus to the larger crime problem. The readers of NIJ reports and the watchers of television news are invited to think about crime in terms of drugs. Likewise, to parole agents in California and elsewhere during the 1980s, drugs, and more specifically crack cocaine, have defined a whole new era for the enterprise.

The empirical logic of this connection, however, should not blind us to the specific links between drug use as a phenomenon and correction's recurrent need to create a convincing account of community control. Drug use today is the surface upon which the problem of controlling the offender in the community is projected. Just as it did in the 1950s, the problem of drug use has provided a material ground for the ideological reconstruction of parole.

Just as industrial work and clinical treatment gave parole supervision practical and epistemological foundations (that is, allowed the risks posed by offenders to be objectified, detected, and responded to), drug use provides moorings for the contemporary parole enterprise. Drug use provides a coherent explanation of why and perhaps when parolees return to crime (just as idleness or psychological complexes did earlier). The flow of positive and negative drug tests provides the register on which to trace the otherwise invisible process of criminal degeneration (as did fiscal irresponsibility, or evasiveness in an interview). Treatment for drug addiction provides a model for controlling criminal degeneration, and abstinence from drugs provides contemporary parole with its "after" picture (in place of the industrial "good worker" or the clinical "well-adjusted person").

Then and Now: The Problem of Drugs in the Clinical and Managerial Eras

The sudden salience of drug abuse for crime seems to raise the potential for a resurgence of the clinical model in parole and in corrections more generally. Indeed, many individuals within the correctional community have viewed the attention to drug abuse as an opportunity to shift back toward a more rehabilitative approach, against what they see as an unfortunate swing to retribution in the 1970s and 1980s. When we focus on method, technique, and strategy, rather than objectives, however, the drug "problem" that emerged in the 1980s offers a very different account of parole practice than that which nurtured the clinical model.

12. In November 1986 only 59 percent tested positive, but the author of that study, Eric Wish, believes that number may have been biased by internal police policies during that month.

One difference is in the drugs problematized now and in the past—not simply their chemical properties, but the social practices that have developed around them. During the 1950s, public fear of opiate use (especially morphine and heroin) and its concentration among the young within the ghettos and barrios of the large cities led to the introduction of new technologies such as group counseling, drug testing, and short-term reconfinement.[13] The heroin crisis ebbed due to the introduction of some improved treatment modalities (like methadone), and the aging of the cohorts involved with heroin, and because society in general, and corrections in particular, got more used to it.

The current drug crisis is driven by cocaine, particularly the highly addictive smokable form known as crack. Six years into the crack crisis no particularly promising treatments have emerged, and while the spread of the drug seems to have slowed, its disintegrative effects on poor communities continue unabated (Currie 1993). Nor does it appear that crack will be a drug with which it is easy to learn to live. By the 1970s many experts were convinced that earlier views of heroin addicts as violent and dangerous were wrong.[14] Crack is currently perceived as the source of aggressive criminality and potentially violent and aberrant behavior.[15]

Whether or not heroin and cocaine pose different organic challenges, they have a different social context, offer different opportunities for technological solutions, and have evoked significant differences in parole strategy. Three points seem particularly important in contrasting the drug control regime in California which developed in the 1950s and continued in modified form until the early 1970s (see chapter three) with the drug control regime that emerged after 1985: (1) Drug use was once seen as defining special individuals out from the poor population as a whole; now it helps define the poor as a criminal population. (2) Testing formerly marked those who were readdicted from those who were not; today it measures a continuum of risk. (3) Heroin addiction, the major drug problem of the past, was seen as a problem that could be treated; cocaine addiction, the major drug problem of today, is seen as a problem that can be, at best, contained.

---

13. The legislature created programs like the Narcotics Treatment and Control Program, and the California Civil Addict's program which came to involve a large proportion of the agents in the state. These programs are discussed in chapter three.

14. This remains a highly contested issue: see McGlothlin (1979), Wish (1982, 1987), Kaplan (1983).

15. This may turn out to be a cyclical phenomenon where drugs are initially seen as leading to violence and then downgraded as their use is more closely studied. It is widely believed by many parole agents that crack addicts are more dangerous than heroin addicts ever were. Doubtless this belief is influenced by the fact that crack addicts today are younger than most of the heroin addicts encountered on parole caseloads.

From Individual to Population

In the 1950s and 1960s, narcotics users were perceived as a special group of individuals involved in crime but set apart from the mainstream of the population. The addict might hang around other criminal activities, like Nelson Algren's heroin-injecting hero Frankie Machine, but he was invested with a special moral significance as a person utterly dominated by the corrupting pleasures of the drug. Drug use provided a "total identity" that remained uniquely individualizing even as the most demonic images of the 1950s gave way to more soothing psychotherapeutic ones (Duster 1970, 87–102).

Unlike heroin, cocaine use today does not define a unique class of offenders so much as a unique social class—the underclass—perceived as criminally at risk. It is not that character formations have been proved irrelevant to chronic illegal drug use by scientific research, but the demographic features of its distribution are deemed more salient.[16] While drug use may help locate a person as belonging to the underclass[17] it does not distinguish an offender as an individual.

From Status to Continuum of Risk

In the clinical era drug use had a dichotomous character. Some agents may have appreciated that some of their parolees could manage their habits and others could not, but the law required almost complete intolerance of drug use. Testing marked a binary opposition between individuals who renewed their use of drugs, and thus needed to be secured in a custodial treatment center/prison, and those who did not and could be safely kept in the community. In Troy Duster's study of correctional treatment of drug users in California during the late 1960s and early 1970s, he observed that exaddict parolees were accorded a special status in the eyes of parole agents which cast their every violation into a special moral dimension:

> Other criminals on parole are far more likely to get away with minor transgressions such as seeing old friends and taking a drink if they simply avoid trouble with the police. The ex-addict on parole sees himself quite correctly in a different situation. His minor transgressions of the same dimension (in his eyes) are treated by the parole agent as a lapse into "drug prone" behavior. (1970, 207)

16. This has been enhanced by the bifurcation of the cocaine consumption market into a crack trade which is associated with the underclass, and a powder trade which was once associated with trendy members of the upper classes. Now that casual use is reportedly declining, cocaine of all sorts is coming to be seen as an underclass drug. Doubtless its negative image is both partial cause and effect of its class reorientation.

17. Crack use is perceived as far more broadly diffused among the poor than heroin. Although (perhaps inaccurately) it is seen as an inner-city and minority problem, it is assumed to be used among all segments of this population, including groups like women, mature men, and young children who were not considered vulnerable to heroin.

The simple fact of drug use today no longer accords the parolee a special status. In the face of evidence that the vast majority of offenders use drugs, even a positive drug test no longer triggers an automatic change in status, but the frequency of use provides a possible tool for risk classification (Wish, Toborg, and Bellassai 1988). Parole agents in California see the number and rapidity of positive drug tests as an important basis for differentiating among all parolees who use drugs. Most agents are unwilling to speak directly about a tolerated level of use, but the sense that drug use must be treated as a continuum of dangers is evident in their practice. The frequency (rather than the fact of) drug use, as charted by the positive tests, builds a highly plausible account of increasing risk and, eventually, the need for revocation. This was explained succinctly by a parole supervisor:

> We usually tolerate drug use to a certain extent, then we run out of options. We have few resources; there is a shortage of tools to deal with these parolees. After a certain number of dirty tests we are going to pick up other delinquencies. The guy may be selling his mom's TV, stealing a carton of cigarettes or a bottle of gin from the liquor store. We come under a lot of pressure to do something about that guy. Up until now that has meant sending them back to prison.

In one sense, the current view of drug use represents a growing sophistication about drugs in corrections. Some politicians talked of zero tolerance in the 1980s, but few penal managers joined the chorus. But if the "status" view of drug use is too expensive to be taken seriously today, the fact that it is now seen as a continuum of risk is not simply realism, it represents a fundamental reinterpretation of drugs as a social phenomenon.

Advocates of aggressive use of drug tests as a predictor do not see them as tools for the clinical diagnosis of the individual, but as indicators of the risk group to which that individual belongs. A recent description (Carver 1986) of the benefits of Washington, D.C.'s program of drug testing as a condition of pre-trial release is exemplary of the new framework in which the drug test is read.

> With the assistance of the National Institute of Justice [sponsored drug testing program], judges in [the District of Columbia] are now much better equipped to *identify* those drug abusing defendants who pose the greatest threat to community safety, and to *monitor* their behavior and *control* their drug abuse while under the court's jurisdiction in a way that *reduces* the risk associated with drug abusers. (Carver 1986, 1, emphasis in original)

From Treatment to Containment

Despite the failure of drug treatment programs to achieve some of the high expectations that were set for them by the 1970s, they succeeded in winning significant control over heroin addicts. Between 1961 and 1972 some 17,800 opiate addicts went through the California Civil Addict Program which was administered by the Department of Corrections and involved hundreds of parole agents in supervising special narcotics caseloads. Although none of the techniques of control used in the program proved to be a silver bullet, subsequent evaluation and research has documented that the program was successful in reducing degree of subsequent drug use and of property crimes by addicts seeking to purchase the drug (McGlothlin, Anglin, and Wilson 1975). After 1970 a major factor in this manageability was the availability of methadone, a substitute opiate which satisfies an addict's chemical need while theoretically not providing the psychological high that makes continued drug use attractive (Kaplan 1983, 213–25). In studies of California addicts, methadone had even more dramatic effects on use and property crime rates than supervision alone (Anglin and McGlothlin 1984).[18]

The profile of cocaine treatment and control is vastly different at this point. The treatment believed to be most effective is a period of inpatient drying out and counseling followed by regular testing and counseling. Inpatient treatment is expensive. Waiting lists for subsidized programs are long, and in some communities parolees are given low priority. No substitute drug (like methadone) or blocking agent (which exists for opiates) has been discovered to provide a quick chemical solution to the cocaine problem.[19]

In the absence of accessible technologies to treat cocaine abuse, the sense of manageability that heroin had for parole in the 1970s has been replaced by a sense of extraordinary challenge. This is exacerbated by the widespread perception that cocaine abusers are younger, more violent, and less interested in treatment than heroin addicts. One veteran supervisor described the difference between the two drugs and the two cohorts of users:

> Rehabilitation is less workable now than in the old days. Now we have more violent parolees. Heroin users in the old days were our main concern. They committed property crimes but they were not particularly violent. They also had more of a will to try to change. The emphasis on self-help is not there anymore. We have younger, more aggressive

18. The major virtue of this approach is the control it promises over the subject. It may not wean the addict from drug dependency, but it mitigates the pathologies that are attendant upon addiction to illegal drugs. Indeed, Kaplan raises, although he rejects as immoral, the possibility of addicting offenders to methadone to make them easier to control on supervision (1983, 218).

19. Methadone's benefits come more from the stabilization of the addict's life than from any direct chemical benefit. One benefit of methadone is that it prevents heroin addicts from undergoing physical symptoms of withdrawal. Addicts can either be maintained on methadone or weaned from dependence altogether. The whole idea of substituting one kind of addiction for another has remained controversial, and it is not clear that a substitute for cocaine would be perceived as useful. Unlike opiates, cocaine does not generate physical withdrawal symptoms.

offenders who abuse cocaine. Their potential for violence is truly frightening.[20]

The methodology of testing in the 1960s also contributed to the sense that
correctional drug control efforts were aimed at curing addiction, and that a
cure was obtainable. Nalline, an opiate derivative with no intoxicating effects, was injected in parolees by physicians, operating in "clinics," who
looked for the telltale pupil dilation in subjects who had used other opiates
within 48 hours (see chapter 3). This gave testing a medical aura which was
appreciated in the 1950s and 1960s when prisons were renamed treatment
centers and classification was called diagnosis. It was also common to refer to
nalline's "anti-narcotic effects" as if it possessed therapeutic powers. In fact,
its physiological effects had no beneficial effect on the subject's opiate dependency.

Contemporary practice relies overwhelmingly on chemical testing of urine,
which has become a cheaper and faster method than it was in the 1960s. The
body produces distinct proteins known as metabolites as it absorbs virtually
any drug (whereas nalline only reacts with opiate use). Chemical tests work by
reacting to the presence of trace amounts of the distinctive metabolites in
urine or blood.[21] Different processes vary in error rate and in cost. Urine testing, the major modality used by corrections, holds none of the medical associations that surrounded nalline. It is handled in scattered sites, rather than
in clinics, it does not require a doctor to be involved, and it creates no changes
in the physiology of the subject.

In the clinical era, drug abuse demarcated a distinct class of offenders for
whom parole had real management solutions. They were, in effect, a source of
support for the whole effort to constitute an effective parole mechanism that
could rely on its own methods. Today drugs have almost the opposite meaning.
They signify the unmanageable circumstances of a great portion of offenders
for whom there is little optimism, and whose situation does little to encourage
faith in parole as an effective tool.

20. The distinction that many parole agents draw between cocaine and heroin users seems to be
driven by three distinct assumptions. First, that heroin users were a more docile lot even when they
were younger. Second, that however volatile heroin users were when they were younger, they are now
older, and since older offenders tend to be less active and violent, heroin users as a class are less active
and violent. Third, because heroin has been around longer and there are more technologies available
for the addict to fall back on, addicts of any age may be less inclined to lose control.

21. Recent methods have been developed which detect metabolites in nails or hair. Since a single
hair may reflect weeks or even months of growth it provides a stored record of drug use during the
period. Tests of urine and blood, in contrast, only reveal drug use over a short-term which varies from
drug to drug. Cocaine is generally undetectable in urine after three days; marijuana may be detected
up to three weeks after the last use.

Drug Testing As A Method of Control

In the absence of new technologies to control cocaine use, drug testing itself has moved to a central position in the performance of control.[22] More than anything else today it provides the material basis for surveillance. It applies to the vast majority of parolees.[23] It justifies and organizes most field contacts and office visits. It serves as the most accessible measure of parolee, and parole agent, performance.

For the agent, drug testing provides an established set of procedures which help to organize his work and give it functional value. Like the revocation procedure discussed above, drug testing is one of the systems that "works." Urine goes in, results come out. The tests provide indicators which are both salient and interpretable.

Testing also allows the agents to gain some control over their caseloads. Whether or not drug testing has any direct effect on a parolee's drug problem, it can, and does, play a critical role in "managing" the parolee's time. It affects not simply those who have severe drug problems, but all of those who are subject to testing.

One of the primary tasks for parole agents today is to create regulating mechanisms for those with no other significant attachments.[24] The sheer amount of open time in the lives of parolees is a major source of risk from the perspective of the agent. Unemployed, living in hotels or shelters, and not belonging to any formal networks, many urban parolees have few such occasions when they must effectively "check in" with the system: these occasions demand self-regulation if they are to be pulled off.

Drug tests provide a particularly efficient way of doing this. They require the parolee to be at home or come into the office to test. Often the agents will be vague as to when they are coming by the parolee's home, thus keeping him home for a longer section of the day. In contrast, when they make an appointment for a parolee to come into the office to test they will often set a precise

22. This is not without precedent during the clinical era. The nalline test was looked on as a kind of therapeutic device, rather than simply as a testing mechanism. This was due in part to its explicitly medical trappings, set in a "clinic" and performed by doctors. Chemical drug testing has a less medical allure, yet it too provides a sense of effectiveness that comes from a technology that is self-sufficient.

23. The parole agent manual authorizes drug testing for parolees with "a documented history of illegal use of controlled substances within five years prior to the present commitment or during incarceration" (Parole and Community Services Division 1987, sec. 1115). This includes arrests or convictions for drug offenses or earlier admissions of drug use in probation or prison reports. In my sample 80 percent of the parolees were subject to testing, although only 45 percent of these ever turned in a positive test over the course of their first year on parole.

24. That was true to a large degree by the late 1960s, but there were a far greater profusion of programs in job training, counseling, and drug treatment. The agent could function as a broker.

time (like 2:15 P.M.), so that a parolee in Los Angeles without a car may have to plan his day around making the right transit connections. Once in the office, the parolee must check in with the staff, often wait an hour for someone to see him, and provide his most recent address, phone number, and law enforcement contacts.

Today's urban poverty provides few opportunities for most parolees to distinguish themselves. Drug testing provides the agent with one of the few available indicators of who is "making a good adjustment" on parole, and who is not, just as work did in an earlier era. Correspondingly, it gives the agent few things about which to make risk distinctions.[25] With little else to go on, many agents recognize adherence to procedure as the best available sign that the parolee is trying to "make his parole" and thus is a worthwhile risk to remain in the community even though a drug test may have been positive. Drug testing provides a regular system of cooperation points, where the parolee can either show his good faith (often phrased as "taking care of business") or demonstrate his lack of commitment to parole compliance.

A regular meeting schedule would accomplish some separation, but visits linked to detection of drugs gives the agent a stronger sign of "cooperation." The parolee has not merely gotten up and arrived at the office, but has done without for several days in order to clean up enough to come in. One regional staff member explained that drug testing "is not really for detection, it is for control. A parolee can always beat the test, but only if he has his own drug habit under control."

A parolee who continues using up to the limits of where a test will be positive is bound to turn in an occasional positive either because of an unannounced test or because human metabolisms are not mechanical. An occasional positive test might only indicate a bad call, but a series of positives indicates a parolee who has given up even appearing to conform. Thus the normal course of drug testing permits a large amount of drug use but catches those parolees whose abandonment of any effort to ward off trouble with the agent indicates serious degeneration. A parolee who no longer cares whether his agent will know he is using probably does not care about the consequences of stealing from his kin or strangers and is thus moving close to burning through the scant resources that sustain him.

Drug testing can also be used for self-regulation by the parolees. From the early days of specialized narcotics control units in California during the mid-1960s agents had noted that some parolees who could not quit drugs could manage to keep it down enough to beat the testing schedule. This helped prevent them from becoming readdicted although they continued to

25. It is axiomatic that one cannot make risk judgments without making distinctions among different levels and types of risk.

use. Eventually this use was destroyed by the imposition of a strict policy requiring reimprisonment for each positive test. Current policy permits the parolee to use the testing regime as a self-control mechanism more readily because of the broad discretion the parole agent has to continue parolees in the community in the face of one or even several positive tests.

The current regime of urine testing also enhances the ability of management to control decision making by providing an easily monitored audit trail.[26] The lab which conducts the chemical analysis generally sends a sheet with the results of each batch of tests directly to the unit supervisor. Each agent is notified by circulating copies of the sheets with her parolees highlighted if there was a positive sample. This means that each supervisor (as well as higher-up administrators) can know as much about a parolee's drug use as the agent does. At the same time, the visibility of positive tests also provides a validation device for the agent's compliance with other procedures like filling out activity reports for each violation or meeting minimum specifications for field contacts.

Summary

Parole officials are surely right when they point to the sudden surge in cocaine use in the mid-1980s as the source of many of their problems.[27] As we shall see in the next chapters the high rate of parolees returned to prison for persistent positive drug tests became a major concern to planners in the California Department of Corrections in 1988 and 1989. At the same time the drug problem provides the vital matrix through which knowledge about the various actors in parole and the exercise of power in parole from all sources is integrated, regulated, validated, and objectified.

Testing fills many of the functions that work and therapy did in earlier parole configurations, yet drug testing, by virtue of its technical qualities, makes possible a much different structure of relationship among parolee, agent, and system. The most important distinction is that the testing system requires little in the way of discourse, communication, or explanation. It is part of a self-contained "truth"-producing system that does not require interpretation of social life in the community. It thus provides the grounds for a parole that is more integrated as a system and less dependent on the community, the professionalism of the agent, or the integrity of the bureaucratic hierarchy. But it is a system with only a tenuous connection to the task of controlling drug use or mitigating the cost to public safety in the community.

26. In current practice, little of this capacity is effectively utilized by management. Partly this is due to major gaps in the technology of information management to be dealt with below.

27. Table 7.1 in the next chapter shows that other states experienced a comparable bulge in parole revocations during this period.

The Enduring Place of the Agent

This chapter has focused on the rise of technologies that provide control without primary reliance on the parole agent, yet the role of the agent remains at the center of parole supervision. Invested with significant legal authority but restrained by a thick network of procedures, the parole agent is the crucial link between parole's historical formation and its potential for reformation.

As noted in chapter one, parole predates the parole agent role by almost four decades. Not until the mid-1930s, when the Depression had knocked out the labor market on which parole had relied so heavily, did the existence of a field staff become a major pillar of parole's claim to effectiveness. The official discourse of the 1930s described the agent as an effective guarantee that private control arrangements, like employment, were actually operational. The role reached its apotheosis in the clinical era of the late 1950s and 1960s. By the time of the 1959 edition of the parole agent manual, the agent had become the essential ingredient in control strategy as the positive pole of a special relationship with the individual parolee.

The legal and political developments of the 1970s stripped the parole agent role of much of its assumed capacities. The determinate sentence law, with its emphasis on uniformity and retribution, offered a conception of penal justice which was inherently unfriendly to individualized judgment and the special role of the agent. Although the sentencing law left parole supervision intact, its ideological influences on the organization of parole were manifest. The New Model, which parole officials promulgated in 1979 as a basis for reinvigorating parole supervision, displaced the agent's relationship to the individual parolee in favor of functional specialization with different agents meeting different needs or problems of the parolee.

Throughout the evolution of the control model in parole the agents have always remained in a precarious position. As the front-line control agents they are as concerned as anyone with having an adequate account of how they are exercising their power and fulfilling their duties. Yet they have the least leverage to endure contradictions between practice and narrative. They must daily confront the capacity or incapacity of their techniques to grasp the tasks they are assigned. Despite these vulnerabilities the role survives because at bottom the agents remain integral to any account of control that is plausible to the public.

The Significance of Casework

The role of the agent was always associated with "casework," a term borrowed from social work and social science discourse which involves the development of expertise on the individual character and circumstances of a troubled person. While casework might involve various ways of collecting information, the essential ingredient has always involved the professional visiting the client (here the parolee) in his or her community setting.

During the clinical era an intensive effort was made to place casework at the very center of parole supervision (Cressey 1959). To succeed under this social worker model of professionalism the agent would have to develop an individualized knowledge of parolees. Unfortunately, the research program never generated the necessary epistemological base. In the end the researchers were among the most eager to demystify the casework premise (Robison and Takagi 1968).

Many agents and supervisors continue to look at casework done in the field as the heart of parole. In their view casework is what allows the agent to really know the parolee, to really influence the parolee. It is what differentiates the parole agent from probation officers, whose decline in status has been paired with climbing caseloads that have made home visits nearly impossible.[28] (It is also what justifies the provision of a state car for each agent's use.)

The importance of the age is also reflected in official discourse. The most recent edition of the parole agent manual also places primary weight for supervision on "contacts with parolees and persons involved with parolees" (Parole and Community Services Division 1987, sec. 1110). It sets specific minimum contact requirements for each type of caseload. High control caseload agents, for parolees with a risk score of 7.5 or above (see discussion of risk scores in chapter four), are to make two face-to-face contacts with the parolee (at least one at his residence) every month, and two contacts with a collateral source (relative, law enforcement, service agency, etc.). Agents on the standard control service caseload need only make one face-to-face contact per month. The specifications do not detail "how" these contacts are to promote control.

The standard view of why the special status of the parole agent remains essential to public security is that the parolee is deterred from committing new crimes by the fear that the parole agent is likely to discover through unannounced visits the fruits, instrumentalities, or confederates of a criminal enterprise in the parolee's home. Every agent with some years in the business has a story about the time they walked in and found weapons, drugs, or money on the table.

Despite the low number of contacts required, many agents believe that the threat of an unpredictable visit is a significant deterrent. As one agent put it: "they believe the agent is an all-seeing eye." Some tricks of the trade do enhance that capacity. Where caseloads are geographically assigned (which some units do), agents may be seen moving about the neighborhood. They like

28. Many recent hires in parole today came from county probation offices which have suffered tremendous budgetary restraints since the property tax limitations of the late 1970s.

to leave their cards in the doors of parolees who live near other scheduled visits.

An alternative view of the utility of casework lies in its capacity to reveal the parolee as he really is. The assumption is that the parolee can prepare himself for office visits psychologically and physically, but an unannounced visit at home will give an undistorted reading of the parolee's situation. Yet even enthusiasts doubt it has much of a control effect on the parolee:

> It provides me with an understanding I can't get sitting in my office. If a parolee comes into my office, without me having knowledge of his community and how he fits in there, I don't know what I'm being confronted with. . . . As far as trouble prevention there seems to be no difference [in whether or not the agent gets out into the field]. At first when I started I was totally into doing casework in the field. Now I have been grounded in the office by the administrative pressure of handling three jobs; I haven't done any real fieldwork for three months. In terms of problems on my caseload I can't see any difference.

Others, like an agent I spoke with who had trained in social work prior to entering corrections work, doubted that their colleagues shared any general sense of what casework means:

> They speak about casework around here but only in a generic sense. Work on a case is casework. But they don't use the casework method. Just look at the activity reports, there is hardly any effort to explain why a decision is being made.

In fact, experience in the field is intermittent. Contact goals are not viewed as imperative, and failing them is not considered as much of a problem as failing to complete a revocation report on time. During the late 1980s the rapid expansion in both parolees and staff made it especially difficult for agents to emphasize casework since they were often being introduced to a new caseload or absorbing extra cases while waiting for new agents.

When the agent does get into the field, the visits tend to be dominated by the needs of other technologies like that of collecting urine samples for drug testing. In most of the visits I made, the collection of urine was the central event. If the parolee was home we would come in and chat with him for several minutes. The agent might look around the house and visit the parolee's room, if he hadn't been to this dwelling before, or for a long time. After a short amount of time the sample container would be brought out and the urine sample taken.

The primary interaction between parolees and the supervision process is really through the office rather than the agent. Parolees come in with or without an appointment in order to undergo drug tests, give a new address, or seek assistance like a bus pass or a welfare hotel room. In many of these visits, the parolee will interact with a parole agent assigned for the day to handle "drop-in" parolees, but even if the official agent of record is available, the visit is more or less the same. A brief check is conducted on items like current address, contacts with police, and employment prospects, usually followed by a trip to the lavatory for a urine sample. Rarely did such interactions as I observed last more than ten minutes.[29]

The Power of Agents

The political and legal developments of the 1970s stripped away much of the ideological context of the agent's role built up during the clinical era; yet it left the agent a powerful legal actor. Parole agents are equipped with legal authority to carry and use firearms; to search places, persons, and property, without the requirements imposed by the Fourth Amendment; to order arrests without probable cause and to confine without bail. In most respects these powers apply to the relationship of parolee and parole agent (in that respect they might equally be described as disabilities of convicted felons under state law).

In some respects, however, these powers extend into the wider community. The power to search applies to households where a parolee is living and businesses where a parolee is working. Albeit less directly, the other powers inevitably affect the parolee's personal support network and the larger community. The ability to arrest, confine, and in some cases reimprison the parolee makes the parole agent a walking court system for those people directly affected by the civil and criminal conduct of the parolee.

One important dimension of that power is the ability it gives parole agents to act in concert with the police to extend police powers. Police regularly contact parole agents to seek their cooperation in searches of parolees. Formally, the parole agent is the one who is supposed to contact the police for assistance in carrying out searches of a parolee's home or property if backup support is needed. But in practice the police usually initiate the interaction in cases where they suspect the parolee has evidence of a crime in his possession, but where the police lack sufficient indicia of probable cause to go in on their own powers. The police also seek parole authority to hold a parolee who has been arrested without bail. Parole agents, in turn, find themselves in need of police assistance in cases where they plan to arrest a parolee who may resist. While

29. If a potential exists for a thicker kind of casework in contemporary parole, it is likely to be among "high control" and "high service" agents who enjoy caseloads that are only supposed to be half the size of the regular ones. High control caseloads are composed of those with the highest risk scores who are supposed to represent the greatest threats to the community. High service caseloads, composed of those with high need scores, are predominantly made up of the mentally ill. Agents in both categories are expected to keep in more frequent contact and provide more special expertise than regular agents. But these agents are often burdened with a higher arrest rate among their cases, which means more time doing revocation reports.

no explicit quid pro quo is made there are powerful incentives for cooperation from both sides.

A second important dimension of parole agent power is the role he can play in enhancing the capacity of family support networks to maintain felons in the community. In those situations where the family members of a parolee are able to establish a relationship of trust with the parole agent he can access the considerable discretionary power latent in the parole function.

A good example is the case of a young woman who lived in the same household as a parolee who was her cousin. A dispute arose in the cramped household between the two, and the parolee threatened to kill her. She got in contact with the parole agent, but was afraid to testify against him personally or have the threat brought out in any hearing. The parolee had recently turned in a positive drug test. The agent brought revocation charges, and he strongly urged that the parolee be returned to prison as a threat to the community without specifying the actual threat. Although a single positive drug test is rarely sanctioned with revocation, the parolee drew seven months.

Family connections can work the other way as well, with the relationship between relative and parole agent working to help the parolee avoid punishment. In one case a parolee had been arrested by the police on suspicion of participating in the gang rape of a young woman. The parolee's mother called the parole agent and claimed that her son was not involved (she also claimed that the young woman was a prostitute). Although the agent was skeptical he remarked that the mother had been good about reporting drug use by her son and had cooperated when the agent had sought to return him to prison to "dry out." The agent promised to call the police and the district attorney and to look into the case. Later the mother promised that the victim would admit to being mistaken about the parolee. The agent discussed the case with the district attorney and proceeded to fax paperwork to the jail to remove the parole hold on the woman's son.

In the absence of direct subsidization of the cost of maintaining the parolee in the household, the most effective tool the parole agent has to conserve the family's social and economic capital is the revocation power, which means the ability to withdraw the parolee from the household. Such interventions can cut both ways. They may pull the parolee out before he does lasting damage to his relationship with his kin. If the intervention results in some respite from pathological processes (e.g., drug use) the felon may return capable of a less rapid burnout. On the other hand, the intervention may simply confirm to the family that the parolee is a permanent loser and is not worthy of family sacrifices.

In either event, the family's confidence in the parole agent's ability and willingness to remove the felon may have an impact on their willingness to take the parolee in the first place. Removing a family member who has "burned out" his welcome is likely to be one of the most taxing and demoralizing experiences a family can go through. One of a parole agent's most attractive faculties from the family's perspective is the ability to bring about a separation of the unwanted family member in a manner which does not require the admission that the separation is desired.

The Role of the Agent in the Future of Parole

It is difficult to say whether the parole agent role remains at the center of supervisory power because of its potential for maximizing control efforts or because of organizational inertia reinforced by a powerful union and an absence of better ideas. It is possible to imagine a future for parole without a strong agent position. Probation departments provide one such model. There, in many cases, declining revenues and huge caseloads have left the probation agent only nominally as caseworkers. Their primary task is to serve as a case-processing center for the county criminal courts. The expanding role of revocation discussed in the next chapter suggests that parole agents might well be reduced to processors for a state sanctioning system that will run parallel to the county criminal courts.

An alternative future lies in reinvigorating parole's traditional role as a situational grant of public power to private members of the community. Such a function requires that power be exercised through agents who are capable of getting to know the individual circumstances of parolees, and who are professional enough to prevent responsiveness to private community needs from clashing with the due process rights of parolees.[30] For the present, the viability of such a role for agents has been diminished by a decline in the capacity of community institutions (formal and informal) to provide social and economic resources for maintaining them in the community. Whether or not a reinvestment in the institutional resources of poor communities will come to be seen as an alternative to the current high level of incarceration remains to be seen.

Conclusion

We have examined each new technology in terms of its local deployment and specific effects. It is now time to consider how they fit together in a plausible model of control. One source of strategic coherence is the set of political and legal demands described in chapter four. They have guided parole development by making clear what parole should *not* be—invisible, unaccountable, contingent. Parole managers since the late 1970s have strived to make the

---

30. It also requires agents who can see beyond their own class circumstances to recognize and support viable lifestyles among their clients that may violate the norms of their own lives (Gordon 1991, 145).

enterprise defendable by making it more visible, more accountable, more deliberate.

A second source of strategic coherence has been the developments in social control in the community. To varying degrees both the industrial and the clinical models of control were applications to corrections of strategies that seemed to be working in the larger society. Corrections as the government of the poor has always been a poorer version of mainstream government, both public and private.

James B. Rule, in his analysis of mass surveillance strategies and technologies for managing large populations, identified three central strategies at the heart of the control exercised in large corporate and public enterprises: (1) methods for efficiently identifying those individuals likely to generate problems so that more intensive surveillance or control can be applied precisely; (2) condensation and standardization of information, and (3) proliferation of contact points where individuals provide new information to the system and can be targeted for control measures (1972, 297).

These developments proceeded apace in the 1980s, especially in private sector enterprises like credit card companies, insurers, and banks, all of whom are faced with the task, not unlike parole's, of monitoring large populations for compliance with a wide array of technical rules All make use of computers and automated record analysis systems to stay on top of a large number of clients and transactions. All seek to attain greater predictive efficiency in knowing where to target control efforts. All seek technical contact points that permit information to accumulate on a regular and easily assimilable basis.

These mechanisms have supplemented and in some ways have come to replace the mass disciplines of industrial society.[31] The disciplines achieved control over large aggregations of bodies by increasing the visibility of individual bodies, the intensity of activity they engaged in, and the coercive regulation of activity. The new techniques of mass surveillance operate by identifying categories of individuals based on their capacity for self-management and permitting individuals variable access to resources and power depending on their risk-group status.[32] While discipline was based in work and extended only indirectly into domestic life, mass surveillance is quintessentially a device for regulating consumption and moves into production from there.[33] Since the underclass is marginal in both categories, it is

31. Here I just note the major features. I have discussed this shift from discipline to management in earlier works (1987, 1988).

32. For different views of the role of disciplinary power today see Cohen (1985), Shearing and Stenning (1983), and O'Malley (1992).

33. That is almost surely to overdraw the contrast. There were various attempts both early and late to extend direct discipline to the household (Donzelot 1978). Likewise there are many ways in which mass surveillance has been used from early on to organize production. In this condensed discussion, however, it is more useful to highlight the contrast.

predictable that the correctional embodiment of each strategy will be weaker than its mainstream analogue. Yet as the world of work disappears altogether for the urban poor, corrections must inevitably turn to consumption-based strategies.

We can see in contemporary parole efforts to follow this mass surveillance model. Drug testing provides standardized information. It may be of predictive value. Above all else it constitutes a ready set of contact points between the agency and parolees who often have few other obligations. The risks and needs score instrument offers some promise of identifying those parolees who require the most attention, and does so in a way that is standardized and compact. Specialized caseloads offer a way to build on the capacities of drug testing and risk evaluation to target parole controls more precisely.

It is easy to see why these mechanisms are attractive to penal managers (Reichman 1986). The vast network of surveillance that surrounds the ordinary transactions of nonconvicted citizens undoubtedly does exert a social control effect, inducing conformity (Gordon 1991, 89), and when control fails, makes it easier to bring the violator to account.[34] This is common knowledge to anyone who has tried to rent a car while running too high a balance on their credit cards or receive medical care without having gone through the regulatory loops required by the heath maintenance organizations many working Americans rely on for health coverage.

While the growth of mass surveillance techniques in the penal system may eventually have significant effects, beneficial and otherwise, intended and unintended, it remains at the moment rather strikingly behind the powers of the commercial and regulatory sectors of the surveillance society (Wilkins 1973).[35]

Private enterprises utilize advanced computer systems that allow millions of transactions to be performed and tracked nationally every day. Even certain branches of the government (typically ones which raise revenue and thus attract scarce public capital, for example, the IRS or California's Division of Motor Vehicles) have achieved considerable rationalization of information management. But the problems for parole in adopting the model of mass surveillance enterprises are more than ones of inadequate capitalization.

34. Gordon talks about the capacity of the system to "discipline . . . to 'traditional values'" (1991, 89); the mass surveillance strategies used by commercial and regulatory organizations seem far more oriented to technocratic aims of system performance.

35. The sectors are not, of course, totally distinct from each other. According to Diana Gordon, criminal justice system information is increasingly being used for commercial and regulatory purposes (1991, 66). Presumably criminal justice operatives could use the information created by commercial and regulatory systems as well. The problem is that their clients are less likely than others to be involved with recorded transactions of that sort. But there is likely to be increasing interaction in the future. If someone somewhere has not already been convicted of a crime with the help of automatic teller machine withdrawal records introduced to destroy an alibi or put the accused near the crime scene, he will be soon.

Rule noted two limiting factors to the growth of mass surveillance. First, few of the systems he surveyed, not withstanding their prodigious information-processing techniques, could survive if rule breaking were the practice of more than a small minority of its clients (he cites 25 percent as a speculative limit). Above this level, Rule estimated, the cost of delivering control would become too great. Second, all of the systems Rule studied relied to a large extent on voluntary cooperation by their clients in contacting the system (Rule 1972, 287–88).

The basic social conditions of parole supervision run square into Rule's limiting factors. The populations of people who use consumer credit, insurance, or vehicle licensing are not preselected for their propensity to break rules. Parolees get to be parolees by committing at least one, and usually more, felonies. In a sample of urban parolees drawn for this study over 70 percent had some violation (mostly minor ones) during the course of their first year on parole. Because of the widespread incidence of violations, it is doubtful that parole can ever become extremely precise in distributing surveillance power.

Parole could, in theory, reduce the level of official deviance by ceasing to count certain kinds of minor violations. Unfortunately those violations that are the most likely to be ignorable, such as drug use or failing to meet appointments, are precisely the ones that are most suitable to the technologies of mass surveillance because they are so closely tied to those technologies. In contrast, those violations that are by general consensus the most important to check are the ones on which parole has no practical hold. Burglaries, robberies, and assaults take place outside the system.[36]

The ability of parole to preemptively identify those offenders who perform the most serious violations is limited. The risk score, largely based on crime severity and past record, is used to distribute more intensive surveillance. But even if the risk score did a better job identifying who will commit robberies, burglaries, and assaults, there is little likelihood that increased surveillance will significantly lower the risks. Even doubling contacts for high control case-loads to four times a month does not provide much of a check on behavior. Planned property crime can simply be done when the parole agent is not likely to come visiting. Violent assaults can happen any time, especially late at night when parole agents are likely to be at home.

The point is not that parole can do nothing to combat serious crime,[37] but that its capacity to deal with crime is tied to "old-fashioned" techniques of individual investigative work and association with law enforcement. It is un-

36. Not surprisingly these violations are detected overwhelmingly by the police. Police arrests were involved in 89.8 percent of drug sales violations, 93.8 percent of property violations, and 90.5 percent of violent violations in my sample.

37. In the latter case close work between parole and police can make a difference. In addition, the use of parole search powers can extend the effectiveness of police.

likely to yield to methods of mass surveillance. The New Model had counted on prediction to justify placing a significant portion of parolees on minimum supervision. In the intervening years the Parole Division has in fact placed few parolees directly on minimum supervision during the first or even second year of parole. While the New Model emphasized careful and strategic distribution of resources, the practice that has developed places more and more parolees in the middle-level control/service caseload which reflects a lack of confidence in the ability of the system to differentiate. Without belief in that ability the technologies assembled by the New Model remain unfulfilled.

Inducement is also a major problem. Most of the enterprises that Rule studied relied on clients to initiate contacts such as credit card purchases, insurance claims, or vehicle license applications. There are two ways to induce voluntary contacts: provide services people want or link controls to services people want. Parole does provide some services and aid including transportation vouchers, housing and food vouchers, and occasional cash advances. These do bring some parolees in some of the time. Skillful agents can stretch them to create as much additional contact as possible (by offering, for example, short-term bus passes or housing vouchers that expire quickly and require an additional contact). These inducements are limited because the conditions are poor and often available from other sources (friends, family, or county public assistance).

The second category of inducements are limited by the marginal economic and social status of the population under supervision in the inner cities. Many surveillance systems attach contacts to other things people want. In California, vehicle registration provides the most effective means of compelling drivers to pay parking fines. When you try to register a vehicle, the system demands the full debt. Similar techniques are used by universities, who hold up diplomas and financial aid to collect overdue book fines, tuition, and other funds. In a New England state studied by Rule, all vehicles entering the turnpike are checked for warrants at the toll booth. Anyone wanting to drive somewhere must submit to contact with the system.

In all these cases surveillance of people is possible because they are engaged in other pursuits which, although unrelated to the aims of surveillance per se, provide contact points for surveillance. Parolees are too often unattached to any continuing social activity which parole can hope to use as a contact point. Parole finds itself in the awkward position of trying to build toll booths where there are no roads. [38]

Despite a concerted effort to develop the technologies of mass surveillance since the 1970s, parole has not yet been able to replicate the development of

---

38. This is perhaps the most important reason why drug testing, of all the technologies we have examined, has emerged as a central organizer of the parole enterprise. It provides an objectified space in which the criminal risk of parolees can be articulated and responded to. Yet even the ubiquity of drug testing has not yielded a stable and plausible model of parole.

an autonomous surveillance capacity analogous to the ones successfully developed in the private sector. In part this has been an institutional problem; implementation has been inconsistent and intermittent. In part this has been a problem of social and economic change, the population parole is charged with managing lack many of the social connections that make modern mass surveillance viable.

Even drug testing, by itself, cannot provide a sustainable practice. Its supporters acknowledge that it can only function in a highly developed institutional infrastructure:

> Testing should be implemented, however, only in programs that have manageable caseloads so that the test results can be used constructively with the person as part of a comprehensive treatment plan.
>
> Any monitoring program, particularly if it includes a potentially controversial urine-testing component, must be carefully planned before it is implemented and subjected to continuing evaluation after it becomes operational. Particular consideration must be given to the actions that will be taken if a drug user fails to comply with program requirements and whether the jurisdiction has the appropriate resources . . . to enforce those actions. (Wish, Toborg, and Bellassai 1988, 6, 17)

Without such an infrastructure, an account of control based on drug testing is not sustainable. Risk leads eventually to reconfinement, which becomes the heart of the program. Like the map of a town that has not been built, the components of a technocratic parole based on automatic eyes and programmed information management do not yet form a credible account of parole.

This stems from two distinct problems. The more easily solved conceptually is the simple undercapitalization of technology for government and especially for government of the poor. A massive investment in computer technology and training for staff will greatly improve the capacity of the correctional system to monitor the populations under its governance. The more intractable problem is the difficulty of deploying such mechanisms on individuals with extremely limited involvements with mainstream economic and social life. Surveillance can to some extent stimulate its own activity, as drug testing does, but in the end this degrades the capacity of mass surveillance to produce rational choices. Without underlying mechanisms of stability and control there is nothing to map.

After all, the well-funded versions of mass surveillance provide only a limited disciplinary effect directly. The clients of these systems do not have to submit to them in the way factory workers did. While they provide incentives for conformity (by tying continuing access to performance) their major task seems to be to identify those subpopulations that are already provided with adequate controls. Rather than disciplining the population, they screen for the well-disciplined. Increasingly primary discipline is a form of self-regulation taught by commercial companies and suburban school systems. But systems of mass surveillance play a role in accrediting the reasonableness of the risk posed by a subgroup and thus improving access to the channels of resources and power which expand opportunity for self-regulation.

In contrast the correctional system may play the opposite role. To the extent that it overcomes the problems of establishing an equipmental base for mass surveillance, the effect may be one of reinforcing the insecurity and isolation of the poor. Diana Gordon describes this potential as an "electronic panopticon" (1991, 1989).[39] Gordon suggests that the success of these new surveillance techniques may produce a lower-cost criminal justice system that will make an exclusion strategy for the poor more politically palatable.

The continuing difficulties of sustaining a plausible account of parole on the model of management takes its toll on those who carry out parole. The perception of "risk" is constantly turned up by the loud signals coming from the political system. Yet the capacity to "manage" it is not plausible to them or to the public. For many, supervision has become just a temporary space between initial release from prison and inevitable return to prison. Their task in such a system is to do the best they can to make sure they can find the parolee when the time comes to arrest him. Increasingly, their credibility as actors is contingent on initiating imprisonment procedures. The result is a system that has shifted from supervision to the mechanics of adjudication and punishment.

39. At least the panopticon was intended to integrate the disreputable and marginal into the larger economy, while the new surveillance aims at cementing their exclusion. Perhaps it would better be called the "electronic leper colony."

PART THREE

Management and Governability

Here is the irony of this tale. Parole, which once operated as a mechanism to control prison inmates with the promise of early release and ultimately relinking them to the social discipline of the community, now functions as a mechanism to secure the borders of communities without social discipline by channeling its least stable members back to prison. Rather than functioning as a "surety" for the disreputable, parole functions as a lower-cost system of incarceration for a population that is increasingly defined as inherently, irredeemably dangerous.[1] There are two major challenges facing this evolving function for parole (and perhaps corrections more broadly).

First, the managerial model of control requires some thresholds of acceptable risk. This is the lesson of mass surveillance technologies. They work on populations whose risk can be predicted and balanced. So long as parolees are seen as indistinguishably dangerous a managerial system tends toward becoming an efficient path to prison.

Second, precisely because parole and other forms of community supervision provide a cheaper path from arrest to imprisonment, they generate increasing costs of incarceration in prisons and jails. They are not alone in this. Other new innovations in crime control like the police drug sweeps initiated in New York (Blumenthal 1992) and Los Angeles (Davis 1990) also generate unacceptable costs of incarceration.

While being as tough as possible on crime remains the most politically viable position in the early 1990s, the fiscal costs of that strategy are setting limits to further prison growth. This puts more pressure than ever on commu-

---

1. This is one of the conclusions to be drawn from the 1992 jury verdict acquitting three officers and failing to convict a fourth charged with beating California parolee Rodney King.

nity supervision sanctions like parole to maintain larger populations at lower costs than full imprisonment.

The following two chapters sketch the scale of this conundrum and explore the innovations being offered to escape it. Chapter seven reviews data on parolees returned to prison in California and a number of other large states. It documents a system whose increasingly efficient managerial abilities are narrowing rather than expanding the base of their account of control. Chapter eight explores three reform efforts popular nationally. All of these continue the basic logic of the managerial model and thus do not seem likely to improve the situation.

CHAPTER SEVEN

Parole and Return to Imprisonment

Parole supervision depends on the plausibility of the account it provides of how men who have proved themselves to be criminally dangerous can be safely controlled in the community. I have argued that the creation of such an account has become progressively more difficult since the 1950s. In the face of a prolonged crisis in the ability of corrections to provide such an account, one of two things might be expected to happen. First, the practice of managing felons in the community could be abandoned completely as an undeliverable promise of security (we would also expect probation to dry up).[1] Second, parole supervision could substitute for its lack of credible measures reimprisoning felons as soon as their behavior manifested anything more than the presumptive dangerousness of all parolees.

It's far from clear why the first option did not happen in California. It came close. When the legislature abolished parole release in 1977 it was believed by many inside the correctional establishment that parole supervision would be eliminated as well. The truncated one-year parole term that most felons were ordered to serve under the original determinate sentence law appeared at best as a compromise designed to appease the large numbers of parole staff who would lose their jobs in a clean sweep. It was assumed the second shoe would drop, however, in the near future. Instead the length of the normal parole sentence was expanded to three years in 1979. Between 1980 and 1990 the California parole population grew 569.5 percent, more than twice as fast as the prison population. This has meant tremendous institutional growth with

1. In this case prison sentences would end completely the period of correctional jurisdiction over an offender until such time as he was again convicted of a crime.

new units opened, new promotions, and new hires—all despite the lack of development of a coherent model of control.

Revocation and the Prison Population

The expansion of parole without the construction of a plausible model of control has created tremendous internal tensions that have pushed the agency toward the second path described above. The growing importance of revocation as a parole activity is powerfully documented in figure 7.1, which represents the percentage of all persons on parole in a particular year who are returned by administrative and judicial actions.

The Revocation Rate Trend

In figure 7.1 we see considerable fluctuation between 1945 and 1980. After initially going up to a peak of 15 percent during the post–World War II recession in California, the rate of return declined to around 10 percent in 1955. That percentage began to go up in the late 1950s and continued to rise until it passed 20 percent in 1964 and 1965. In the mid-1960s the top management of the Parole Division sought to bring the return rate down. After a brief rise in the percentage between 1970 and 1971 the rate declined to its lowest level in the series in 1975.

This fluctuation, however, operated within a range of 10 percent for more

Figure 7.1. Parolee return rates, 1945–1987. *Source:* Messinger et al. 1988.

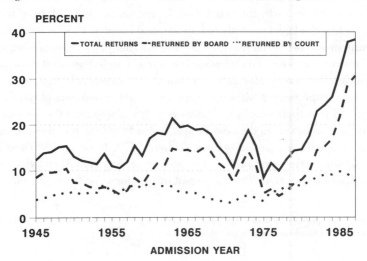

than 30 years. This pattern altered in 1980 when the rate passed 20 percent, from where it continued to go up at a historically unprecedented rate. In 1987 the rate passed twice the postwar upper limit. In 1990 the rate reached an astounding 56 percent (California Department of Corrections 1991, tables 6 and 7). Notice that this does not mean that half the people released every year to parole are eventually returned to prison. It means that at present more than half of all persons experiencing parole during the year are returned to prison at some point during that year (and this ratio does not include in either side the large numbers who have absconded altogether from supervision which we will discuss below).[2] The point is simply that California parole is as much in the business of sending people to prison as it is in the business of managing people on the street, and the trend is clearly toward it being more and more of a system for imprisonment.

The role of parole is even more evident when the total rate of return is broken down, as it is in figure 7.1, into the rate of returns with a new court sentence and the rate of returns of those whose parole has been administratively revoked by the Board of Prison Terms. As the figure shows, the rate of court returns went up in the late 1970s and 1980s. In 1990 nearly 14.4 percent of all parolees that year were sent back via the courts with a new term (California Department of Corrections 1991, tables 6 and 7). But the rate of increase has been relatively moderate compared to the rate of Board returns which reached 41.4 percent in 1990. The contribution of the regular court and prosecutorial system to the increasing rate of parolees returning to prison seems to be marginal (Messinger et al. 1988, 5).

Thus while the tendency to return parolees to prison may reflect a general trend toward more punitive policies in the criminal justice system, which is also evident at the front end of the system in the courts, parole is imprisoning at a substantially higher rate.[3] With virtually half of all people on parole sent

2. Following the method of Messinger et al. (1988), I have calculated the revocation rate as the ratio of the total number of adult felon parolees returned to prison during the calendar year by the total number of adult felons experiencing parole during that year. The latter number is attained by taking the total number of adult felon parolees in good standing on December 31 of the previous year and adding the total number of adult felons released to parole during the calendar year. This is a slight variation from Messinger et al., who used the population as of January 1 of the year in question. Since the difference is slight I do not differentiate the figures in the text, but all numbers before 1988 are based on Messinger et al. This base rate provides a picture of the total population at risk of experiencing a revocation. In fact, many of these individuals will be discharged before the year is out (or even very old), but this number provides the maximum figure exposed.

3. It appears that whatever drives the revocation rate moves primarily through the Board rather than the court system. The Board in turn has tended to ratify the revocation recommendations of local parole units. Returns to prison ordered by the Board are tightly linked (especially since 1977) to the use made by parole agents and supervisors of their discretion over whether or not to report violations to the Board.

back to prison in recent years, the decision of whether to seek revocation in the face of a violation has become one of the most persistent and demanding problems for parole staff.

Revocation as a Percentage of Admissions

The transformation of parole into an imprisonment system has had a substantial effect on California's already growing prison population. In 1990 half of all admissions of adult felons to California prisons (51 percent) came from parolees being returned by either administrative or judicial process. Most of these, 38 percent of almost all such admissions, were parolees returned by the Board or pending Board action (California Department of Corrections 1991, table 4A).

Since 1988 when the impact of parole actions on prison populations was highlighted by Sheldon Messinger and his colleagues (Messinger et al. 1988), the response of parole to violation behavior which does not independently result in a new criminal conviction has been a central concern of the corrections system and state government more generally (California Department of Corrections 1988; Blue Ribbon Commission 1990; Legislative Analyst 1988–1989). Pressure has been mounting to save prison space by keeping more parolees on the street. Some moderation in the revocation pattern discussed in this chapter may be expected as a result.

The National Pattern

Nationally the rate of adults on parole or mandatory supervision grew at 62.3 percent from 1979 to 1988, a somewhat slower rate than prison population rates during the same period which grew 83.4 percent (Bureau of Justice Statistics 1990a, tables 6.77 and 6.43).[4] As tables 7.1 and 7.2 show, however, the contribution of parolees or mandatory releasees returned to prison varies considerably from state to state.

With over 40,000 individuals on parole in 1990 California made up over 10 percent of all the individuals on parole in the United States during the same year. Even considering its huge population base, California stands out with 237 individuals on parole for every 100,000 people. Nine other jurisdictions

4. The terms parolees here encompasses those released to supervision by discretionary action of an administrative board as well as those, such as in California, who are supervised for a mandatory period following completion of their determinate sentence. Other work, including *The Sourcebook of Criminal Justice Statistics* (Bureau of Justice Statistics 1977a–1991a), uses the term parole to refer only to the former and uses the phrase "mandatory supervision" for the latter. Whether there are differences in the revocation pattern of states which have eliminated parole release will be explored below.

Table 7.1   Parole Revocation Rates for Selected States, 1978–1989

State	1978	1979	1980	1981	1982	1983	1984	1985	1986	1987	1988	1989
All states	7	6	NA	11	12	12	NA	13	14	16	17	18
CA	**19**	NA	**13**	**13**	**18**	**19**	**21**	**23**	**32**	**38**	**41**	**39**
FL	4	3	NA	2	15	11	**24**	**11**	**13**	**16**	**18**	**26**
AZ	**10**	7	7	8	**12**	**11**	**15**	**18**	**19**	**21**	**16**	**15**
IL	NA	NA	14	13	**16**	**16**	12	**16**	**18**	**15**	**9**	**14**
NY	NA	7	9	10	10	11	10	6	8	8	10	9
WA	5	3	4	4	4	18	NA	8	6	3	2	4
TX	8	6	8	7	13	12	9	13	14	13	13	13
NJ	9	11	10	7	6	7	9	9	9	9	8	8
PA	8	7	7	9	10	10	10	10	3	4	4	4
MI	NA	11	9	9	10	11	16	15	15	17	16	17

Sources: 1978–1983 and 1986–1989 data from *Sourcebook of Criminal Justice Statistics* (Bureau of Justice Statistics, 1980–1985, 1987–1990). 1984 data from *Parole and Probation, 1984* (Bureau of Justice Statistics), table 6. 1985 data from *Corrections Populations in the United States* (Bureau of Justice Statistics), table 5.10a. Bold type indicates determinate sentencing law in effect during that year.

have higher rates, but only Texas, with over 67,000 individuals on parole, has larger absolute numbers on parole.[5]

The data in table 7.1 comparing California's revocation rate with the next five largest states in terms of correctional populations, and several other selected states, demonstrate that California's rate is far higher than any other state or jurisdiction by several magnitudes. Most of these states experienced increases in their revocation rates during the 1980s, but with some exceptions these increases have been slow and inconsistent compared with California's rapid and steady increase.

While other states are sending a smaller percentage of their parolees back to prison each year, these numbers are having a large effect on their prison populations. Nationwide nineteen states, including California, had parole returns accounting for more than a quarter of prison admissions in 1990, and many more clustered between 20 and 25 percent (Bureau of Justice Statistics 1991a, table 6.57). We see in table 7.2 that most of the larger states experienced some increase in the proportion of their prison admissions composed of individuals who violated their parole or mandatory supervision, but with the exception of Texas, in no other state has the reimprisonment of parolees had such a significant effect on the prison population as it has in California.[6]

At the very least these tables ought to bring us back to the humbling truth

5. The other jurisdictions with their rate per 100,000 are New York, 314; Pennsylvania, 251; Rhode Island, 508; the District of Columbia, 824; Kentucky, 248; Mississippi, 265; Tennessee, 262; Texas, 656; and Washington, 311 (National Institute of Justice, 1991).

6. Note that table 7.2 does not disaggregate those parolees returned by administrative action from those returned by new court commitment as table 7.1 does.

Table 7.2   Parolees Returned to Prison as a Percentage of Total Prison Admissions for Selected States and Selected Years, 1974–1989

State	1974	1976	1978	1980	1982	1983	1984	1985	1986	1987	1988	1989
All states	12	15	15	16	17	19	22	22	24	25	27	29
CA	19	23	**21**	**21**	**27**	**31**	**38**	**42**	**49**	**53**	**58**	**59**
FL	12	11	14	16	10	8	**10**	**6**	**5**	**3**	**3**	**2**
AZ	9	8	**18**	**10**	**17**	**12**	**12**	**18**	**17**	**19**	**17**	**13**
IL	6	9	**27**	**31**	**29**	**30**	**30**	**30**	**31**	**29**	**20**	**25**
NY	23	19	21	24	23	25	29	14	17	17	20	19
WA	23	29	28	28	23	29	**30**	**20**	**18**	**12**	**6**	**10**
TX	8	10	13	16	20	23	29	31	32	34	38	41
NJ	30	26	30	30	18	21	29	30	30	28	27	25
PA	7	13	19	20	21	24	24	27	29	33	36	29
MI	14	16	18	17	17	30	24	24	20	19	18	20

Sources: 1978–1983 and 1986–1989 data from *Sourcebook of Criminal Justice Statistics* (Bureau of Justice Statistics, 1980–1985, 1987–1990). 1984 data from *Parole and Probation, 1984* (Bureau of Justice Statistics), table 6. 1985 data from *Corrections Populations in the United States* (Bureau of Justice Statistics), table 5.10a. Bold type indicates determinate sentencing law in effect during that year.

that it is very difficult to isolate specific factors that, taken alone, drive punishment (Zimring and Hawkins 1991). Thus, if it is true that declining employment opportunity has been felt in California, it has surely been felt even more in rust belt states like Illinois, Michigan, New York, and New Jersey. It should not make much sense on this account that Pennsylvania in 1989 had the same revocation rate as Washington, or that Arizona's was only slightly lower than Michigan's.

Likewise, the shift to determinate sentencing in six of the eleven states represented in tables 7.1 and 7.2 has no consistent effect on parole revocations. In some states, like Illinois, the beginning of determinate sentencing corresponded to a rapid rise in the proportion of revocations among total prison admissions, from 9 percent in the year before determinate sentencing was adopted to 28 percent immediately afterwards. Yet in others, like Florida, the adoption of determinate sentencing in 1984 was followed by a rapid decline in the proportion of revocations among prison admissions. This reflects both the wide variation in policies grouped under the phrase "determinate sentencing" and the interaction of political demands with the narrative process of constructing an adequate account of control in corrections.

One argument of this book has been that penal policy while responsive to both social conditions and political conditions always responds from within an existing account of control. If we miss the role of this account as an interpretive matrix in which social and political pressures are given a context and a basis for practical adjustment and attempt to isolate specific changes, for example, the decline in employment opportunities at the lower end of the labor market, or new political demands reflected in sentencing law, we must find confusion in this table. While no comprehensive account can be provided here for the outcomes in even these eleven states (let alone the other thirty-nine and the federal government) it may be useful to take a look at three: Texas, Illinois, and Florida, to get a feel for the interaction of factors that played a role in California.

TEXAS

Texas continues to release most of its felons through the discretionary action of the parole board.[7] Once released on parole they are subject to supervision and required to meet specified conditions of parole for the remainder of their maximum term.[8] If parole is revoked the parolee is returned to prison for up to the period remaining between the release date and the maximum sentence. There is no reduction for time served on parole.[9]

Texas has experienced one of the fastest growing parole populations in the country. Between 1983 and 1988 its parole population increased by 143 percent (in comparison the prison population increased 46.9 percent, and the probation population increased 32.9 percent) (Texas Criminal Justice Division 1990, 5). Texas has also experienced a dramatic increase in the percentage of prison admissions composed of parole violators going from 8 percent in 1974 to 41 percent in 1989, with most of this increase spread out evenly over the period. Unlike in California, however, Texas's parole revocation rate has increased only slightly since the late 1970s.

One factor in Texas is the existence of federal court order mandating capacity restrictions. While California expanded capacity by building prisons at a brisk pace throughout the 1980s, Texas did not. In order to avoid confrontation with the federal courts Texas has shifted prisoners to parole and probation. Thus, the increasing proportion of prison admissions coming from parole revocation reflects the size of the overall parole population and the effort to utilize probation rather than imprisonment by the committing courts. If regular court commitments to prison decrease, even if the parole portion stays the same, the proportion of parolees among all prison admissions will change.

In a careful study of survival probabilities for successive parole release cohorts between 1984 and 1987 over three years following first release, William A. Kelly and Sheldon Ekland-Olson concluded that prison overcrowding was

7. Texas Code of Criminal Procedure, article 42.18 (Vernon's 1993).

8. Ibid., sec. 8(a). Texas provides for mandatory supervision for all those not released on discretionary parole. These prisoners are released automatically following completion of their maximum sentence as reduced by good-time credits and are then subject to parole supervision for the period of that reduction.

9. Ibid., sec. 14. The Board of Pardons and Paroles may continue a parolee in the community despite finding them guilty of violating parole.

increasing the rate of both parole releases and parole revocations (1991, 619). Several processes appear to have been at work in Texas including an increase in the proportion of higher-risk offenders in the succeeding parole release cohorts, the use of technical violations to respond to public fear of crime, and possibly reduced deterrence when parolees realized that they would face shorter parole revocation terms if they were caught. Texas has also aggressively pursued alternatives to reimprisonment for parole violators. Parolees who violate the conditions of parole may be sanctioned by increasing their supervision, placing them temporarily in a residential custody situation, or simply increasing the level of supervision (Texas Criminal Justice Division 1990).

ILLINOIS

Illinois abolished parole release and adopted a form of determinate sentencing which became effective in February 1978.[10] Under the determinate sentence laws, judges sentence from a range established by the legislature for five categories of crime severity. These ranges are wide, for example, four to fifteen years for a class 1 felony. Once set and upheld against motions for a new sentence and appeals (which are provided for) the term is reduced only by the application of two types of "good time" credits. All prisoners avoiding disciplinary problems receive day-for-day reduction.[11] Meritorious credits of up to sixty days a year can also be given at the discretion of the Department of Corrections to reward particularly outstanding actions.

Following the expiration of the sentence less good-time deductions, prisoners are obligated to serve a period of mandatory release supervision in the community. The length of this term is a basic sentence established for each category (ranging from three years for the most serious categories to one year for the least) plus the period of accumulated good time.[12] An administrative body, the Prisoner Review Board, may discharge the prisoner from parole if it determines that he is likely to remain crime-free without supervision.[13]

During this term of community supervision the parolee may be returned to prison by action of the Prisoner Review Board, following a hearing, for committing a new crime or violating a condition of parole. The maximum period of confinement is the total parole period.[14]

While Illinois, like much of the rest of the nation, has experienced a gar-

10. Illinois Revised Statutes, chap. 38, sec. 1005-8-1 (d).

11. The Department of Corrections has no discretion over the allotment of these credits which can be deducted only by action of the Prisoner Review Board, an independent agency which is responsible for setting conditions of mandatory release and handling revocations as well. See Illinois Revised Statutes, chap. 38, sec. 1003-3-9 (Smith-Hurd 1992).

12. Ibid., sec. 1005-8-1 (d).

13. Ibid., sec. 1003-3-8.

14. Ibid., sec. 1003-3-9 (3)(i)(B).

gantuan increase in its prison population since the mid-1970s (a whopping increase of 276 percent between 1974 and 1989),[15] it does not appear that determinate sentencing has by itself been a cause.[16] Indeed, the prison population increased on average by more than 25 percent between 1974 and 1978 (under the indeterminate sentencing system), and it increased on average only 8 percent a year from 1978 to 1989 (under the determinate sentencing system).

Table 7.1 does not permit a comparison of Illinois's revocation rate under the Board of Pardons and Paroles, which had the revocation authority under the indeterminate sentencing system, and the Board of Prisoner Review which has the authority under the determinate sentencing system. Since the new arrangements have been in effect the rate has fluctuated moderately, starting at 14 percent in 1978, peaking at 18 percent in 1986, and dropping again to 14 percent in 1989.

A considerable change in the proportion of prison admissions accounted for by releasees being returned can be seen in table 7.2.[17] In 1976 parolees being returned to prison accounted for less than 10 percent of the prison admissions that year. In 1978 they accounted for 27 percent. However, since then the proportion has remained rather steady, reaching a peak of 31 percent in 1980 and again in 1986, then dropping to 25 percent in 1989.

Without knowing more about how the discretion to initiate revocations is managed by supervision officers in Illinois, it is impossible to learn much from the statutes and the numbers. While Illinois has experienced virtually the same level of prison population growth as California, it appears to have come from the regular court commitment process to a far greater extent than in California.

While the determinate sentence laws adopted in Illinois and California are remarkably different, the discourse of reform in both states shared many of the same features hostile to traditional parole models: distrust of discretion, skepticism about rehabilitation, an emphasis on punishment. Illinois also suffers from many of the same economic challenges as face California but even more so. This underlines the fact that these external pressures do not themselves determine the governability of the parole situation.

15. Calculated from the Bureau of Justice Statistics's *Sourcebook of Criminal Justice Statistics* (1978a and 1991a).

16. Casper (1984) suggests that determinate sentencing in Illinois should be expected to increase the prison population based on evidence showing that parole release may have been used as a relief valve for prison crowding in the past. He did not have sufficient data on post-1978 population changes to confirm this.

17. Note that even though it is unlikely that many people sentenced under the new law would have been released by the end of 1978 (and thus exposed to revocation for any part of that year) the new Board of Prisoner Review took over all revocation authority immediately and prisoners sentenced under the previous system were given the option of having it applied to them.

FLORIDA

In 1983 Florida adopted a sentencing guidelines law which abolished parole release for most classes of offenders.[18] Under the new law judges must sentence a convicted felon to a term within a narrow range. Any departures from the range must be supported by explicitly referenced mitigating or aggravating circumstances.[19] The ranges are calculated using a formula which takes into account both offense severity and the prior record of the offender.

Like other determinate sentencing approaches Florida stressed a sentencing system that would be uniform, fair, and focused on the goal of punishment (Spitzmiller 1984). But following the lead of Minnesota, Florida instructed the sentencing commission it created to consider the limited resources available for expanding prison capacity. In the legislative findings section of the guidelines bill this point is made strongly: "State government can no longer afford an uncritical and continuing escalation in capital outlay for prison construction at the expense of other competing social and economic priorities."[20] The bill specifically encouraged the "increased use of noncustodial alternatives" to alleviate crowding. The result of this new policy is evident in population numbers. Between 1974 and 1984 (the first year of the guidelines) the prison population went up 145 percent, or approximately 14 percent a year. Between 1984 and 1989 the prison population went up 37 percent, or an average of 7 percent a year.

Florida has gone farther in limiting parole. The relatively few felons subject to indeterminate sentences are still placed in parole supervision under the old laws.[21] Those felons sentenced under the new guidelines are released at the end of their sentence less the accumulation of good-time credits and special prison crowding reduction credits.[22] Only those convicted of a violent crime *and* who have previously served at least one felony term are subject to supervision following release.[23] Prisoners released onto parole supervision are subject to conditions set by the parole commission and to revocation for violations of these conditions for up to the length of their gain-time reduction from their original sentence.[24]

The data in table 7.1 show that the parole revocation rate more than doubled in the first year after the guidelines went into effect. It is difficult to

18. For an analysis of the development of the Florida law see Spitzmiller (1984).

19. Florida Rules of Criminal Procedure, rule 3.701 (West 1993).

20. Laws of Florida, chap. 83-131, sec. 1 (Joint Legislative Management Committee, Tallahassee, 1983).

21. The 1983 law called upon the sentencing commission to consider eliminating parole altogether. The date of its repeal pending the review was initially set at 1985, but it has been extended until it is currently scheduled to lapse in 1993.

22. Florida Code of Criminal Procedure and Corrections, sec. 994.291 (1) (West 1993).

23. Ibid., sec. 947.1405.

24. Ibid., sec. 947.141.

tell whether this was a result of the new law, informal reaction to the new law, or other factors altogether. The rate quickly returned to its previous level and then began climbing again. But as can be seen in table 7.2, the effects of a higher revocation rate have been neutralized, and more, by the reduction in the number of persons subject to a supervision.

A Closer Look at the California Experience

The percentage of parolees returned to prison through administrative action every year may be taken to be the function of several different factors: the incidence of behaviors that count as violations, the instruments through which violations may be detected, and the policy toward violations once they are detected. We examine each in turn.

The Incidence of Violation Behavior

Violations of parole in California can occur in three different ways: new crimes, technical violations, and disobedience of parole instructions. Perhaps the most intuitive place to look for clues to the rapid increase in parole revocations is at crime. Looking at reported crime the nation as a whole experienced a minor increase in crime, while California experienced a significant drop (11.1 percent; Bureau of Criminal Statistics and Special Services 1990, 1).[25]

Looking at specific crime categories, the picture both nationally and in California was more complicated in the 1980s. During the first half of the decade all categories of reported crime went down in the nation and in California. Starting in the middle of the decade, however, violent crimes began to go up sharply (ibid., 6). Property crimes went down in California throughout the decade. Nationally property crimes went down slightly, with a large dip in the early 1980s and a rise starting in 1984 (7).

These moderate fluctuations cannot explain California's high revocation rate. It is possible, of course, that parolees have been generating a disproportionate amount of these crimes. Since the parole population by definition is composed of convicted felons it is not surprising that they should be more criminally engaged than other portions of the population. Nonetheless data assembled by the Department of Corrections in 1989 strongly suggest that the number of arrests of parolees has not changed significantly in the 1980s (California Department of Corrections 1989b, chart 17). As a percentage of felons on parole those arrested for violent crimes made up 7.5 percent in 1980 and

25. Despite a surge in robberies and assaults in 1985 and 1986 nationwide victimization rates for virtually all categories of crime went down during the 1980s, continuing a trend that seems to have begun in the mid-1970s (Bureau of Justice Statistics 1990a, table 3.3).

5.8 percent in 1988; 9.2 percent of all felons on parole experienced an arrest for a property offense in 1980 compared with 8.8 percent in 1988. Only drug arrests showed a significant increase. Only around 4.1 percent of felons on parole were arrested for drug offenses in 1980, while 15.6 percent were arrested for drug use in 1988 (California Department of Corrections 1989b, chart 17).

Violation Decision Making Inside the Parole Process

Whether the violation was discovered by a parole agent or through an arrest for a new crime, the immediate issue for parole staff is whether or not to report the violation to the Board, a decision tantamount to revocation of parole. That may come at one of two different points, depending on the discovery mode. For those whose violations are discovered by the parole agent, typically after a string of positive drug tests, the decision will take place before the parolee is arrested. The agent and the supervisor will meet and "conference the case." The agent will summarize the situation. If the parolee has not had many previous positives, if he has not yet tried a treatment program, and if he has been maintaining regular contact with the agent, the decision will often be to continue on parole, with either an increase in testing frequency or a requirement that the parolee pursue a drug treatment program, or both.

These decisions come closer than any others to the clinical model of parole as individualized justice. The conference between agent and supervisor will involve a discussion of the parolee's character, circumstances, and performance. Usually this will take place after positive tests have continued in the face of threats by the parole agent and promises by the parolee to "clean up." In such a situation the parole agent often feels that his or her credibility is on the line. If a decision is made to "continue on parole" it will often be presented to the parolee as a situation in which the supervisor wanted to send the parolee back to prison but has been held off for one last time by the efforts of the parole agent to get the parolee one last chance (although this is the opposite of the actual roles in the conference). The supervisor may well come into the parole agent's office where the parolee is waiting and make clear how close the parolee is to returning to prison.

For those violations defined by a police arrest, the decision-making process follows the arrest and looks far different. Formally the police are supposed to contact the parole agent, who in consultation with the supervisor has the authority to place a special parole hold on the parolee which prevents the parolee from obtaining regular release by bail or on his own recognizance. The fiction is that the parole staff are requesting the police to hold the parolee. In practice the police are usually the ones who are seeking a way to hold the parolee.

Frequently the police call and speak to a parole officer on duty who has no relationship to the parolee but who generally approves the hold.

The parole agent's active role in a police arrest situation begins after the parolee has already been placed under a parole hold. The clinical quality described above is gone, and the parole agent takes on something much more akin to the role of the assistant district attorney, responding to the police, gathering facts, deciding whether the case should be pursued, and selling that decision to the supervising district attorney.

Since the parolee is already in custody the due process clock is running (see chapter four). In order to meet the ultimate deadline of a timely hearing, the internal guidelines of the Parole Division require a report to be filed with the hearing officer within two weeks. The agent's report must be prepared well before that. This pressure to decide quickly is exacerbated by the overcrowding of the county jails. In San Francisco, Oakland, and Los Angeles, jail rules require inmates kept under parole authority to be transferred to state prison within a few days or be released automatically.

Parole unit staff have the authority to remove parole holds, thus permitting parolees to obtain normal pre-trial release from detention, but this option is rarely exercised. In theory parole hold decisions call for a full investigation of the facts of the case and an appraisal of the parolee's dangerousness to the community if released. In practice parole agents are extremely reluctant to take responsibility for placing a parolee whom the police have charged with almost any crime back on the streets.

Responsibility for revocation has long been split between the Board and the parole supervision staff. Before the changes in constitutional and statutory law during the 1970s, the bulk of this responsibility lay with the Board. The Board required parole agents to report all but the most trivial violations of the conditions of parole, and the Board decided whether the violation required a return to prison.

Under the law as it now stands, the Board and the higher echelons of the Parole Division can, if they wish, provide specific guidelines for revocation. While some pressure is now being brought to bear on these organizations to take up this authority (discussed in chapter eight), at present they have allowed tremendous discretion to remain with the unit level staff. Only a limited set of serious violations are made matters of mandatory reporting to the Board. Since the late 1970s much of the effective power over whether or not a parolee will be returned to prison is held by the parole staff, predominantly at the local unit level.

A recent study of parole violations conducted by Department of Corrections staff estimated that only 11 percent of all the revocations in 1986 were mandatory report violations (California Department of Corrections 1988, 20). The regional and central administration of the Parole Division have thus far issued only general objectives for revocation rather than specific guidelines. Review of specific decisions is perfunctory and reversal of the decisions made at the unit level uncommon.

The Department's study argued strongly that decision making at the unit level is the most significant causal factor in explaining the rapid rise of California parole revocations during the 1980s. They found that from 1980 to 1984 slightly more than half of all parolees arrested each year (for all crimes) were continued on parole at the unit level without being reported to the Board of Prison Terms. Starting in 1985, the ratio began to change rapidly toward greater revocation. By 1988 only about one arrested parolee was continued on parole for every ten sent to the Board to face revocation.

The Exercise of Discretion at the Unit Level

In this section the logic of revocation decision making in contemporary parole will be explored further by examining the violations discovered in a sample of inner-city parolees from Los Angeles, Oakland, and San Francisco over the course of one year following their release from prison, and correlating the decisions parole agents made with theoretically salient aspects of the parolees' records, circumstances, and behaviors. The sample cannot serve as a comprehensive picture of violation decisions across the state, comparable to the revocation data presented above. At best, it provides a picture of how decisions to revoke are arrived at in the hardest pressed areas of the state. The social conditions which are thought to underlie both the growth of crime and the rise of a harsher parole policy are to be found in these communities.

The sample is also limited in providing information on only one year. Without a series of such years one cannot easily determine whether the patterns observed belong to a trend of any kind. They cannot, for that reason, be used to show what is driving the growth in revocations over time, although they may point toward fruitful areas for further research in that area. The main purpose of this analysis, however, is to shed light on the implicit account of parole control that parole staff draw upon in the practice of revocation.

In the chapters above it was suggested that parole supervision has undergone important historical redistributions around changing accounts or models of control which expressed in practical elements a more or less satisfying interpretation of the risks posed by released prisoners, the factors tending to exacerbate or reduce such risk, and the elements of a strategy capable of controlling it. The managerial model in contemporary parole has placed revocation at the very center of the practice. As suggested in chapters four and six, much of the attractiveness of revocation is explainable in terms of new legal demands and new technologies which have developed revocation practice into an efficient system with readily accessible means and objectives. What remains to be explored here is whether these external factors are complemented by the development of an internal logic of revocation practice that can ground parole work in the same way that industrial discipline and clinical examination did for earlier epochs.

Offense Type and Disposition

The data in table 7.3 suggest that there is considerable variation in the treatment of different types of offenses.[26] Reporting to the Board is rare in the case of drug use, but virtually certain in cases of property or violence offenses.

It is useful to distinguish two types of parole violations. Some violations are based on conduct that would be violations of the criminal law whether or not a person was on parole. Robberies, thefts, assaults, and driving under the influence, as well as less serious traffic offenses, are all punishable under the penal provisions of California law for all citizens. Other violations are based on conduct that would not be punishable were it not for the status of being on parole. This is true of violations for absconding or evading supervision, or possession of certain types of weapons (for example, knives with blades exceeding two and one-half inches in length). It is also true of drug use violations based on positive drug tests. Although drug testing is used by a variety of private and public authorities outside of the parole context, it is never linked to criminal penalties.

Traditionally the second sort of violations have been called "technical," since they involve conduct which offends the technical conditions of parole, rather than criminal prohibitions. Yet this terminology is ambiguous since all parole violations are based on the conditions of parole rather than criminal statutes. Thus a person accused of theft may be acquitted by the criminal process and revoked by the parole process due to different rules of evidence or standards of proof. Today the Department of Corrections usually reserves the term "technical" for those offenses, like absconding, that have no correlate outside of parole (and other supervision statuses like probation). Here the term "status" offense will be used in distinction to "criminal" offense. Status offenses, as we see in table 4, are far less likely to be reported to the Board than criminal offenses, a difference statistically significant at the 99 percent confidence level.

The data in tables 7.3 and 7.4 suggest that while parole agents have discretion to resolve criminal violation cases at the local level they rarely exercise it. When confronted with crimes, parole agents and their supervisors over-

26. The term "continue on parole" (COP) refers to a decision *not* to reverse parole.

Table 7.3   Disposition by Violation Type
(in percent)

| Type of Violation | Disposition | | |
	COP	Board	Total
Drug use	81.0	19.0	100.0
Drug sale	9.6	90.4	100.0
Absconding	25.0	75.0	100.0
Weapons	20.0	80.0	100.0
Property	12.5	87.5	100.0
Violence	12.5	87.5	100.0
Other	58.3	41.7	100.0
Total sample	47.0	53.0	100.0

$N = 385$ $P < .01$

Table 7.4   Disposition by Whether the Violation
Was a Status or Criminal Offense (in percent)

| Violation Type | Disposition | | |
	COP	Board	Total
Status	65.0	35.0	100.0
Criminal	20.5	79.5	100.0
Total sample	47.0	53.0	100.0

$N = 385$ $P < .01$

whelmingly pursue a revocation hearing. In some cases they may not feel that imprisonment is essential, but they clearly feel that the Board must be given the opportunity (and hence the responsibility) to make this decision. The only violations where parole agents and their unit supervisors exercised their discretion to resolve significant numbers of cases without the Board's intervention were drug use and absconding.

Demographic and Social Factors

Demographic factors shed little light on which drug users go to the Board. No doubt the small sample size hinders the detection of subtle effects, but cross tabulations of age, race, and gender against disposition for drug use violations failed to yield any statistically significant differences. Gender alone of the three suggested some trend, with women being less likely to be returned to prison. While this is consistent with a large literature on gender and punishment (Daley 1989) the number of women in the sample was far too small to allow much further analysis of this difference. Social factors, such as the pa-

Table 7.5   Disposition in Drug Use Violations by
Whether the Parolee Was Homeless (in percent)

Homeless at Time of Violation	Disposition		
	COP	Board	Total
No	83.3	16.7	100.0
Yes	16.7	83.3	100.0
Total sample	80.9	19.1	100.0

$N = 168$ $P < .01$

rolee's living situation and employment, had moderate, although statistically significant, effects on disposition in drug use cases.

Parolees with no stable residence during the thirty days prior to the discovery of the violation were more likely to be reported to the Board than all other drug abuse violators, a difference statistically significant at the 99 percent confidence level. Yet the small number of homeless cases requires caution in viewing the evidence.[27]

My observations suggest strongly that the confidence a parole agent has in the parolee's domestic partners (especially family or significant other) is important in deciding the agent's response to drug use. If a parole agent believes that the partners are genuinely motivated in preventing the parolee from becoming readdicted, the agent will be more likely to support a decision to continue on parole, especially if the partners are prepared to help financially or logistically with getting the parolee into and through a drug treatment program.

While such differences appear to drop out in relationship categories like kin, they do show up for those with the most unstable residential situations. This may reflect the greater risk that those parolees without a home are involved in other offenses in addition to drug use. It is also related to the practical needs of parole supervision. Parole agents need to know where to find a parolee if they have to arrest him. Since a positive drug test is almost always taken as a serious warning sign of "deterioration" it raises the chances that a need for making an arrest will arise sooner or later. If the location of the parolee is likely to be difficult to determine, the agent may just decide to make it sooner.

Observations during fieldwork also suggested rather strongly that whether the parolee had a job or not was a major influence on the parole agent's determination of how to respond to drug use. While denying that a parolee with a

27. A second reason for caution in interpreting the data here is the inadequacy of the domestic situation code to capture the salient differences in parolees' lives. As suggested in chapter four, differences in domestic situations tend to get washed out when they are aggregated into large categories such as those used here.

job was exempt from being returned to prison for drug use, most parole agents acknowledged that they would "work" with an employed parolee who was using drugs in order to prevent his reincarceration. As long as a parolee was not showing signs of full-blown addiction (a consistent series of positive tests taken every few days suggesting daily use of cocaine or heroin), it was doubtful that a parolee would be returned to prison.

Several factors go into this reasoning. The fact that the parolee has an income from work reduces somewhat the likelihood that drug use will lead to further crime. (Most agents believe, however, that readdiction is sure to push the user beyond what he can afford from salary and in all likelihood will lead to termination from the job due to absenteeism and related problems.) The fact that the parolee is working increases that chance that deterioration will be checked by pressure from the employer, peers, or family members dependent on the earnings.

The most important consideration is the relative merits of keeping the parolee in the community now while he has a job, versus having him back in the community in two or three months after a prison hiatus that may have ended the employment opportunity. Parole agents know that while the Board will send a drug user back to prison, they will rarely give him more than several months. As long as there appears to be any chance of stabilizing the parolee while he is still working there is very little to be gained by a return to prison.

An initial look at the influence of income source on decisions in drug use cases shows results that run counter to the tendencies observed during field-work. The differences are not statistically significant, but surprising. It appears as if those with welfare income are the least likely to be referred to the Board.

A larger difference between those with jobs and those without a known income source emerges when the number of prior offenses is controlled. The differences are not statistically different, but they suggest that employed drug users may have been disproportionately represented among the multiple offense drug users precisely because they were considered a better risk.

It is also possible that subtler effects of income were missed by the coding strategy for income source. Employment for the year was coded as the type characterizing the majority of time spent in the community. Thus a person who was employed for his first two months on release, but who was then revoked for the remaining ten months, would be coded as employed for the year. This coding method obviously loses a sense of stability in employment that may be important to agents. (The same is probably true for the domestic situation variable as well.)

While weakness in the coding of both domestic situation and income source probably obscures some of the effects these social variables have on the violation decision process, it is also possible that they simply play less of a role in practice than they do in the self-understanding of parole agents. That self-understanding remains grounded in some of the enduring notions of normalization inherited from the industrial and clinical models of parole. The hardening of poverty in the urban areas from which this sample is drawn, as discussed in chapter four, may well undermine the ability of parole agents to rely much on these factors.

Where full-time regular employment is rare it cannot function as the central tool of differentiation that it did during the apotheosis of the disciplinary model during the Second World War when the fact of being unemployed might have clearly indicated a bad attitude toward noncriminal ways of life. The fact that a parolee has not obtained regular employment in the late 1980s and early 1990s tells the agent little about the parolee's character or motivations. In a situation where families are hard pressed to sustain their most marginal members it is difficult to place much confidence in the parolee's support network to provide a bulwark against readdiction and crime. Indeed, families sometimes ask the parole agent to intervene and, if necessary, remove from the community a parolee whose readdiction to drugs threatens to overwhelm the family's limited resources.

Likewise, the narrow ledge of survival on which many parolees are balanced makes it imperative that the parolee retain the support and interest of those in the community who have an interest in him: his parents, relatives, friends, those whom Stack (1974) calls the kin. Any indication that his support is in danger of being exhausted sets alarm bells off in a parole agent's head. Even without a legal requirement of support in the community as a condition for release, parole relies overwhelmingly on voluntarily supplied family solidarity. The data in table 7.6 suggest that complaints from family and other people in the immediate environment of the parolee (known as "collateral sources" or simply "collaterals") are taken seriously in determining the response to violations.

Table 7.6 Disposition in Drug Use Violations by Whether There has been a Collateral Complaint against the Parolee (in percent)

	Disposition		
Collateral Complaint	COP	Board	Total
No	82.4	17.6	100.0
Yes	55.6	44.4	100.0
Total sample	81.0	19.0	100.0

$N = 168$ $P < .05$

The collateral complaint variable in table 7.6 is defined as "yes" when a parole agent has received a complaint from a civilian third party about the parolee within the thirty days up to and including the date that the violation was discovered. When a parent, spouse, or housemate of the parolee complains about his conduct, the agent takes this as a strong signal that intervention may be necessary to prevent the relationship from being unalterably compromised. Thus even a minor violation, like drug use, when coupled with expressions of concern by kin can result in return to prison. Although such complaints are infrequently made, they greatly increase the likelihood of a parolee being revoked for drug use, a result significant at the 95 percent confidence level.

While collateral complaints indicate that parole remains responsive to the signals sent by the community about its capacity to tolerate a parolee's behavior, the relative insignificance of their numbers suggests the limits of rationalizing decision making on such a basis.[28] If the social world of the underclass is increasingly less illuminated by the normative logic of work and community, parole agents who are seeking effective predictors of future behavior must rely more and more on the light that parole itself is able to throw on the parolee.

Supervision Factors

Faced with the daunting task of evaluating the "adjustment" of parolees in a social setting which provides few opportunities for differentiating, parole agents must home in on even minimal signals that a parolee is capable of self-management in the community. In many cases the parolee's compliance with supervision requirements is the only opportunity for evaluating his capacity to successfully carry out social interactions. Parole is itself one of the most important theaters in which the social performance of the parolee is evaluated against a shared understanding of normative adequacy. This is especially true at a time when other potential theaters of life, such as work and family, are often closed off to parolees.

A dichotomous "cooperation" variable was created by examining the thirty-day period prior to the discovery of a violation for indications in the parole agent's notes that the parolee showed up for testing and other supervisory functions, including attending required sessions at the Parole Outpatient Clinic or keeping appointments with other agencies referred by the parole agent.

28. The relative paucity of collateral inputs may also speak to the insufficiency of time for and encouragement of fieldwork by parole agents, and to the lack of rapport between community and parole staff. It remains to be considered whether a redirection of parole strategy might not be able to generate greater response from the community.

Table 7.7 Disposition in Drug Use Violations by
Parolee Cooperation (in percent)

Cooperation	Disposition		
	COP	Board	Total
No	39.1	60.9	100.0
Yes	87.6	12.4	100.0
Total sample	81.0	19.0	100.0

$N = 168$ $P < .01$

As shown in table 7.7 drug violators with a record of cooperating in the
month before their violation were more than twice as likely to be continued on
parole than those who had been only marginally complying, a result significant at the 99 percent confidence level. In the imploded social world of the
inner-city parolee, parole functions such as drug testing, agent contacts, or
parole outpatient clinic meetings are some of the most significant institutional
requirements available. It is not surprising that those parolees who are unable
or unwilling to negotiate those minimal bureaucratic constraints are deemed
very poor risks, and thus reincarcerated.

The data show that most drug offenses are resolved at the local unit level
without revoking parole. The parolee is often warned about future penalties
should use continue. The frequency of testing is usually increased. If several
positive tests have come in over a long period the parolee may be ordered to
bring in slips from drug programs he has applied for or evidence of attending
self-help groups like Cocaine Anonymous. But in the end the violation is dismissed without reimprisonment and without review by the Board of Prison
Terms.

The 20 percent of drug use violations in the sample that did result in a report to the Board disproportionately came from parolees who had raised their
visibility through repeated violations or through arrests. Visibility is important because it raises the chance that the parole agent's response will be noted
and perhaps criticized by others (for instance, the supervisor or the police).
Not surprisingly, visibility increases the chance that the agent's response will
adhere more closely to the path which is perceived as most widely acceptable.
In the context of the late 1980s that came to mean return to prison.

Social factors, like the parolee's domestic situation and employment prospects, play a role by selecting out those who pose the greatest risk. This in
effect is strongest with respect to housing because that is more available than
work. Even the very poor will not easily turn away kin who are faced with
homelessness as an alternative (Rossi 1989, 37–38). The parolee who is
homeless, or constantly shifting from one friend or family member to another,

Table 7.8   Logit Estimation on Likelihood of Drug Violation
Being Reported to the Board of Prison Terms

Variable	Coefficient	Significance
No income	−.09	No
Homeless	1.73	No
Multiple drug violations	.67	No
Collateral	.98	No
Cooperation	−2.70	99%
Arrest	1.78	95%
Constant	−.88	No

$N = 168$ $P < .01$
Log likelihood $= -63.6$

demonstrates that he is dangerously depleting the private resources available to him. Although in some social policy contexts this might indicate the need for greater public assistance, in the present correctional context it calls for a more punitive response. Employment is far more marginal in its significance, mainly because its scarcity in the poor communities to which most of the parolees in this study returned robs it of much distinguishing power as a variable.

Parole agents appear to place primary reliance on parole performance itself. In a social world which provides little functional surety for parolees, a record of compliance is a minimum requirement of trust. Those parolees who fail to "take care of business," as supervision responsibilities are often referred to, go back to prison in a far higher proportion.[29]

Indication of the relative strength of these factors is provided through logit analysis, a method of multivariate analysis often recommended where a dichotomous dependent variable makes ordinary least-squares regression unreliable. In a logit model the dependent variable is the logarithm of the odds that a particular choice will be made (Pindyck and Rubinfeld 1981, 288). Here the dependent variable is whether or not the violation was reported to the Board. The equation estimates the contribution of each independent variable to the likelihood of the case going to the Board. Interpretation of the cardinal value of logit coefficients is extremely complicated. In table 7.8 they are presented mainly to suggest the relative weight of the factors cross-tabulated with disposition.

A positive coefficient indicates that a parolee for whom the relevant characteristic is applicable is more likely to be reported for a drug use violation. A

29. The phrase "taking care of business" suggests an analogy to the disciplinary model of parole. Yet with the diminished employment opportunities in the communities to which most parolees return, parole itself has replaced the labor market as the domain for control and judgment.

negative coefficient indicates that a parolee with the relevant characteristic is less likely to be reported. Since logit analysis controls for all independent variables simultaneously it provides a comparative indication of salience.

The strong effect associated with the cooperation variable suggests that parole agents rely heavily on criteria that they can control and interpret with little or no help from the community. Arrest also remains a strong factor, suggesting that where the agent does look to outside indicators it is primarily to other law enforcement sources. None of the other factors were statistically significant. If they have an effect on decision making it is too subtle to be estimated with confidence in a sample of this size.

Strains in the Management Model

Parole today finds itself once again under increasing pressure to redefine itself. The proximate cause in this case is the link between parole revocation decisions and California's prison population made irretrievably visible and public with the publication by Messinger and his colleagues of their data showing how large the parole contribution to the prison population had become (Messinger et al. 1988). Significant in any event, this finding was particularly relevant because of the astounding rise in California's prison population, from 22,500 inmates in 1979 to 86,000 in 1989 (Blue Ribbon Commission 1990, 2). This point has been subsequently echoed in stronger form by other bodies examining the prison population situation:

> It is increasingly apparent that parole violators are one of the principle forces driving the overcrowding of California prisons. (California Department of Corrections 1988, 14)

> This high rate of return has aggravated prison overcrowding and has had a major impact on CDC [California Department of Corrections] operations and costs. (Legislative Analyst 1988–1989, 643)

> Parole violations are a significant and dramatically increasing contributing factor to prison population increases. (Blue Ribbon Commission 1990, 24)

Along with these pronouncements have come increasing demands that parole do something to stem the flow of parolees back to prison. While not uniformly critical of parole, much of this discourse views the evolution of meaningful standards to regulate parole discretion as the solution to the revocation problem.

Conclusion

The expansion of the populations under supervision is combining with the internal dynamics of the parole model to generate a tightening feedback loop between supervision and incarceration, as a large number of drug and property offenders who would not have been incarcerated during the 1970s are entering the prison system (Zimring and Hawkins 1991).[30] This flow of offenders into the prison system who have not necessarily committed especially violent crimes, but who are disreputable in terms of their connections with the community, has two aspects.

The first involves the relationship of parole to parolees and their communities. Often these are very short sentences (Messinger and Berecochea 1990). Still, once in the system they compel innumerable iterations of a decision process that is structured toward returning individuals to incarceration. A system that was once for so long oriented by the idea of reintegration of prisoners into the community is now oriented toward isolating and containing this population. The population of parolees in California, over sixty thousand in 1990, represents a group whose risk of imprisonment is incredibly high. As Messinger and Berecochea (1990) put it:

> The court imprisonment rate per 100,000 of *this* population-at-risk [parolees] is, well, mind-blowing; under current conditions, it represents a veritable ready-pool for arrest, conviction and (re)commitment to prison. When one adds to this rate the even higher rate of return generated by the board, the result is very, very considerable. (18)

This pool is becoming the place of concentration for California's correctional resources and attention.

The second involves the relationship of parole to its own procedures. As the social crisis has made it more and more difficult for parole work to be organized by the logic of the community, the work of parole has come to be more and more oriented by its own internal processes. The most well-organized and adequately resourced of these processes are revocation procedures. This development represents the success of parole in adopting revocation as a model of parole practice. Faced with legal, political, and economic changes that severely undermined its traditional strategies, parole in the 1980s reorganized itself around the technologies and imperatives of revocation.

Parole has managed to assemble a pool of technologies and procedures that permit it to operate rationally within the prevailing norms of public exercises of power. Drawing on the requirements of due process imposed in *Morrissey v. Brewer* (see chapter four), parole has refocused its attention on the routinized processing of violation cases. These requirements impose clear standards for effective implementation which are successfully transmitted and monitored by a command and control structure that did not even exist before 1972 but has been successfully grafted onto the structure of local, regional, and central management.

---

30. See *New York Times* editorial (1991).

In its own way this concentration and punishment model is consonant with the prevailing ideology of crime and its control. Just as the industrial and clinical models were successful because they were able to fit into the ideologies of crime and its control that predominated in earlier days, the current managerial model achieves through its revocation function a satisfying interpretive fit with the current notion that custody is the necessary and sufficient solution to criminal risk while at the same time meeting the managerial impetus to define and meet performance standards.

The problem is not that frequent recourse to revocation fails to fit with the managerial model for parole practice: indeed, for the reasons outlined above, revocation provides for a parole program which fits well with prevailing ideas about crime and corrections. The immediate crisis is generated by the fact that the political system cannot accept the fiscal and social implications of the new correctional system to which parole has adapted itself. Parole has been successful in transforming itself from a system of rehabilitative discipline to one of risk management and now finds itself criticized for that accomplishment.

CHAPTER EIGHT

Penal Postmodernism: Power without Narrative

In the late 1970s the question was whether parole should survive. Correctional managers turned to the problem of building and running more prisons, while parole focused on proving it could do something useful. To many, inside and outside, it seemed that the enterprise drifted along without a positive vision of what control was and how to achieve it. At this writing in the early 1990s, with recognition growing in state capitals that it will take spending money in new supervised release programs to save money on the prison side of the budget, there is a new opportunity to innovate. The question is how to shape a coherent parole practice in the face of today's circumstances. This will take more than a new vision, it will require rebuilding the strategies that anchored parole for its first three-quarters of a century, or replacing them with a new set of strategies.

Generally, it is only in retrospect that one can understand the transformation of an institution. Looking at the current strategies being played out today in parole, and corrections more generally, it is impossible to know whether they offer a distinction that will make a difference in the long run. In the short run, we are free to draw on our analysis of how the power to punish is exercised, in at least one large parole system today, and to speculate on how the current strategies of reform are likely to change the way power is exercised. In this chapter we review some of the approaches that are currently being touted as possible solutions.

Guidelines

In the technical sense used today, "guidelines" refers to a more or less comprehensive set of rules which decision makers apply in order to arrive at a decision, such as the number of months to sentence a person convicted of first-degree burglary (Gottfredson and Gottfredson 1984). An example are the new Federal Sentencing Guidelines, which provide a highly detailed and rigid procedure by which federal trial courts are to set prison sentences (U.S. Sentencing Commission 1987). The rules define how the basic offense, the offender's criminal history, and various mitigating and aggravating factors are to be combined in arriving at a cell of a sentencing grid which sets a specifiable range (for example, eighteen to twenty-four months). [1]

Guidelines in the sentencing function are appealing because of their capacity to replace individualized discretion with predetermined and explicit decision rules capable of being defended and monitored. Their popularity grew immensely during the 1970s, as indeterminate sentencing systems became discredited. Although several distinct formats for determinate sentencing [2] were developed during the 1970s, today the "guidelines" approach has emerged as the most popular and has become virtually synonymous with determinate sentencing. [3]

When the determinate sentence law was first put into effect in California in 1977, there was little reason to contemplate guidelines for parole revocation decisions, since the maximum revocation was for six months, and the maximum parole period for most felons was a year. Since 1979 the revocation period has been extended to a year, and the maximum parole period extended to four years. In recent years, with costs of prison growth increasingly visible, and the role of parole revocations in driving prison population growth apparent, a number of guideline strategies have been discussed and deployed in California.

Guidelines for Board of Prison Terms Revocation Sentences

The Board conducts hearings as the "neutral and detached" hearing body required by *Morrissey v. Brewer* for parole revocations. The hearings are bifur-

---

1. Sentencing is not the only criminal justice function to undergo guidelining. Pre-trial release decisions in many states and in the federal system are subject to guidelines. Outside the penal system guidelines enter into innumerable administrative decisions in hiring, admissions, and the like. The private sector has also increasingly subjected its front-line service workers to fairly rigid guideline-like procedures which you will discover if you try to get something special done at, for example, a bank or an insurance company.

2. Even before determinate sentencing reform started, guidelines were being implemented as methods for making parole release more rational.

3. California's determinate sentencing system might be considered a modified guidelines approach. It established a presumptive sentence for each offense, which the judge can raise or lower for various aggravating and mitigating circumstances. Other systems, like Indiana's which permits a judge to select a sentence from within a wide range, may be considered a determinate sentencing system but not a guidelines system.

cated into a guilt phase and a dispositional phase.[4] In the first part, they determine if the parolee is "responsible" (i.e., guilty) for the charges in the revocation complaint. In the second part, "responsible" parolees are sentenced under the Board's statutory authority to revoke parole for up to twelve months.[5]

In May 1988 the Board of Prison Terms adopted "Parole Revocation Guidelines" to regulate its authority to sentence parolees to revocation terms in the second, or dispositional, phase of the parole revocation hearings. Although the logic of the guidelines is grounded in the imperative of uniformity in punishment, the initial impetus toward developing the guidelines came from the legislative budgeting process. In the words of one senior Board administrator, "bed pressures not 'just deserts'" mandated the guidelines. The 1987–1988 report of the Legislative Analyst openly discussed prison-use reduction as one path the legislature might need to take to control costs.[6] Behind the scenes, the staff saw the Board's revocation sentences as an important part of the prison population problem.

The Legislative Analyst's staff believed that a guidelines system would bring down costs by reducing the use of maximum revocation terms. They believed that some of the deputy commissioners who preside over hearings were handing out maximum revocation sentences for minor violations, in a manner wildly inconsistent with the decisions of a majority of their colleagues. Another expected benefit of guidelines would be greater efficiency in screening (revocation plea bargaining) because parolees would know in advance the likely terms to be imposed on a finding of responsibility.

Within the Board, the guidelines issue was seen as a lever to place blame on the Board for what was essentially a combined crisis of legislative irresponsibility, depleted county finances, and parole supervision. The Board's administrators also worried that guidelines would ultimately tie up Board discretion to handle publicized offenders in a way which would rebound on public anxieties, to the ultimate detriment of efforts to decrease prison populations.

The guidelines that were eventually implemented defined appropriate sentence ranges for all offenses, but left discretion to adjust sentences for the individual parolee. They established three offense levels. Type I violations, those involving technical conditions of parole, those "primarily injurious to

---

4. The Board employs thirty-four deputy commissioners who conduct the hearings in two-person panels. Board members themselves occasionally participate in revocation hearings, although their main task is making release decisions concerning felons sentenced to life imprisonment.

5. Both phases are semiadversarial; see the discussion in chapter five.

6. The Analyst's office is a research arm of the legislature, similar to the General Accounting Office on the federal level. They have played an important role in recent years in focusing attention on the costs of imprisonment, a subject that elected officials have been reluctant to engage.

the parolee and/or the parole process" (Board of Prison Terms 1988, 1), were to receive terms of up to four months. Type II violations, those involving misdemeanor criminal offenses and nonviolent felonies, as well as multiple or repeated violations of a Type I nature, were to receive terms of five to nine months. Type III violations, those involving violence or major felonies, were to receive up to twelve months.

The guidelines permit adjustment up or down, based on the "risk the parolee poses to the community," defined broadly as "the number and nature of the commitment offenses, prior criminal history and the adjustment on current and previous parole status" (Board of Prison Terms 1988, 3).[7] This determination is wholly unstructured, although the guidelines urge deputy commissioners to document their reasoning.

While there is no systematic evaluation of the effects of the guidelines available, it is unlikely that they will do much to ease prison overcrowding. Even if they reduce the number of individual cases where the sentence is quite outside the norm, the effects are likely to be very marginal (especially given the fact that the maximum term regardless of the guidelines is twelve months). As long as new candidates are being rapidly accumulated for those bed spaces, shortening terms will not provide much new slack in the population demand. Indeed, shorter sentences are part of the present prison population crisis.[8] Such rapid turnover raises transaction costs involved in processing and reduces the opportunities for parolees returned to prison to benefit from any treatment programs within the institutions.

Guidelines for Parole Agents and Supervisors

In 1989 the Parole Division developed provisional guidelines for unit-level staff on three distinct decision points: arrest holds, violation reports, and parole discharges.[9] They were circulated to unit supervisors as additions to the official Parole Operations Manual, in a memorandum in April 1989 ("the memo" hereafter). Like the Board, the Parole Division offered no explicit indication that the guidelines were intended to have any effect on the number of revocations (and through that on prison population). Instead, the issue was framed in terms of improving the decision-making process by eliminating "*differences* in decision making [that] are increasing as the number of units increase" (Parole and Community Services Division 1989, 1, *emphasis*

7. There is no formula for calculating criminal history as there is in many other guideline sentencing systems.

8. The utility of controlling the Board's discretion was further reduced by the introduction, at virtually the same time, of a law permitting prisoners serving revocation sentences to receive good-time credits, effectively halving most revocation terms.

9. As of the date of this report the guidelines had become final.

added). Unlike the Board's guidelines, however, the memo avoided terms like "equity and uniformity." "Differences" provided a more neutral focus, while leaving unclear exactly what the problem of "difference" was.

Once again an important impetus appears to have come from the Legislative Analyst's office. Its report on the 1988–1989 budget focused direct attention on the Parole Division's role in the prison population crisis.

> [California Department of Correction's] reports suggest that parole staff decisions to refer more parole violators to the BPT [Board of Prison Terms] for revocation, instead of continuing to supervise them in the community, play a much larger role in the increase [of prison population]. Because the BPT in recent years has revoked the parole of over 95% of the parolees referred to it for revocation, the Parole Division's decision to refer parolees to the BPT is tantamount to a decision to return them to prison.
>
> Conversations with parole staff during field visits suggest that many technical parole violators are referred to the BPT for revocation because parole agents are reluctant to assume the risk of allowing troublesome parolees to remain in the community given the currently limited options and controls for managing them in the community. (Legislative Analyst 1988–1989, 645–46)

The report stopped just short of explicitly criticizing the Division for overuse of revocation. It implied that more resources in the community might be a necessary corollary to cutting prison spending, but at the same time the report hinted strongly that internal changes were needed, including taking more responsibility at all levels of parole for the cost of revocations.

The cover letter of the memo sent out to all regional administrators suggested the significance of parole unit decision making without specifically labeling the situation a problem per se:

> Unit supervisors make a large number of significant case decisions regarding parolees on a daily basis (there were about 100,000 violations handled at the unit level during calendar year 1988). Unit supervisors decide if a parole hold is to be maintained, the disposition of parole violations and whether most parolees will be discharged or retained on parole. (Parole and Community Services Division 1989, 1)

There is little doubt, however, that as a result of the Legislative Analyst's report, as well as independent academic research (Messinger et al. 1988), the Parole Division understood that it might come under attack for the prison overcrowding problem and intended the memo as a way of staying ahead of criticism.

The first decision point involved parole hold decisions. As discussed in chapter seven, when a parole agent is alerted that one of his parolees has been arrested by the police, the customary practice is for the agent to approve a parole hold, which prevents the parolee from obtaining pre-trial release. Afterwards the hold may be lifted if the agent and supervisor determine that the charges are unfounded, or that the parolee should be continued on parole.

Once the parolee is in custody, however, the deadline for filing a formal revocation report is linked to the parolee's due process right for notice, and timely hearing approaches fast. Typically the agent must decide within three or four days whether to lift the hold or send the parolee on toward revocation. A number of observers inside the Division began to feel that parole holds were encouraging agents to move inexorably toward revocation. If the process could be interrupted, by dropping the hold under conditions which provided reasonable control over the parolee while a final decision on the alleged violation was made, a larger number of violations might ultimately be handled at the unit level without referral to the Board (and a return to prison).

The parole hold index innovation was first developed in Los Angeles. The basic idea was borrowed from the forms used to process pre-trial release on "own recognizance" bonds. For each yes/no question, the index provides a numeric point score. Higher scores indicate a better release risk. A score of nineteen or above is deemed "appropriate to recommend hold removal" (Parole and Community Services Division 1989, 6). The score is not mandatory; the parole agent utilizing the index may override its recommendation. The index sheet provides a space for explaining any overrides. [10]

From the time of its introduction in Los Angeles many agents have taken umbrage at the index, and the agent's union waged a partially successful struggle against it. Many expressed the view that the worksheet was an insult to the agents' professional capacity to evaluate their parolees. In fact, the designers of the index did not believe in the power of its mechanical scoring to replace parole agent expertise, but they hoped that the process of working through the sheet would compel the agents to perform a more thorough consideration of the individual case than they assumed was taking place. The designers also believed it would provide legitimation for agents to make release decisions by placing official sanction on the idea that risk assessment doesn't mean avoiding all risks. They also believed that by making the process more visible the index might permit comparisons between units to be easily made. Publishing such comparisons might create its own pressure on those units where an especially high number of parole holds were being left on by making comparative statistics available. [11]

10. The supervisor is required to review the work sheet and must approve any recommendation prior to any action being taken.

11. Several months after the memo was circulated a grievance was taken by the union to the chief administrator of the Parole Division, who decided that each region would have discretion over whether to implement the index.

The second decision point covered in the memo was violation decisions. As suggested by the Legislative Analyst's report (discussed in chapter seven), reports to the Board are tantamount to return to prison. Indeed, since most parolees facing revocation will spend a month or more in a prison prior to formal revocation, reporting would push prison admissions all by itself even if the Board released a higher percentage after the hearing. The memo seems to address itself specifically to the "reluctance" of unit-level parole operatives to assume the risk of keeping some violators in the community.

> Recommendation of revocation of parole is only one control method available to parole staff. Unit supervisors should consider application of progressive sanctions to resolve parole violations. Referral to the [Board of Prison Terms] for revocation action shall be reserved for cases where there is a threat to public safety or the parolee cannot be managed safely in the community. (Parole and Community Services Division 1989, 7)

The memo is careful, however, not to really establish any authority for taking a risk with a parolee. Only those who are not "a threat to public safety" are to be continued on parole. But public safety has been the operational standard over the course of a decade in which the percentage of violators reported to the Board has gone up many times.

The violation guidelines are glosses on the basic standard set out in the parole agent manual which calls for referral to the Board where the "[p]arolee is a danger to person or property of others" (Parole and Community Services Division 1987, sec. 1320). They go farther only by spelling out what concrete community alternatives neutralize the apparent risk of the violative behavior. For example, the guidelines provide that a parolee who commits a violation of the technical rules of parole (primarily the rules requiring regular reporting and obeying the instructions of the parole officer) should be continued on parole if the parolee "has made an otherwise good parole adjustment[, the parolee's] violations are minor[, and] a control/treatment program is available" (Parole and Community Services Division 1987, 7).

Most agents could accurately claim that these are the standards they already use. If they have a high rate of technical violators going back to prison it is precisely because most of them have not made a good parole adjustment, and whether or not the particular violation before them is minor, there is no effective control/treatment program available that can negate the fear that more serious violations will follow.

The third decision point covered in the memo was discharges. For most nonlife prisoners convicted of a crime committed after 31 December 1988, discharge takes place automatically after thirteen months of "continuous parole" (parole not interrupted by suspension or revocation) unless the Board of

Prison Terms orders their retention. For all but specified violent felonies[12] the power to retain has been delegated to the unit level of the Division.[13]

Discharging has an indirect but important relationship to the revocation problem, because it helps determine the size of the population at risk of being revoked. The practice in most regions has been to retain all parolees who violate parole (even with a technical or minor drug violation) and others who have not violated parole but have a very serious or notorious commitment offense. So long as a parolee remains on parole, he remains vulnerable to failing a drug test or breaching some other condition of parole, which may result in a return to prison.

The memo introduced new guidelines for this unit-level discretion to discharge. These factors stop far short of dictating the outcome in any case. Indeed, they may be best seen as increasing discretion to discharge, even where occasional or early violations of parole are involved. Before introduction of the guidelines, the practice was to treat any violation, including a positive drug test, as grounds for continuation on parole. The discharge guidelines offer a less stringent test for early discharge for parolees who are

1. First termer[s] with no prior convictions.
2. Legally self-supporting or self sufficient.
3. Currently drug free.
4. [Have a] stable residence. (Parole and Community Services Division 1987, 9)

Crucially, the new guidelines define parolees as "currently drug free" even though they had positive drug tests six months earlier, thereby preventing an occasional positive drug test from keeping a parolee under supervision for years even if he is otherwise well adjusted. In practice, the requirements that the parolee be self-sufficient and have a stable residence are likely to exclude many parolees who belong to the most distressed segments of the urban underclass.

Formal Constraints on Power and Their Limits

The deployments of guidelines technology in the Board of Prison Terms and the Parole Division have shared two noteworthy features. First, both guidelines were initiated in response to budgetary pressures over prison crowding

12. Murder, mayhem, rape, sodomy by force, oral copulation, child molestation, arson, most residential robberies, and large-scale fraud. See California Penal Code, sec. 667.5 (West 1993).

13. Supervisors, acting on the recommendation of the agents, have the power to send the file for formal retention by the Board (a pro forma function) or allow the thirteenth month to elapse with no action.

rather than to the process values like uniformity, equity, or bureaucratic conformity, despite their association with these values. Second, both stop far short of determining outcomes to the degree of criminal sentencing guidelines such as those in California, Minnesota, or the new federal system. Evaluating whether tighter guidelines in the revocation process would improve it involves deciding whether the revocation process ought to adopt the model and the objectives of criminal sentencing.

Yet both agencies differ from each other as they do from the criminal courts. The Board is closest to the model of a court. The bulk of its business, handled by its deputy commissioners, involves adjudicating cases of parole violation, and then sentencing those found guilty.

Parole supervision decisions like whether to report a violation, whether to keep parolees accused of violations confined, and whether to discharge them have corollaries in court functions, but in purpose they stand far removed from the criminal process. Under Section 3000 of the California Penal Code parole is distinguished as a period "immediately following incarceration" intended to enhance "public safety" by providing for the "supervision of and surveillance" of parolees, as well as counseling. In contrast, Section 1170 of the Code defines the purposes of imprisonment for crime as "punishment," a purpose "best served by terms proportionate to the seriousness of the offense with provision for uniformity."

It is not surprising, then, that the Board has come far closer to developing guidelines which resemble those used in criminal sentencing. The Board's guidelines appear to treat the problem of setting the revocation terms as one fully comparable to the retributive posture established for California sentencing courts under Section 1160. However, they also reserve a large discretion (as much as possible within the narrow twelve-month range) under the theme of parolee risk to incapacitate dangerous parolees. This may seem contradictory, but it reflects the Board's concern that it be able to handle the occasional politically charged case. Guidelines here may not be very consequential, but they are fully compatible with the Board's organization. In fact, the staff managers who administer the operation of the Board view the guidelines as largely a functional mechanism in an organization that acts through multiple, independent panels at sites all over the state.

Perhaps the most startling aspect of the Board's guidelines is that a period of twelve months is viewed as a dangerously wide discretion to begin with. Since the adoption of Senate Bill 16 in 1988, the large majority of parolee violators are eligible to receive good-time credits which effectively cut their sentence in half. Thus the operational space for most revocation decisions is six months. In contrast, the Adult Authority (the predecessor to the Board of Prison Terms) had the legal authority to resentence a parole violator to the maximum of the original sentence (which for many felons was life). That guidelines appear a natural solution to managing such a comparatively small amount of discretion suggests how difficult it has become to exercise the power to punish in a way which satisfies the demand that power be just and rational.

The Parole Division's provisional guidelines avoid any overt identification with the themes of punishment, equity, or uniformity. Instead they are couched in the language of closing the performance gaps among units. The Division's guidelines also work with a very different structure than the Board's guidelines. The Board's guidelines are mechanical decision rules (although with a large escape clause). The Division's are clarifications (at best) of broad substantive standards like "danger to public safety" or "good adjustment."

It is difficult to see how parole supervision operations could operate with mechanical decision rules under their present self-understanding. While most agents and supervisors claim no confidence in the capacity of parole supervision to effectively reform parolees, most continue to believe that they can make accurate assessments of how dangerous a parolee is. The idea remains powerful within parole that an agent capable of evaluating the comprehensive picture is the ideal decision maker. Given this orientation it is not surprising that the application of mechanical decision rules is unwelcome. Indeed, it is a tribute to the power of guidelines as a political technology that it is even seriously applied in the parole context.

It is possible to imagine a parole system that has completely abandoned the model of individualization, as some large-scale probation departments essentially have done. Decisions in such a system might be fully operationalized in a guidelines structure. In today's parole setting, however, guidelines are likely to be useful only in initiating a process of rationalization that will truly affect practice (if it does at all) primarily through encouraging effectiveness.

Intensive Supervision

Intensive probation supervision has been studied in Georgia, New Jersey, Illinois, and Massachusetts (Petersilia 1987). Intensive parole supervision has been tried in Massachusetts (Massachusetts Parole Board 1987), Wisconsin (Department of Health and Social Services 1989), and recently in California with the Substance Abuse Revocation Diversion program (Parole and Community Services Division 1988). The renewal of interest in intensive supervision programs (ISPs) appears in some respects to be a revitalization of the Progressive tradition of casework, which has waned in much of contemporary parole (as well as probation). While carefully avoiding terms like "rehabilitation," most ISPs have emphasized the power of supervision to make a positive difference in the behavior of offenders (Gordon 1991, 106).

More or Different?

If the intensive supervision movement, like drug treatment, offers a way to
link up with modern punishment's historical reliance on strategies of normalization, it is also bristling with features that suggest a different overall configuration. Much of what ISPs have to offer over conventional penal strategies lies
in better organization, more resources, and the capacity to screen for a less
troubled class of clients, rather than in having better means of normalizing.
With their emphasis on comprehensive surveillance and rapid return to prison
for failures, they offer themselves as "tough" measures which can both control
and punish crime (Gordon 1991, 98).

ROUTINIZATION OF THE EXERCISE OF POWER
Earlier experiments in intensive supervision made little effort to control and
monitor what supervision agents actually did (see chapter three). The assumption was that more was better, but no attempt was made to control the process
of supervision. In response to general criticisms of the effectiveness of parole
and probation in the 1970s, regular parole and probation programs have
sought to achieve higher levels of specificity in supervision by setting minimum requirements for field contacts, drug tests, and other control strategies.
These specifications, however, tend to be honored on an ad hoc basis.

In contrast, the new ISP programs place considerable emphasis on setting
and achieving specific control goals.[14] Program participants are required to
be contacted twenty times per month during the first phase of the New Jersey
program, twelve of which are to be in person by the agent (Pearson 1987, 35).
Specifications are also set for other control strategies, like drug testing, cur-
few compliance checks, and employment verification.

Most of the new programs place a tremendous emphasis on auditing to create a written record of compliance. The target objective is one contact a day
through the parole agent, his assistant, or others in the community or in service agencies that have been mobilized. In both Georgia and California supervision is handled in agent teams, a feature that, whatever its other virtues,
creates greater accountability than exists when an agent is working alone.

PRECISE CONTROLS OVER DAILY LIFE
In the 1950s, parole and probation conditions provided a vast array of specific
controls on the behavior of supervised subjects. Typically those under supervision were required to work and maintain a stable residence, and obtain
agent approval before driving a car, contracting debts, or getting married or

---

14. Lawrence Bennett has argued that the accountability factor is the primary distinction of the new
programs and an important component in their acceptance by judges and the public (Bennett 1988).

divorced. Many of these rules were selectively enforced. Instead of seeking rigorous requirements agents would use evidence of violations of these conditions to revoke parole or probation if they had decided on other grounds that the offender was too dangerous to remain in the community.

In the 1970s many of these conditions were eliminated in an effort to create a more realistic control strategy. As we have seen, much of that realism was generated by the deteriorating social and economic conditions among the urban poor. Even major conditions, like work and stable residence, were gradually downplayed. In 1977 they were eliminated due to new sentencing laws that provided for release on parole regardless of whether a program in the community had been arranged.

ISPs seem to mark a reversal of this trend away from normalization. All of them emphasize rigorous structuring of daily activities, monitored through frequent contacts, electronic surveillance, and daily logs. The most significant emphasis is placed on employment. In most programs, parolees must be employed or in school full time to remain in the program. In some cases unemployed parolees will be maintained but must document daily employment searches beginning at a specific time and verified periodically by the agents. Such activities can in themselves provide some of the social control effect of work inasmuch as they simply occupy time, create conformity promoting contacts with the mainstream of economic life, and help make the subject accountable for his activities (Gordon 1991, 117). In addition, many require the parolees to perform specified amounts of community service under supervision and to participate in drug treatment programs and curfews.

In all programs a conscious effort is made to fill the daily life of parolees with a network of rules, not simply crime-related rules, but rules about appointments, work, treatment participation, and the like.[15] While in most conventional parole supervision, noncriminal acts are only selectively punished, SARD and other ISP programs strive for a "no violation without sanction policy."

The rules communicate an intent to hold the parolee responsible for all actions, but they also are designed to constitute "early warnings" of disintegrating commitment to the program. Rules enforcing conventional life-style, like curfews and the requirement of employment, force a confrontation with the parolee well before his conduct has reached a criminal state.

Mobilizing Private Social Control in the Community

Parole and probation have always interacted with private forces in the community. Agents have been expected to interact with spouses and parents. Regular

15. One exception is an experimental program in Milwaukee studied by Walter Dickey (1990). There the original intention of creating a tighter rule structure was deliberately replaced by a regime of less rules, on the grounds that rules only created more opportunities for failure.

employment was a bona fide requirement for parole through the 1950s at least. Supervision added private members of the community as legally empowered third parties along with state and offender. They effectively participated in the machinery of punishment, which was to take their concerns and interests into account in making parole decisions. But this role of private power was attenuated in the 1960s and 1970s (see chapters four and five). Current ISP programs have reintroduced it.[16]

The most developed program of this sort is in New Jersey (Pearson 1987, 40; Gordon 1991). To get into the program (and out of prison), inmates must line up both "a community sponsor" and, if possible, "network team support." The sponsor must be a citizen in good standing with the law, willing to accept physical custody of the parolee for at least the first 180 days of release. During that time, he must cooperate actively in helping the parolee to make good on the program, including providing the agents with information on the parolee's compliance. The "team members" are expected to oversee the parolee in some particular aspect of his program (like community service work) or help with a resource (like providing transportation). Both sponsor and team members sign the inmate's application and must be approved by the panel considering admissions (Pearson 1987, 32).[17]

In California there is no specific work requirement, but agents are expected to engage their parolees in treatment programs, to find them housing in special residences contracted to the Division, and the like. Other service workers, and volunteer members of the community, will be mobilized to help fill the parolee's days with interactions that monitor compliance and provide feedback to the parolee. The intent is to provide what one ISP planner aptly called an "artificial support system" for parolees.

> Some people like you and I have a natural support system through our jobs and families. We will try to give them the same thing through a program that will create continuous contact.

Other ISP programs that do not require specific commitments from private employers or other community members seek to mobilize the community's self-protective capacities. Local law enforcement is notified of each parolee in the area and under some programs agrees to make regular contacts. Other formal and informal authority figures are notified when this is relevant. In Wis-

16. Diana Gordon views this reintroduction of private power as a threatening expansion of penal controls into society: "The primary institutions of society—work, family, neighborhood—become sites of penal control, annexed to the justice system in a way that recalls Foucault's image of the "carceral archipelago'" (1991, 144). This presupposes that there are strong "institutions of society" available to penal clients or agencies, an assumption that does not appear sustainable in light of the significant impoverishment of underclass communities (a phenomenon which Gordon is fully sensitive to in the rest of her book).

17. Georgia initially required such a collateral commitment but has backed away from making it a mandatory feature.

consin's program, which includes more serious offenders than many of the other ISP programs, agents regularly contact community members who might have special security concerns:

> [A program agent] notified elementary school officials, the school's parent/teacher association and the local neighborhood association that a convicted child molester had moved into the neighborhood. Photographs of the offender were made available to these groups and they were asked to report contacts they or their children might have with the offender. (Department of Health and Social Services 1989, 4)[18]

Harkening back to the earliest days of parole, and earlier to the recognizance bond, ISP programs involve building a direct link between the community directly touched by the presence of the offender and the state's power to punish.

NORMALIZING JUDGMENT

Some ISP programs also include elements that harken back to the nineteenth-century disciplinary schemas that Michel Foucault described as "normalizing" judgment.[19] In contrast to juridical judgments, which focus on whether or not laws have been broken, normalizing judgments in Foucault's sense focus on adherence to norms within everyday life. Rather than targeting power in response to breaches of the rules, a regime of normalizing judgments targets power to the successive improvement of performance. Thus in the "École Militaire" in eighteenth-century France, a whole set of variations in dress, responsibilities, and burdens were imposed; as students graduated from one rank to another the regimen of life improved (Foucault 1977, 181). A very similar scheme was employed by Zebulon Brockway at Elmira (Rothman 1980, 34).

Both New Jersey and Illinois structure their programs in terms of ranked phases through which the parolee passes on the way to release or return to conventional supervision. Each successive phase involves less intrusive surveillance requirements. New Jersey also highlights daily performance by mandating that participants keep a daily diary of everything they have done and how it advances their program (Pearson 1987).

BACK TO THE FUTURE?

Intensive supervision programs are geared toward managing parolees in an environment denuded of background social control institutions. In commu-

18. The state's evaluation report goes on to relate this to the enforcement of essentially private rules as described in the section above. "Since this client's supervisory rules prohibited him from associating with children or approaching school property, this technique is an example of how surveillance can be increased without direct agent/client contact" (Department of Health and Social Services 1989, 4).

19. "The perpetual penality that traverses all points and supervises every instant in the disciplinary institutions compares, differentiates, hierarchizes, homogenizes, excludes. In short, it *normalizes*" (Foucault 1977, 183).

nities without work or traditional social roles it is hard for penal managers to define normality, let alone seek to enforce it. The new programs suggest two different kinds of response to this bleak situation.

First, those programs that require an offender to already have a job placement or the commitment of community sponsors before they can be admitted operate as screening mechanisms to keep out all but those offenders with the least risk and the best resources for self-management. Harkening back to the Elizabethan recognizance bond (Samaha 1981), they favor the better-off, but also place a greater control burden on them. They rationalize the expenditure of state resources for social control with the capacity of certain elements in communities to provide for their own.[20] Not surprisingly such programs are highly exclusionary. Georgia's ISP is 68 percent white (Petersilia 1987, 14). Presumably those who belong to the most disempowered and divested elements of the society will continue to be controlled primarily through frequent recourse to incarceration.

Second, instead of seeking to back up or mobilize private social control, some programs, like Wisconsin's or California's, seek to provide it directly; they reach out for reinforcement to the realms of work and family only on an attenuated basis when these are available. These programs are open to those without available private resources, but it remains unclear how far states will go in creating the infrastructure for control, including treatment programs, expensive surveillance technology, vocational assistance, and education. Building a substitute support system is likely to be expensive, and unless the programs result in the parolee obtaining adequate employment and housing that they can keep once they complete the program, the effects are likely to be temporary.

Unlike the classical nineteenth- and early twentieth-century disciplinary sanctions, these programs cannot work off the potent controlling force of the labor market and the community—indeed, they must replicate these on an artificial basis.[21] Earlier intensive supervision efforts disciplined offenders in

20. While the disciplinary mechanisms Foucault described used "normalizing" judgments as part of a coercive apparatus aimed at reshaping the individual subject, the techniques of current ISP programs that appear to mimic elements of what Foucault called "Panopticism" are aimed not at normalizing but at screening those who in effect are already normal, that is, have conventional attachments.

21. A recent *New York Times* feature (Lee 1990) notes the rapid increase in nonacademic-related rules in schools. The justification for rules such as those banning excessive jewelry, expensive clothes, and beepers is the link of those behaviors to such publicized evils as the drug culture. But Lee points out their resonance with a broad sense that "the home and neighborhood are dysfunctional and chaotic . . . [thus] the school must be a model of function and discipline." Progressive education imagined that schools transformed society by developing individual aptitude and judgment. Contemporary education, at least that directed at the inner cities, instead seeks to invest directly in the infrastructure of community social control. In quite the same way new intermediate-level criminal sanctions seek to provide a comprehensive set of controls which introduce the kinds of background controls that were traditionally provided by private social relations in communities which are perceived as vacuums of control.

order to reintegrate them into ongoing social institutions that required and reinforced discipline—the factory, the military, the educational system. Today discipline is harnessed to the aim of "stabilization." Success will be measured in the days or weeks over which eventual return to prison is delayed.

On one level, the absence of an aspiration toward eliminating crime is a reflection of conservative political discourse on the crime issue. But even below the level of explanation, the methods reflect a pragmatic orientation toward minimizing risks that cannot be realistically eliminated. The point is not to secure the parolee to an existing set of controlling institutions, like the labor market or the family, but to build a permanent infrastructure to which parolees can be temporarily restrained. Once "under control," ISP parolees in California and Wisconsin are returned, not to private sector social control, but to regular low-intensity supervision. Thus while gesturing toward the past of "rehabilitation" they point toward a grimmer future of acceptable risk, what Diana Gordon calls "social adjustment" (Gordon 1991, 116).

Investment in this kind of infrastructure is likely to be viewed as worthwhile by correctional administrators facing the staggering costs of prison construction and operation. The biggest problems are likely to be political. ISPs run afoul of the punitive political discourse about crime and are vulnerable to enduring the less eligibility principle discussed below. Services like employment, treatment, and stabilized residence are resources badly needed by many other non-offenders in the communities of the urban poor. Nonetheless, in the absence of any better-fitting accounts of control that can deal with the severe limits on system costs, we can well expect these techniques in whole or part to be further introduced into regular parole and probation (Gordon 1991, 131).

Drug Treatment

One of the strongest recommendations made by the recent Blue Ribbon Commission report on inmate population management was to develop a "substance abuse strategy to systematically and aggressively deal with substance abusing offenders while they are under correctional supervision" (1990, 74). More specifically, the Commission recommended that "intermediate sanctions" be developed to handle parolees in the community that are "at risk of returning to prison" (79). The Commission proposed a range of strategies for parole including specialized caseloads, substance abuse treatment facilities inside prisons, more community treatment openings, and specialized custody units for parolees violated on drug abuse grounds.

The emphasis which the Parole Division and the Blue Ribbon Commission have given to combating drug use among parolees no doubt reflects the widespread public concern in California and the United States as a whole about drugs, particularly the violence associated with drug marketing. At the same

Table 8.1   Percentage of Felons on Parole
Revoked by the Parole Board by Violation Types.
1971–1972 and 1987

Violation	1971–1972	1987
Violence	2.4	5.4
Property	1.0	5.4
Drugs	2.7	7.2
Absconding	1.1	3.9
Alcohol	.6	0.0
DUI	0.0	.7
Technical	.4	9.9
Total	7.8	32.5

Sources: 1971–72 from Star, Berecochea, ard
Petrocchi (1978); 1987 from Department of Carrections (1988).

Note: Data from 1971–72 include the violatioms
of male parolees only: at that time there was a separate parole board for women. The 1987 data included men and women. Women made up 7 6
percent of the parole population in 1986.

DUI = Driving Under the Influence.

time it also represents a strong need felt by those who manage the power to punish to have some way to incorporate the normalizing element of penality which has been so important to modern punishment from its inception. In the absence of a strategy for normalization, penal managers must either opt for continuing growth in incarceration or expressly acknowedging that the state sets some limit to its responsibility for guaranteeing public security. Increasingly both options are impossible.

Two points of caution arise from the analysis of parole supervision and revocation in chapter seven and earlier. First, there should be no illusions that the creation of a large-scale drug treatment and control apparatus in the community can do more than *slow* the growth of parole revocations.

According to the data in table 8.1, the Parole Division would continue to send more than a quarter of all parolees back to prison every year even if the state ceased to revoke any parolees where drug use was the only charge, while drug violations have increased. This is also true of parolees returned for absconding and other "technical" breaches of the supervision process,[22] who made up over a third of revocations in 1987. Some of them may indeed be drug abusers seeking to avoid detection, but they are precisely the ones least likely

---

22. Markedly since the early 1970s, so have violent and property offenses. These parolees are unlikely to be perceived as acceptable candidates for nonincarcerative treatment.

to cooperate with a treatment regime. Those that are not altogether excluded by treatment-oriented programs will find themselves occupying the heaviest custody end of the treatment continuum.

Second, as the Blue Ribbon Commission recognized, drug abuse is really a community rather than a corrections problem (1990, 73). Even assuming that treatment in a correctional context is no less effective than voluntary treatment, the former faces the same grave difficulties as the latter in seeking to control the self-destructive patterns of people living in impoverished and disempowered communities.[23] To its credit, the Commission faced the fact that making a real difference in this social context means providing significant help in employment, housing, and social services (75).

While this has always been a part of correctional aspirations, it has also always been checked by the potent force of the "less eligibility" principle, which holds that conditions among the punished must always be worse than the conditions among the least well-off among the law-abiding, lest perverse incentives be created. While I believe there are compelling reasons in our contemporary situation to relax this supposed axiom of penal-political economy, the political obstacles to large-scale investment in the social well-being of felons are formidable.[24]

Without such investment, however, the construction of a drug treatment and control apparatus in the community will lead to the creation of low-intensity prisons within our large urban areas. This may be cheaper and more palatable than building more prisons. Yet realistically it brings us no closer to evolving a model of "reintegration." It will permit parole agents to make less costly custody decisions, but it provides no real incentives for parolees to take responsibility for the construction of viable noncriminal lives.

Conclusion: Are We Postmodern?

In the midst of change, it is difficult to see what larger structures are being constructed through the operation of short-term strategies and tactical innovations driven by the immediate pressures of management. For at least the last two centuries the power to punish has been exercised as a form of normalization, with the labor market as its original and definitive model. Through all the eras at which we have looked—industrial, clinical, and most recently managerial—the correctional effect has sought to make felons submit to the rhythm of normal life in urban society, especially labor. These changes have remained within a recognizably "modern" understanding of punishment. Do the current strains and changes bode any deeper transformation?

23. Indeed, in poor communities the drug culture may be a very important mode of organization. See Williams (1989).

24. The applicability of the less eligibility principle is considered further in chapter nine.

Like postmodernists in architecture, postmodernists in corrections must define themselves by what they are not. Much of contemporary penal innovation takes the form of a nostalgia for the trappings of a disciplinary society. A good example are the "boot camps" which have been established in many states to give youthful offenders shock treatment in rigorous discipline modeled directly on military training (Kane 1989). Boot camps are attractive because their obsession with order, physical fitness, and rigid rules of decorum present such a stark contrast with the seeming malaise and disorganization of both regular penal institutions and the larger world of urban poverty to which the former are increasingly a kind of adjunct. But there is little reason to believe that these oases of discipline can function effectively in a social world that offers little resonance.

Many aspects of the innovations we have examined share with the boot camp a wistful quality that is unlikely to provide a real alternative model for the power to punish. Yet at a deeper level these programs offer two features which begin to point toward the elements of a postmodern strategy in penality.

First, all the new innovations share a commitment to a rigorous auditing of penal power. In contrast to the broad discretion over punishment which penal modernism created, contemporary innovations stress precise controls and documentation over the decision making of correctional actors. For example, the guidelines composed by the Parole Division and the Board of Prison Terms automatically create a record of decision making which can be easily assimilated by automatic data-processing technologies. The new intensive supervision programs operate through specifications which require actions to be taken at regular intervals. In both cases the procedures are offered as having prescriptive or deterrent functions, but they also allow a greater managerial control over the exercise of the power to punish.

Second, most contemporary innovations share an emphasis on the creation of a correctional infrastructure in the community to which subjects can be attached in the absence of traditional structures of private social control. Drug treatment centers, and intensive supervision programs, allow parolees to be "stabilized" without the high-cost alternative of prison, and without creating real niches for them in the community. Some work by admitting only those prisoners with good resources for self-management in the community and then lending the state's power to punish to those resources. Others assemble "artificial support networks," but in both cases the idea is to build the capacity of corrections to provide a stable pattern for offenders who cannot be counted on simply to be absorbed into the labor market or any other system of disciplinary controls.

I argued in chapter six that efforts to improve the basic rationality of penal control are hampered by the unique problems of the population which parole in particular and corrections more generally seek to control. In the new technologies being tried and discussed today, we see the beginnings of a solution to that problem by making power more efficient and more self-reliant. It remains to be seen if these elements can coalesce into a practically successful strategy of control. For example, we do not yet know if drug treatment will prove "stabilizing" to the current drug-using population.[25] There also remain powerful political problems about the relationships between punishment, security, and social class in a society where the norm of equal justice is in increasing tension with the demand to control crime risks at an acceptable fiscal cost. These problems will be taken up in the concluding chapter.

25. Much of the research on which the Blue Ribbon Commission based its recommendations dealt with heroin addiction and its treatment.

Dangerous Classes, Laboring Classes, Underclasses

When you got nothing, you got nothing to lose. You're invisible now, you got no secrets to conceal.

Bob Dylan, "Like a Rolling Stone," 1965[1]

Caseworkers used to be viewed as spies, checking to make sure there was no man in the house. Now, the welfare mothers say, the system has gone to the opposite extreme, leaving them in isolation.

New York Times, 6 July 1992, A11

The most memorable words of the Fourteenth Amendment seem to speak only in the negative about government:

No State shall make or enforce any law which shall abridge the privileges or immunities of citizens of the United States; nor shall any State deprive any person of life, liberty, or property, without due process of law; nor deny to any person within its jurisdiction the equal protection of the laws.

Yet they have had the greatest consequences for the positive development of government in America. Through diverse legal doctrines developed in a great range of social struggles these words have been read to demand an integration of the various forms of government, and thus an integration into a common political society. They are to politics what Shema[2] is in the Jewish liturgy—a foundational statement of monotheism.

This admittedly sweeping picture is likely to bring the word "federalism" to the lips of any student of constitutional law. It is true that from the very start judges strove to restrain the most nationalist readings of this amendment. In the *"Slaughterhouse Cases"*[3] the Supreme Court reasoned that the framers of the Fourteenth Amendment intended to preserve a distinct realm of privileges associated with state citizenship, and meant to protect only a limited set belonging to national citizenship. A century later, despite significant steps toward enlarging the Fourteenth Amendment to its original horizons, in *Miliken*

1. Copyright 1965 by M. Witmark and Sons.
2. Deut. 6:4.
3. 16 Wall. 36 (1873).

v. Bradley[4] the Supreme Court held that municipal boundaries were a barrier to the Fourteenth Amendment right to attend public schools untainted by racial segregation.

Still, few would deny that since the 1930s the Supreme Court has imposed on government actors at all levels and with all functions, from school districts to the military to state penal systems, an obligation to respect a common body of citizenship (and human) rights. Thus while real separations remain between federal, state, and even local governments, they must subject their exercise of power to a unified set of norms.

This normative integration of government has been true to the central meaning of the amendment to its framers. It is doubtful that they worried about the racial distribution of elementary school classes, or the number of rat hairs allowed in hamburgers at the Santa Clara County Jail (although constitutional ruling on these subjects may be appropriate), but at the very forefront of their minds was the mission of abolishing the separate governments of slavery and freedom that had existed within the United States until 1865.

Common citizenship does not necessarily mean equality of economic or social result. Some among the framers of the Fourteenth Amendment, like Thaddeus Stevens, might have welcomed the opportunity to enact a commitment to that kind of equality. What the majority of supporters of the amendment surely agreed on was a fully open market society where those of even the lowest classes would have the legal opportunity to enter every domain of economic life.[5] This was a commitment to mobility less hindered by geography or status.

The historical program toward a common government[6] of life has had its most ambiguous legacy with respect to the poor in America. Neither the Warren nor Burger Courts recognized special Fourteenth Amendment protection for the poor.[7] The political commitment of the national government during the 1960s and 1970s to dismantle the social barriers around poverty has proved fleeting. The formation of intractable poverty zones in our metropolitan areas over the last several decades poses fundamental questions about the leg-

4. 418 U.S. 717 (1974).

5. It is clear that in time the boundaries between social and economic life have blurred to an extent that the framers never dreamed of. Yet even the narrow kind of economic equality which they specifically intended is endangered by the hardening spatial segregation of our metropolitan areas and the formation of poverty zones.

6. The movement toward a common political society has not only been one of litigation. During the 1930s and 1940s the labor movement achieved great strides in transforming the government of work and of retirement. During the 1950s and 1960s the civil rights movement pushed Congress to legislate greater equality in commercial life.

7. In a number of cases they found different doctrinal grounds for approving the claims of selected groups of the poor, like welfare recipients, the children of illegal aliens, or poor voters, to be governed more or less in the same way as others. See Goldberg v. Kelly, 397 U.S. 254 (1970).

acy of common citizenship won in the Civil War and constitutionalized by the great amendments which followed it.

Those persons with stable positions in the labor market are largely governed by the federal and state governments, which as ineffective as they may be at least acknowledge an obligation to assure their security and well-being. The practical regulation of daily life for these classes takes the forms of mass surveillance described in chapter six. Even where these largely private systems do not acknowledge formal legal rights, they often yield reliable expectations and relative security that are essential preconditions for effective political participation (Michelman 1969).

In contrast, today's "underclass" finds itself virtually ignored by the state and federal government, except as a demonized other for use in the electoral process. In a very real sense the penal system, along with the welfare system, has become the predominant government of the poor. We would not be far off if we speculated that on any given day at least half the young males in the underclass population are under the custody of the penal system.[8] There is virtually not a household in the zones of hardened poverty where someone is not under custody at some point.

It is a peculiar form of government.[9] Politically it is bereft of self-government rights. Legally it involves diminutions of the general constitutional protections against searches and seizures by the police. Beyond the formal institutions of government, however, the situation gets even grimmer. The poverty zones are left unsecured and unregulated by the postindustrial economy and its forms of mass surveillance.[10] As their involvement with the labor market has been attenuated and their involvement with the criminal justice

8. I base this on Mauer's (1989) estimate that a quarter of all young African-American men are in custody on a daily basis. The base for Mauer's calculation was all African-American men between the ages of nineteen and twenty-nine without taking class into account. Since the African-American experience with crime today varies tremendously based on class (W. J. Wilson 1987; Jaynes and Williams 1988) it is fair to assume that among the smaller underclass population the custody figure would be much higher. A recent study in Baltimore found 56 percent of African-American men between 18 and 35 were either in the custody of the criminal justice system or wanted on a warrant (Terry 1992a).

9. The Civil Rights Act of 1866, which served as the blueprint for the Fourteenth Amendment in demanding equal treatment by government of all citizens, recognized criminal conviction as an appropriate basis for power to be exercised in fundamentally different ways. Since the 1930s the Supreme Court has created protections for criminal defendants and even convicts, but i has continued to recognize criminal conviction as a status which lessens the applicability of most other rights to equal government.

10. Gary Marx argues that through new techniques of surveillance society itself is becoming "the functional alternative to prison" (1988, 221). But even this image splits in two. The communities of the middle and upper classes may become more like the prisons that reformers since Bentham have dreamed of: light structures that use surveillance to replace confinement and punishment. The communities of the poor are becoming analogues to the worst of actual prison conditions: they are dumping grounds for the marginal contained within borders maintained by geographic isolation and threats of punishment.

system intensified, the new urban poor are being separated into a distinct political society (as the term "underclass" itself seems to express). In the course of human events, such divisions of political society have invariably lead to revolutions, civil wars, and genocides.

The Return of the Dangerous Classes

The emerging cycle in which the formation of an underclass without a regular connection to the labor market helps to define the very poor as a dangerous class, and their perceived dangerousness reinforces their isolation, threatens an unprecedented regression in our political-economic history. According to contemporary students of urban history, American cities were far more dangerous places in terms of careless accidents and violent assaults before 1860 and became steadily less dangerous through the Second World War (Lane 1979; Monkkonen 1975). That historic process, linked to a variety of processes including industrialization and the disciplines of the labor market, is in danger of being reversed.

From Dangerous Classes to Working Classes

In the early nineteenth century as the population of urban poor expanded, they came to be seen as a "dangerous class," inherently vicious and criminal (Chevalier 1973; Katz 1989). To the worried gentry, the poor were not simply the current losers in a continuing economic tourney, but a distinct and separate race of humans fated to a different and more gruesome destiny than the higher-born.

For instance, the term "proletariat," which came back into descriptive use during the 1830s and 1840s (it was originally an historical term designating the lowest class of Roman society), was not used so much in an economic as in a biological sense:

> It is used in this latter way in Balzac, where the proletariat is a race rather than a class and the word connotes a savage and barbarous way of living and dying rather than an occupational distribution or economic characteristic. (Chevalier 1973, 364)

To the social commentators of the early nineteenth century the degradation of the slums was something quite different than the mere privations of poverty, they were the result of the uncontrolled and monstrous desires of the poor themselves.

> When the proletarian . . . aspires to quaff the cup of pleasure reserved for the wealthy and well-to-do class instead of mitigating his poverty by sobriety and thrift, when he seeks not merely to moisten his lips at this cup but to slake his thirst from it to the point of intoxication in an [ex-

cess] of foolish pride, his degradation is the deeper for his desire to rise above himself. (Fregier, quoted in Chevalier 1973, 364)

The dangerous classes of the nineteenth century included both laboring and criminal classes. It is not that the more privileged classes doubted that there was any difference between the two. Honest laborers could be distinguished from the "vicious" by such traits as "industriousness," "thrift," and "sobriety" (Chevalier 1973, 364). Yet the high risk that the worker could fall into the state of viciousness through accidental injury, bad luck, or hard times was always present and highlighted after 1848 by periodic economic crises and waves of violent class struggle.

From this perspective it was obvious that two very different regimes of control must exist for the dangerous classes and for the respectable classes, with the working class largely relegated to the former. It was only with the growth of the social and political position of the industrial working classes in the second half of the nineteenth century (with 1848 as a crucial watershed, at least for Europe) that elites began to negotiate a distinct but respectable place for the working class within a formally common political society (Garland 1985; Painter 1987).[11] It was precisely to answer the rising demands for access and security by the working class that new technologies (progenitors of our new social control mechanisms) like social welfare, accident compensation, unemployment insurance, and pensions were implemented as reforms (Garland 1985).

The great wave of penal reform at the end of the nineteenth century, when community supervision sanctions like parole and probation were introduced, belongs to this great transformation of government and citizenship experienced in much of Europe and North America (Rothman 1980). George Rusche and Otto Kirchheimer (1939) point to these reforms as marking the emergence of even the criminal as a potentially valuable asset to the population who must be integrated and made available to the ever-enlarging labor market. The task of modern penality was to separate from among the convicted those whose crimes could be understood as the result of remediable misfortunes to return them to society, while identifying and isolating those who were intrinsically criminal.

It has often been pointed out that the notion that it is undesirable to waste the social capital invested in members of society was one of the motivating forces in early social insurance programs. It also underlay the policy of crime prevention which the writers of the Enlightenment

11. In Britain this was marked legally by the extension of suffrage to the propertyless. While this had been accomplished in the United States much earlier, the needs of American workers for practical relief had lagged far behind Europe. In the early twentieth century the threats to working-class family security, accidental injury or death and unemployment, became part of the rational political agenda.

had earlier recommended as the best way to stop infringements upon property rights. (Rusche and Kirchheimer 1939, 140)

Advocates for the adoption of parole in California argued along similar lines during the 1880s that the fixed prison sentence compromised the potential to rescue "those who are not criminal by nature":

> There is a large class, at least in California, who are not criminals by nature, but who are too weak to resist temptation when exposed to it. Owing to conditions, the causes of which it might be difficult, perhaps useless, to fathom, many young men grow up in this State without a trade or habits of labor and industry. They mingle with vicious companions, and in some evil hour a crime is planned and executed. Arrested and hurried to prison, many of them are lodged in the State Prison before their parents or friends are aware of their arrest. (California Penal Commission 1887, 79)

The relationship between penal reform and the integration of political society continued for much of the twentieth century. The Second World War encouraged the view that the economy could use every hand, including those behind bars or recently released, and thus spurred a wave of new reforms, including California's important 1944 restructuring. In the postwar period the growth of the clinical orientation in corrections presupposed that the major reason for recidivism was the inability of released offenders to adjust to the demands of ordinary life, and thus assumed that there was a demand for even the most deviant.

Since the 1970s we have experienced a reversal of this historic development. The collapse of the power of the working class to demand improvements in their income and security, combined with the growing economic irrelevance of the urban poor, has driven a return to a more exclusionary role for punishment. Separated from the edges of the working classes by hardened economic and geographical borders, those members of the underclass committed to state prison no longer provide a coherent target for the strategies of integration and normalization.

In the introduction to a recent book on the social condition of a critical component of this new underclass, young African-American men in the poverty zones of America's cities, Jewelle Taylor Gibbs described the way that this population is represented in terms that resonate with representation of the nineteenth-century Parisian poor in the writings of Sue, Hugo, and Balzac:[12]

---

12. See Chevalier (1973). Chevalier would be amused to know that the contemporary American version of the Parisian gentry that snapped up Hugo's novels are now lining up to see "Les Miz" (adapted from Hugo's *Les Miserables*) at the theater, and reading books like Tom Wolfe's *Bonfire of the Vanities*, which frankly portrays the underclass as a depraved population that corrupts government and endangers society.

Black males are portrayed by the mass media in a limited number of roles, most of them deviant, dangerous, and dysfunctional. This constant barrage of predominantly disturbing images inevitably contributes to the public's negative stereotypes of black men, particularly of those who are perceived as young, hostile, and impulsive. Even the presumably positive images of blacks as athletes and entertainers project them as animal-like or childlike in their aggressiveness, sensuality, "natural rhythm," and uninhibited expressiveness. Clearly, the message says: if they entertain you, enjoy them (at a safe distance); if they serve you, patronize them (and don't forget to leave a tip); if they threaten you, avoid them (don't ride on the subway). Thus, young black males are stereotyped by the five "d's": dumb, deprived, dangerous, deviant, and disturbed. (1988, 2–3)

From Working Classes to Underclasses: Some International Comparisons

While Gibb and other commentators on the underclass controversy focus on the specific history of African-Americans, there is reason to believe that the return of dangerous classes is a worldwide phenomenon linked to disempowerment of the industrial working classes in the face of a new global economy.

One particularly powerful example of the link between this is taking place in the African township of Sebokeng in the industrial Vaal Triangle region of South Africa (Keller 1992). The township has a long history as a center for struggle against the apartheid government (and consequent repression). The area achieved international attention after 1984 when its residents launched a rent and utility tax strike against the white South African government that lasted seven years, during which they survived without even basic municipal services like garbage pickup. More recently the area has been struck by the violent confrontation between members of the African National Congress and the rival Inkatha Freedom Party (with perhaps a third role played by the police) that are terrorizing other townships all over South Africa.

Yet the violence operating in Sebokeng today appears to observers to be fundamentally different than the legacy of political violence. Local residents refer to the youth involved as "com-tsotsi," a play on the separate words "comrade," for political activists, and "tsotsi," for thug. Their activities include attacks on the township's service personnel and infrastructure, car hijacking, and other forms of "terrorizing local residents" (Keller 1992).

There are elements of political rationality in the violence. It is often directed toward government personnel or at impeding the operation of local government. But while most political violence implies a struggle over who will control government, the situation in Sebokeng is seen by at least some outside observers as one of "ungovernability." Keller, describing the opinion of local observers, characterizes the violence as "a kind of wild mutiny of a lost generation raised to adolescence without prospects or discipline" (1992). [13] The contextual differences in history and demography between South Africa and the United States cannot be minimized. Yet several features of the Sebokeng situation operate as well in the American situation and may help us understand it. [14]

The manifestations of violence among the Sebokeng youth, especially the highly public hijackings and destruction of automobiles, is strikingly similar to activities in both the United States and Great Britain. Car theft on the highway at gun point ("carjacking") has become a significant menace for both urban and suburban residents over the last several years in many large cities (Terry 1992b).

In Newark a new and bizarrely destructive version of teenage "joyriding" has taken hold in the city's large poverty zones. Young men of twelve and older find cars in the neighborhoods or on raids to the suburbs. The cars are driven on "thrill" rides, the imaginary basis of which seems to come from movies like *The Road Warrior* (Warner Bros. 1982). The ride usually ends only when the car has been destroyed in a series of movie stunt−like maneuvers, often involving deliberately crashing into police cars or other symbols of municipal power.

Something similar is happening in Britain. There, the practice of "hotting," that is, stealing high-powered sports cars and then enacting destructive "hot rod" races in front of public housing complexes, has become so common in the last several years that parliament enacted new language to its automobile theft laws to punish it. These events have often led, as they have in the American and South African contexts, to violent altercations with the police. Britain has also experienced an epidemic of violent disorders at soccer matches by the younger generation of the former working classes who are born on the dole and face a lifetime cut off from the prospects of economic advancement (Schmidt 1992). The racist attacks on immigrants by unemployed German and French youths follow a comparable pattern.

This public youth violence, reminiscent of the descriptions of the "dangerous classes" of the preindustrial city, is developing in communities that

13. This interpretation of the situation is generally countered by local black leaders who suggest that the situation has been exaggerated by white authorities to justify the continuing "economic" apartheid in which nearby white townships with much greater wealth have no financial responsibility to support services in the black townships. Others, however, acknowledge that at least some of the violence has gone beyond the political and entered a stage of pure opportunism.

14. In both places a history of racism has generated a social control problem so great that even black-controlled governments may not be able to stem it.

have in common the breakdown of once thriving industrial economies and the idling of much of their populations. Young men in these communities are growing up without the kind of positive and sustained contact with the disciplinary logic of factories and schools that was associated with the historic decline of violence in industrializing cities a century ago (Lane 1979).

The kinds of mechanisms that allow a community to integrate its youth into the civil order are related to its capacity to reintegrate felons after incarceration. The critical medium in each case is the economic base of adult workers. Without a renewal of this economic base urban societies across the globe may have to live with a constant pattern of urban violence and the prospect of lifelong penal involvement for whole portions of their population.

"Securing" the Underclass

Security is the great commodity of our time. Several whole service industries now vie to mitigate our risks. Life, health, and accident insurance guard us against accidents and disease. Credit cards guard us against shortfalls in income. Government is virtually defined by the problem of managing the security of the population through unemployment insurance, social security, workers' compensation, and Keynesian management of central banking (Foucault 1978; Ewald 1986; Burchell et al. 1991).

For those outside the limited access environments in which these new security mechanisms proliferate, the hard edge of traditional social control remains the predominantly experienced means of security. But this apparatus of security is decidedly ambiguous. Its aim is both to secure the underclass and to secure others against it. In the face of declining public spending on most forms of social support for the poor, criminal justice is one of the few programs left that takes tax dollars from relatively better-off communities and their governments, and spends them on relatively poorer communities and their governments (even if only to lock them up). But increasingly these resources are used to contain rather than to control the crime problem in the underclass.

In the short term the fact that the penal system has become the predominant form of investment in the security of the underclass has resulted in unprecedented growth of the population under correctional management. In the long term this process will have to confront the demands of the middle classes for lower taxes and more services in their communities. How long will suburban voters continue to support funding a public safety system that is duplicative or even irrelevant to the security many now obtain from the private market in the form of safer addresses, surveillance equipment, and private guards?

In charting a course between the pressure to keep costs down while maintaining the appearance of vigilance toward public safety, correctional managers are likely to find themselves moving in one of two directions. Here these choices are drawn out in intentionally exaggerated form to express the value choices which are likely to be down played in actual policy making.

The Waste Management Model

It is distasteful to an extreme to use such an expression. Yet in a culture for which work remains the overriding source of personal worth, the fate of a class excluded from the labor market is to be treated as a kind of toxic waste. Waste management, however, is not meant simply as a polemical label: it names a whole set of technologies that have arisen primarily around the control of environmental pollution, but which have an increasingly broad influence.

FLEXIBLE ACCUMULATION IN CORRECTIONS

It is not difficult to imagine how this model applies to managing the criminal risks of the underclass. It requires the acknowledgement that many of the young men who encounter the criminal justice system will likely become its lifetime clients (Duster 1987). It follows that methods must be deployed to allow this population to be maintained securely at the lowest possible cost. This calls for restructuring our current dependence on large monolithic prisons.

One model of restructuring is what some economists call "flexible accumulation" (Harvey 1990). The large economic structures which aimed at securing the position of the society as a whole are broken up into more mobile units of capital which maximize profits for some while leaving workers, consumers, and communities in a highly precarious position.

Following this logic we should expect to see a breakup of the huge penal systems built up in the 1980s (Cohen 1985, 84). Long prison sentences, while meeting short-term demands for protection, are an expensive proposition whose costs fall all too equally on society. Expensive techniques of discipline, training, or normalization are not warranted if the basic assumption is that there is no realistic potential to alter the offender's status as toxic waste.[15]

One result of this development is the growth of parole and probation populations themselves, for they represent a much lower level of investment or operating costs. Supposedly "intensive" versions of both parole and probation

15. Andrew Scull (1977) predicted a decade ago that the fiscal crisis of the state would result in a "de-carceration" of many offenders back to the community. His work has been widely criticized for missing the politics of crime control that would drive states to unprecedented levels of spending on prisons in the 1980s, but his analysis of the basic economic pressures remains compelling if delayed.

are being touted today as capable of playing an even larger role in the system (Morris and Tonry 1990).[16]

CONCENTRATION ZONES

We must be clear about the potential class consequences of this strategy. The containment sites of this "toxic waste" will be the communities of the underclass. That is where parolees and probationers will be required to live. That is where the drug treatment centers, halfway houses, and other quasi prisons will be built. This will, of course, help ensure that underclass communities are perceived as dysfunctional and dangerous communities. The countervailing potential for such installations to provide added security to these communities will likely be limited by the pressure to keep costs down. The more the criminal justice apparatus becomes associated with services for the poor, the less appeal it will have to taxpayers.[17]

Correctional workers themselves are one important source of resistance to the waste management model. The parole agent has more sustained contact with offenders and with the communities of the poor than virtually any other operative in our criminal justice system. Unlike police officers, they establish relations with particular people within the community.[18] Unlike public defenders or prison guards, they deal with more than the offender's physical location or legal status. Few people in parole, whether interested in law enforcement or social work, like to think of themselves as human waste managers who apply rational methods to distributing dangerous bodies as if they were baggage managers at a busy airport. Indeed, the current high rate of returns to prison represents in large part the commitment of supervision staff to fulfill the rhetoric of public safety in the poorest communities of the state.

Like the calls to legalize drugs, the claims that we are relying too heavily on incarceration must be interrogated to ensure that behind their appeal of greater efficiency is not a willingness to abandon the poor. The fate of the waste management model hangs ultimately on whether it is politically viable. A senior parole manager framed the question tellingly: "Are we willing to go back to the world of Oliver Twist, with beggars and pickpockets roaming the streets, robbing and doing their scams so long as they don't offend proper peo-

16. This trend has its critics. Many doubt that community supervision can make any significant difference in real security (see the editorial in the *New Republic*, "Race Against Time: Our Response to the Conflagration in L.A."). But whether the common political society will continue to invest in the security of the urban poor is already in question here.

17. A lack of taxpayer sophistication as to the social distribution of criminal risk (and thus the benefits of incapacitation) partly explains the willingness to fund the prison-building boom in the 1980s.

18. The recent interest in "community policing" strategies may increase the role of police as brokers of community social control (Skolnick and Bailey 1986).

ple?" Perhaps the jury in the Rodney King case, and the broad indifference that reemerged only weeks after the civil disorders in Los Angeles following that verdict, already provide an answer of sorts.

The Enrichment Choice[19]

> For a century we labored to settle and to subdue a continent. For a half century, we called upon unbounded invention and untiring industry to create an order of plenty for all our people. . . . The Challenge of the next half century is whether we have the wisdom to use that wealth to enrich and elevate our national life—to advance the quality of American civilization.
>
> Lyndon Johnson, 1964

There is little reason to believe that corrections can remedy a situation driven by the very absence of the infrastructure of social discipline on which it has historically depended. At best, corrections can bring a measure of good government to the poor, but it cannot, at least within the constraints of the larger American political economy, substitute for the regulation and security provided by the private labor market. A solution in any comprehensive sense awaits reinvestment of social capital in institutions or enterprises that allow for the creation of networks of social control.[20]

For its part the parole apparatus has, since the 1950s, steadily moved away from reliance on the community in search of technologies that would permit it to operate independently. As a consequence parole has been less accessible as a tool of intervention for private citizens in the community. In short, the exchange mechanism between penal system and community that once existed has broken down in both directions.

MAKING THE GOVERNMENT OF THE POOR MORE RESPONSIVE
An enrichment strategy must first seek to reestablish an interlocutory relationship with the community of the poor. Since the 1950s corrections has sought to create its own techniques that would permit it to function rationally and effectively without the community as a reliable source of power or intelligibility. These techniques have worked important changes in parole (see

19. I take this name from one of the proposals made by the Kerner Commission in its 1968 report. The enrichment option called for a massive infusion of capital and attention to inner-city poor communities.

20. Writing in 1992 this does not seem as farfetched a possibility as it did in the late 1980s when this project began. A broad consensus seems to be developing in policy circles that the government must take a role in facilitating or making new investments in the poverty zones. However, this has yet to produce consensus political support (DeParle 1991; Bush 1991).

chapters three and six), but the promise of an autonomous process has not been fulfilled.

As early as the mid-1960s Paul Takagi saw the internal functioning of the parole system as strained by the gap between the formal evaluation system and the staff's ability to affect the outcomes evaluated (1967, 3–6). Faced with the discovery of a violation of parole conditions, agents and supervisors must make a decision on their own without being able to rely on either the community or the new social control technologies of mass surveillance to fully justify the result. One way to handle that is to stop trying to make differentiations and send all violators to custody when the question of risk is seriously raised. That practice explains, in part, the unprecedented rise in revocation rates during the 1980s.

Within contemporary practice there are hints of what an enrichment strategy could look like. The best agents learn something like night vision. They perceive distinctions in the danger posed by different people whose situations look indistinguishably grim to most of us. Instead of looking at typical inner-city parolees as poorly adjusted because they have no job and live in a weekly hotel room provided by general assistance, these agents look for evidence of integrity and self-control within the limited range of life activities available to the parolees and visible to the agent.

Many of the most savvy recognize that the historical focus on normality defined by the common demands of the labor market must be replaced by a sensitivity to viability. One domain for observing viability is the parole experience itself which generates its own rather limited world of involvements; parolees must show up for tests and appointments and give prompt notice of a new address (even if it changes weekly), for example. The analysis of unit-level discretion in chapter seven suggested that many agents do take the performance of parole functions into account in deciding how to respond to a violation.

Efforts now underway to build a larger infrastructure of control options like drug treatment and job training will expand this capacity to differentiate. Even if they fail at their primary goals, such programs will help by supplying richer and more complicated fields of interactions with which to engage and evaluate the parolee.

Another place agents can look for signs of viability is in the relationship between a parolee and what Stack (1974) calls his kin. These networks of friends and family vary tremendously in their willingness or capacity to help support the parolee. In some cases, kin are involved with drug abuse and crime themselves. In many others, their own economic and social situations are too marginal to balance the additional problems of a released offender.

Although a majority of the inner-city parolees live with their kin, the practical difficulties in using knowledge of these networks in parole decision making are serious. It requires confidence in knowledge that is not easily standardized. The best agents learn to understand the viability of kin networks and to cultivate the ones that are most positive. Development of this knowledge as a source of substantive rationality in parole is hampered by the demands for formal rationality in evaluation, by large caseloads, and by the lack of resources available to even the strongest kin networks.

These problems represent different kinds of challenges. It is possible to relax some of the demand for formal rationality in decision making by giving unit staff a positive basis for the discretion they already have. Some observers have argued for less centralization of authority in parole, not based on the clinical model of the agent as healer, but on a pragmatic appreciation that the field level can develop the best sense of what distinctions matter in communities stripped of traditional indicators (W. Dickey).[21]

Investing Penal Resources in Community Discipline

While the waste management model stresses containment and isolation, the enrichment choice looks toward discipline and self-governance. Innovations like the "boot camp" are gestures in this direction. But as argued above, they seem more aimed at simulating the imagery of social discipline than providing real experiences that link up with viable life courses through society.

The primary vehicle for doing more within corrections is to reinvigorate the role of work within punishment. A growing body of policy experts now call for the dismantling of the welfare system in America, which seems to subsidize idleness and despair, in favor of some form of guaranteed but obligatory work (Kaus 1993). Liberals and conservatives find common ground in stressing that government rewards ought to be tied to work, school, or some other involvement with the world of commerce. If the largely female population supported by welfare requires the discipline of labor, how much more so is the need of the largely male felon population?

Revitalized prison industries are one approach which is being called for. Currently inmates in California and elsewhere spend large portions of their time in virtual lock down because there are few activities to coordinate them outside of their cells. Any attempt to reinvest in profit-making prison industries would generate opposition from both business and labor.

Given the grim prospects that released prisoners have of obtaining paid employment, we must also consider the potential of community service labor. One of the most intractable problems of contemporary parole supervision is simply the huge wasteland of empty time in the lives of so many underclass

21. To some extent, however, formalization is driven by constitutional due process and will not be easily reversed. There are ways to create more room for maneuver, like dropping more parole holds while charges are pending, but they will require risk taking that may not be politically possible.

men. Community service work could fill that space. A more comprehensive network of service obligations would also expand the necessity for contact with observers and thus the plausibility of a control system based on compliance with behavioral standards. While California's existing sentencing law would have to be amended to make work an actual condition of parole, participation in community service could be made an alternative to reincarceration for those who violate the conditions of parole.

The system could also do much more to subsidize the burdens of willing and responsible kin. Under our present system we spend thousands of dollars to care for and control imprisoned felons and then immediately after release return the burden to the family with minimal assistance. Such families must choose between turning their back on their kin or taking responsibility for a person who may have serious problems with drug abuse, violence, and predatory behavior.

A fund to subsidize the first-year expenses of families, or other kin networks, that agree to take in a released prisoner could begin to rebuild the kind of effective exchange that once existed between parole and community. Funded providers might be expected to take more responsibility for policing the conduct of the parolee, including joint participation in drug treatment or other programs. At the same time their interpretation of the parolee's conduct would be given more weight in making violation decisions.

Creative agents in units across the state of California have developed their own ideas for rebuilding the reciprocity between parole and community: reading centers to address the high illiteracy rates not only among parolees but within their communities; community service programs that allow voluntary work as an alternative to incarceration for certain violations; and subsidized housing that would build in surveillance and security.

In the long term, only direct reinvestment in poor communities will make a difference in rebuilding a capacity for community social control, but it is also possible to imagine ways in which a broader public policy of reinvestment in the underclass could be positively enhanced by the control resources of corrections. It is no secret that employers consider members of the underclass, especially men, to be unreliable workers. They would rather hire recent immigrants with little English than native African-American or Hispanic men from the inner city (Levine 1990; Kirschenman and Neckerman 1991). Parole might provide a kind of subsidization of control against this bias—a "surety" that those under supervision will not abuse drugs, and that if they do, they will be removed from the community with far greater rapidity than is possible through the regular criminal justice process.

A return to the paternalistic excesses of the parole conditions that were handed down in the 1950s, when parole agents could demand control over the details of life like marriage, driving, and job choice, is neither likely nor desirable. Those controls were dependent on the norms of an industrial economy which are simply not available. Indeed, what is really needed is the ability to begin to identify and support viable life choices without the support of society-wide norms. In short, an understanding of the normal distinct from the discipline of the labor market is essential.

The Burden of Less Eligibility

Any move to enrich the power of communities through the criminal justice system is likely to bump into the venerable principle of "less eligibility." That principle, developed during the eighteenth century, holds that "the inmate's standard of life must be lower than that of 'free laborers' outside" (Garland 1985, 11). Born with the prison itself, less eligibility has always carried a potent logic of deterrence. If conditions in prison are allowed to rise above those of the bottom tier of laborers, the disincentive against crime would not exist. Yet as a staggering proportion of the public investment in community security is channeled through the power to punish, the principle of "less eligibility" has returned with a vengeance.

The cut of less eligibility is especially deep at times like the present when the living standards of those in the underclass, working poor, and welfare poor are deteriorating. It is difficult, under such circumstances, for penal programs not to be driven to the meanest level of provision, delivered in a harsh and stigmatizing manner. In such a form penality cannot hope to deliver the kinds of services necessary for establishing the infrastructure of the new, mass-surveillance, social control techniques discussed above.

The utilitarian logic of the "less eligibility" principle focuses on the choices of individual subjects who choose between crime and the available alternatives to crime. However, as involvement with criminal justice becomes a virtual certainty for the young males trapped in communities of hardened urban poverty, the logic of less eligibility has become increasingly incoherent and destructive.

Much of the incentive structure presumed by "less eligibility" applies to a situation where the state's penal apparatus operates relative to a stronger disciplinary labor market as a minor part of the overall ensemble of community security; it is inapposite to the social control vacuum of the inner cities today. Indeed, where penal control has become the government of the poor it cannot be effective simply by providing negative incentives. In such circumstances it no longer makes sense to focus on individual incentives at all.

Its current effect is not to sustain deterrence, but to support the very different logic which I have called "waste management." For many parolees who survive by standing in food lines and getting welfare hotel vouchers every few days, prison already carries precious little deterrence value. Some assured me with great seriousness that prison was a safer and more ordered environment than the shelters—a good place to go when they just did not have the energy level necessary to survive in the hustle of the street.

Choosing between a New Reconstruction and a New Civil War

The line between war and crime has always been a tenuous one. Foucault (1977) argued that before the end of the eighteenth century punishment remained very much a form of battle, although ritualized and predetermined. Since the birth of the prison, penal discourse has emphasized that modern punishment is a tool of social policy rather than a sovereign prerogative. At the end of the nineteenth century punishment began to individualize the criminal in response to growing revolutionary strains in society (Garland 1985). The wayward delinquent was substituted for the dangerous class, thereby legitimizing the status of the poor in society.

Today the rise of the underclass and the increasing stratification of society are once again blurring the lines between punishment and war. What stigma can criminal justice hold in communities where a quarter or a half of the young men are in some form of criminal custody every day (Mauer 1990; Terry 1992a)? The rising level of violence in the inner city portends a war of all against all very different from revolution or crime. As Jerome Skolnick (1989) has noted, the young men who join drug gangs today are in much the same position as the rioters who set fires in America's urban ghettos a generation ago.[22]

The public discourse that arose in response to the riots of the 1960s, such as the *Moynihan Report* (see Rainwater and Yancey 1967), the *Kerner Commission Report,* and the *President's Commission on Law Enforcement and Administration of Justice,* chose to view disorder as a civil matter requiring political solutions rather than individual aberrations to be dealt with through the logic of deterrence. They believed that only a national commitment to reconstruct the poverty zones could prevent our becoming two nations once again.

The visions of the late 1960s never even came close to being implemented. National politics shifted, and a different approach, one centered on imprisonment and emphasizing punishment, deterrence, and incapacitation became predominant. After twenty years of implementation, it is difficult to evaluate the success of this conservative strategy. Victimization rates after rising in the late 1970s have declined by approximately 25 percent (Bastian 1992, 4; Bureau of Justice Statistics 1992, 8). Yet to the extent that this may be fairly attributed to punishment (as opposed to demographic changes), it has come at

22. Skolnick's point was validated by the shift from gang violence to civil disorder which took place in Los Angeles during May 1992.

considerable cost. The prison population has increased six times more than the victimization rate has declined (8). Moreover, if the analysis presented in this book is generalizable, there is every reason to believe that most who leave prison will return to crime and eventually prison.

Perhaps the sheer scale of imprisonment today (Zimring and Hawkins 1991) will compel us to consider the social context of corrections. Articulating the relationship between the prison and the social context is a task that has fallen for much of the last century to parole. But whatever we call it now—mandatory supervision, community corrections, etc.—we must confront the limits of less eligibility and the deterrence model. Individual sanctions can be applied effectively only in a context that provides a viable normative framework for choice. In the long run we can control crime only if we can restore the context of economic opportunity and common political destiny against which modern punishment has been intelligible and manageable.

REFERENCES

Ackerman, Bruce. 1991. *We the People. Vol. 1, Foundations*. Cambridge: Harvard University Press.

Algren, Nelson. 1949. *The Man With The Golden Arm*. New York: Doubleday.

Allen, Francis A. 1981. *The Decline of the Rehabilitative Ideal: Penal Policy and Social Purpose*. New Haven: Yale University Press.

American Friends Service Committee. 1972. *Struggle For Justice: A Report on Crime and Punishment in America*. New York: Hill and Wang.

Anderson, Elijah. 1985. "Race and Neighborhood Transition." In *The New Urban Reality*. Washington, D.C.: Brookings Institution, 99–128.

Anglin, M. D., and W. C. McGlothlin. 1984. "Outcome of Narcotic Addict Treatment in California." In *Drug Abuse Treatment Evaluation: Strategies, Progress, and Prospects*. Rockville, Md.: National Institute on Drug Abuse.

Argow, Walter. 1935. "A Criminal Liability Index for Predicting the Possibility of Rehabilitation." *Journal of Criminal Law and Criminology* 26:561–77.

Attorney General. 1939. *Survey of Release Procedures. Vol. 4, Parole*. Washington, D.C.: United States Department of Justice.

Auletta, Ken. 1982. *The Underclass*. New York: Random House.

Baird, S. Christopher. 1981. "Probation and Parole Classification: The Wisconsin Model." *Corrections Today* May–June (1981): 36–41.

Barnes, Harry E. 1944. *Prisons in Wartime: Report on the Progress of the State Prison War Program Under the Government Division of the War Production Board*. Washington, D.C.: War Production Board.

Bastian, Lisa. 1992. *Criminal Victimiztion in 1991*. Washington, D.C.: United States Department of Justice.

Bates, Sanford. 1942. "On the Uses of Parole Restrictions." *Journal of the American Institute of Criminal Law and Criminology* 33:435.

Bell, Daniel. 1973. *The Coming of Post-Industrial Society*. New York: Basic Books.

Bennett, Lawrence. 1988. *Practice in Search of a Theory: The Case of Intensive Supervision*. Washington, D.C.: National Institute of Justice.

269

Berecochea, John. E. 1982. "The Origins and Early Development of Parole in California."
Ph.D. dissertation, University of California, Berkeley.

Berk, Richard J., Kenneth J. Lenihan, and Peter H. Rossi. 1980. "Crime and Poverty:
Some Experimental Evidence From Ex-Offenders." *American Sociological Review*
45:766.

Blue Ribbon Commission on Inmate Population Management. 1990. *Final Report*. Sacramento: State of California.

Bluestone, Barry, and Bennet Harrison. 1982. *The Deindustrialization of America*. New
York: Basic Books.

Blumenthal, Ralph. 1992. "Brown Says Community Policing Will Endure." *New York
Times*, 6 August 1992.

Blumstein, Alfred. 1993. "1992 Presidential Address: Making Rationality Relevant."
Criminology 31:1–16.

Board of Prison Terms. 1988. *Parole Revocation Guidelines*. Sacramento: State of California.

Bohnstedt, Marvin. 1979. *Classification Instrument Dissemination Project: General Information*. Sacramento: American Justice Institute with the National Council on Crime
and Delinquency.

Bound, John, and Richard B. Freeman. 1991. *What Went Wrong? The Erosion of Relative
Earnings and Employment Among Young Black Men in the 1980s* Working Paper 3778.
Cambridge, Mass.: National Bureau of Economic Research.

Braly, Malcolm. 1976. *False Starts: A Memoir of San Quentin and Other Prisons*. Boston:
Little, Brown.

Bright, Charles. 1992. "History of Jackson Prison." Unpublished manuscript.

Brown, Phil. 1985. *The Transfer of Care: Psychiatric Deinstitutionalization and Its After-
math*. London: Routledge.

Burchell, Graham, Colin Gordon, and Peter Miller, eds. 1991. *The Foucault Effect:
Studies in Governmentality*. Chicago: University of Chicago Press.

Bureau of Criminal Statistics and Special Services. 1990. *Crime in California and the
United States*. Sacramento: California Department of Justice.

Bureau of Justice Statistics. 1977a–1991a. *Sourcebook of Criminal Justice Statistics*.
Washington, D.C.: United States Department of Justice.

———. 1985b. *Bulletin: Parole and Probation, 1984*. Washington, D.C.: United States
Department of Justice.

———. 1989b. *Bulletin: Probation and Parole 1988*. Washington, D.C.: United States
Department of Justice.

———. 1991b. *Correctional Populations in the United States, 1988*. Washington, D.C.:
United States Department of Justice.

———. 1992. *National Update, July 1992*. Washington, D.C.: United States Department
of Justice.

Bureau of Labor Statistics. 1989. *Geographic Profile of Employment and Unemployment,
1988*. Washington, D.C.: United States Department of Labor.

Burgess, Ernest W. 1936. "Protecting the Public by Parole and Parole Prediction." *Journal of Criminal Law and Criminology* 27:491–502.

———. 1974. *The Basic Writings of Ernest W. Burgess*. Edited by Donald J. Bogue. Chicago: Community and Family Study Center, University of Chicago.

Burkhardt, Walter, and Arthur Sathmary. 1963. *Narcotic Treatment-Control Project,
Phases I and II*. Sacramento: California Department of Corrections.

Bush, George. 1991. "University of Michigan Commencement Address: The Challenge to Build a Good Society." *Michigan Alumnus* May–June: 42.

California Department of Corrections. 1989a. *Short-Term Inmate Report: Parole Violators and New Commitments*. Sacramento: Department of Corrections.

———. 1989b. *Short-Term Inmate Report*. Unpublished supplemental tables.

———. 1991. *California Prisoners and Parolees, 1990*. Sacramento: Youth and Adult Correctional Agency.

California Penological Commission. 1887. *Penology*. Sacramento: Superintendent of State Printing.

Canguilhem, George. 1989. *The Normal and the Pathological*. New York: Zone Books.

Carver, John. 1986. "Drugs and Crime: Controlling Use and Reducing Risk Through Testing." In *Research in Action*. Washington, D.C.: National Institute of Justice.

Casper, Jonathan D. 1984. "Determinate Sentencing and Prison Crowding in Illinois." *University of Illinois Law Review* 1984:231.

Cavender, Gray. 1982. *Parole, A Critical Analysis*. Port Washington, N.Y.: Kennikat Press.

Chamberlin, Henry Barrett. 1936. "Concerning Parole in Illinois." *Journal of Criminal Law and Criminology* 26:487–516.

Chevalier, Louis. 1973. *Laboring Classes and Dangerous Classes in Paris During the First Half of the 19th Century*. Princeton: Princeton University Press.

Clear, Todd R., and Kenneth W. Gallagher. 1985. "Probation and Parole Supervision: A Review of Current Classification Practices." *Crime and Delinquency* 31:423–43.

Clemmer, Donald. 1940. *The Prison Community*. New York: Holt, Rhinehart and Winston, 1958.

Clevenger, L. Stanley, and John M. Stanton. 1960. "Should an Inmate Have a Job Before Being Released on Parole?" *NPPA Journal* 6:159.

Cohen, Michael D., James G. March, and Johan P. Olsen. 1976. "People Problems, Solutions and the Ambiguity of Relevance." In James G. March and Johan P. Olsen, *Ambiguity and Choice in Organizations*. Oslo: Universitetsforlaget.

Cohen, Stanley. 1985. *Visions of Social Control*. New York: Oxford University Press.

Conrad, D. V. 1975. "Parole Revocation and Indeterminate Sentencing—The California Experience." *New England Journal on Prison Law* 2:15–26.

Cressey, Donald. 1959. "Professional Correctional Work and Professional Work in Correction." *NPPA Journal* 5:1–15.

Crowley, D. A. 1975. "The Later History of Frankpledge." *Bulletin of the Institute of Historical Research* 48:1–15.

Currie, Elliot. 1987. *Confronting Crime*. New York: Pantheon.

———. 1993. *The Reckoning: Drugs, the Cities, and the American Future*. New York: Hill and Wang.

Daley, Kathleen. 1989. "Criminal Justice Ideals and Practices in Different Voices: Some Feminist Questions About Justice." *International Journal of the Sociology of Law* 17: 1–18.

Data Analysis Unit. 1988. *California Prisoners and Parolees 1986*. Sacramento: Youth and Adult Correctional Agency.

Davis, Kenneth Culp. 1969. *Discretionary Justice: A Preliminary Inquiry*. Baton Rouge: Louisiana State University Press.

Davis, Mike. 1990. *City of Quartz: Excavating the Future in Los Angeles*. London: Verso.

———. 1992 "The L.A. Inferno." *Socialist Review* 22 (1): 57.

deCourcy Hinds, Michael. 1991 "Michigan Faces Painful Choices in Cutting Budget." *New York Times*, 23 January 1991.

DeParle, Jason. 1991. "Ideas to Aid Poor Abound But Consensus is Wanting." *New York Times*, 29 January 1991.

Department of Health and Social Services Wisconsin. 1989. *Reducing Criminal Risk: An Evaluation of the High Risk Offender Intensive Supervision Project*. Milwaukee: Wisconsin Department of Health and Social Services.

Deukmeijian, George. 1990. "State of the State Address." 1990. Sacramento: State of California.

Dickey, Walter J. 1992. "From the Bottom Up: Parole Supervision in Milwaukee." Unpublished manuscript.

DiIulio, John J., Jr. 1987. *Governing Prisons: A Comparative Study of Correctional Management*. New York: Free Press.

Donzelot, Jacques. 1978. *The Policing of Families*. New York: Pantheon.

Douglas, Mary. 1966. *Purity and Danger: An Analysis of the Concepts of Pollution and Taboo*. London: Routledge and Kegan Paul.

Douglas, Mary, and Aaron Wildavsky. 1982. *Risk and Culture: An Essay on the Selection of Technical and Environmental Dangers*. Berkeley and Los Angeles: University of California Press.

Dumm, Thomas. 1987. *Democracy and Punishment: Disciplinary Origins of the United States*. Madison: University of Wisconsin Press.

Duster, Troy. 1970. *The Legislation of Morality: Law, Drugs, and Moral Judgment*. New York: Free Press.

———. 1987. "Crime, Youth Unemployment, and the Black Underclass." *Crime and Delinquency* 33:300.

Editorial. 1942. "Prisons and Parole in War Time." *Journal of the American Society of Criminal Law and Criminology* 32:648–49.

———. 1991. "The Prices of Punishment." *New York Times*, 25 February 1991.

Edwards, Richard. 1979. *Contested Terrain: The Transformation of the Workplace in the Twentieth Century*. New York: Basic Books.

Elias, Norbert. 1978. *The History of Manners*. New York: Pantheon.

Ewald, François. 1986. *L'État Providence*. Paris: Grasset.

Farge, Arlette, and Michel Foucault. 1982. *Le Désordre des familles: Lettres de cachet des Archives de la Bastille au XVIIIe siècle*. Paris: Gallimard.

Feeley, Malcolm, Roseanne Greenspan, Richard Berk, and Jerome Skolnick. 1988. *Courts, Probation, and Street Drug Crime: Report on the Targeted Urban Crime and Narcotics Task Force*. Berkeley: Center for the Study of Law and Society.

Finnegan, William. 1990. "Out There." *New Yorker* 66 (30): 51; 66 (31): 60.

Fletcher, George. 1978. *Rethinking Criminal Law*. Boston: Little, Brown.

Foucault, Michel. 1977. *Discipline and Punish: The Birth of the Prison*. New York: Pantheon.

———. 1978. *The History of Sexuality. Vol. 1, An Introduction*. New York: Pantheon.

———. 1979. *Power, Truth, Strategy*. Sydney, Australia: Feral Press.

Freeman, Richard B., and Harry J. Holzer. 1985. *The Black Youth Unemployment Crisis*. Chicago: University of Chicago Press.

Fussell, Paul. 1975. *The Great War and Modern Memory*. New York: Oxford University Press.

Garland, David. 1985. *Punishment and Welfare*. Brookfield, Vt.: Gower.

————. 1990. *Punishment and Modern Society: A Study in Social Theory*. Chicago: University of Chicago Press.

Gibbs, Jewelle Taylor, ed. 1988. *Young, Black, and Male in America: An Endangered Species*. Dover, Mass.: Auburn House Publishing.

Glueck, Sheldon, and Eleanor Glueck. 1930. *Five Hundred Criminal Careers*. New York: Knopf.

Gordon, Diana. 1991. *The Justice Juggernaut: Fighting Street Crime, Controlling Citizens*. New Brunswick, N.J.: Rutgers University Press.

Gottfredson, Michael R., and Don M. Gottfredson. 1984. "Guidelines for Incarceration Decisions: A Partisan Review." *University of Illinois Law Forum* 1984:291–317.

Grant, J. Douglas, and Marguerite Q. Grant. 1952. "A Group Dynamics Approach to The Treatment of Nonconformists in the Navy." *Annals of the American Academy of Political and Social Science* 322:126.

Greenberg, David. 1977. "Delinquency and the Age Structure of Society." *Contemporary Crises* 1:189–223.

Gurr, Ted R. 1981. "Historical Trends in Violent Crime: A Critical Review of the Evidence." In *Crime and Justice: An Annual Review of Research*. Vol. 3. Chicago: University of Chicago Press.

Harrison, Bennet, and Barry Bluestone. 1988. *The Great U-Turn: Corporate Restructuring and the Polarizing of America*. New York: Basic Books.

Hart, H. L. A. 1968. *Punishment and Responsibility: Essays in the Philosophy of Law*. Oxford: Oxford University Press.

Harvey, David. 1990. *The Condition of Post-Modernity*. Cambridge: Basil Blackwell.

Havel, Joan. 1965. *Special Intensive Parole Unit, Phase Four*. Sacramento: California Department of Corrections.

Havel, Joan, and Elaine Sulka. 1962. *Special Intensive Parole Unit, Phase Three*. Sacramento: California Department of Corrections.

Hay, Douglas, and Francis Snyder. 1990. "Using the Criminal Law, 1750–1850: Policing, Private Prosecution, and the State." In *Policing and Prosecution in Britain, 1750–1850*. New York: Oxford University Press, 3–52.

Heacox, Frank L. 1917. "A Study of One Year's Parole Violators Returned to Auburn Prison." *Journal of Criminal Law and Criminology* 8:233–58.

Hentig, Hans von. 1942. "Degrees of Parole Violation and Graded Remedial Measures." *Journal of the American Institute of Criminal Law and Criminology* 33:363–71.

Heydebrand, Wolf. 1979. "The Technocratic Administration of Justice." *Research in Law and Sociology* 2:29.

Heydebrand, Wolf, and Carroll Seron. 1990. *Rationalizing Justice: The Political Economy of Federal District Courts*. Albany: State University of New York Press.

Himelson, Alfred N. 1968. "When Treatment Failed: A Study of the Attempt of a Public Service Organization to Change the Behavior of an Intransigent Population." Ph.D. dissertation, University of California, Los Angeles.

Himelson, Alfred, and Blanche Thoma. 1968. *Narcotic Treatment and Control Program, Phase II*. Sacramento: California Department of Corrections.

Hindle, Brooke, and Steven Lubar. 1989. *Engines of Change: The American Industrial Revolution, 1790–1860*. Washington, D.C.: Smithsonian Institution Press.

Hirsch, Andrew von. 1976. *Doing Justice: The Choice of Punishments*. New York: Basic Books.

Hirsch, Andrew von, and Kathleen J. Hanrahan. 1979. *The Question of Parole: Retention, Reform, or Abolition*. Cambridge, Mass.: Ballenger.

Hobsbawm, Eric. 1989. "Labour in the Great City." In *Politics for a Rational Left: Political Writing, 1977-1988*. London: Verso.

Holzer, Harry J. 1991. "The Spatial Mismatch Hypothesis: What Has the Evidence Shown? *Urban Studies* 28:105–22.

Hoover, Gary, Alta Campbell, and Patrick J. Spain. 1990. *Hoover's Handbook: Profiles of Over 500 Major Corporations, 1991*. Emeryville, Calif.: Publishers Group West.

Ignatieff, Michael. 1978. *A Just Measure of Pain: The Penitentiary in the Industrial Revolution*. London: Penguin Books.

———. 1983. "State, Civil Society and Total Institutions: A Critique of Recent Histories of Punishment." In *Social Control and the State*. Oxford: Oxford University Press.

Irwin, John. 1968. *The Felon*. Berkeley and Los Angeles: University of California Press.

Jahoda, M. 1982. *Employment and Unemployment: A Social Psychological Analysis*. Cambridge: Cambridge University Press.

Jahoda, M., P. F. Lazarsfeld, and H. Ziesel. 1933. *Marienthal: The Sociography of an Unemployed Community*. London: Tavistock Publications, 1972.

Jankowski, Louis. 1991. *Probation and Parole, 1990*. Washington, D.C.: United States Department of Justice.

Janowitz, Morris. 1978. *The Last Half Century*. Chicago: University of Chicago Press.

Jaynes, Gerald D., and Robin M. Williams, Jr., eds. *A Common Destiny: Blacks and American Society*. 1988. Washington, D.C.: National Academy Press.

Jencks, Christopher. 1991. "Is the American Underclass Growing?" In *The Urban Underclass*. Washington, D.C.: Brookings Institution, 28–100.

Johnson, Lyndon. 1964. "University of Michigan Commencement Address: A Battle to Build the Great Society." *Michigan Alumnus* May–June (1991): 25.

Jones, Maxwell. 1953. *The Therapeutic Community: A New Treatment Method in Psychiatry*. New York: Basic Books.

Kadish, Sanford. 1961. "The Advocate and the Expert-Counsel in the Peno-Correctional Process." *Minnesota Law Review* 45:803.

Kane, Francis F. 1917. "Drugs and Crime." *Journal of the American Institute of Criminal Law and Criminology* 8:502.

Kane, Joseph. 1989. "Shock Incarceration: A Dose of Discipline for First Offenders." *Time*, 16 October 1989, 17.

Kaplan, John. 1983. *The Hardest Drug: Heroin and Public Policy*. Chicago: University of Chicago Press.

Kasarda, John. 1985. "Urban Change and Minority Opportunities." In *The New Urban Reality*. Washington, D.C.: Brookings Institution, 33–68.

———. 1988. "Jobs, Migration, and Emerging Urban Mismatches." In *Urban Change and Poverty*. Washington, D.C.: National Academy Press, 148–93.

Katz, Michael. 1989. *The Undeserving Poor: From the War on Poverty to the War on Welfare*. New York: Pantheon.

Kaus, Mickey. 1993. *The End of Equality*. New York: Basic Books.

Keller, Bill. 1992. "Sebokeng Journal: Bullied by Its Own Young, the Township Festers." *New York Times*, 31 July 1992.

Kelly, William R., and Sheldon Ekland-Olson. 1991. "The Response of the Criminal Justice System to Prison Overcrowding: Recidivism Patterns among Four Successive Parole Cohorts." *Law and Society Review* 25:601–20.

Kerner Commission. 1968. *The Kerner Report*. New York: Pantheon, 1988.

Kirschenman, Joleen, and Kathryn M. Neckerman. 1991, "'We'd Love to Hire Them, But . . . ': The Meaning of Race for Employers." In *The Urban Underclass*. Washington, D.C.: Brookings Institution, 203–32.

Kuhn, Thomas. 1962. *The Structure of Scientific Revolutions*. Chicago: University of Chicago Press.

Lagoy, Stephen P., Frederick A. Hussey, and John H. Kramer. 1979. "The Prosecutorial Function and Its Relation to Determinate Sentence Structures." In *The Prosecutor*. Beverly Hills: Sage, 209–37.

Lane, Roger. 1967. *Policing the City: Boston, 1822–1885*. Cambridge: Harvard University Press.

———. 1979. *Violent Death in the City*. Cambridge: Harvard University Press.

———. 1986. *The Roots of Violence: Black Philadelphia, 1890–1960*. Cambridge: Harvard University Press.

Langan, Patrick A. 1991. *Race and Prisoners Admitted to State and Federal Institutions, 1926–1986*. Washington, D.C.: United States Department of Justice.

Lears, Jackson. 1981. *No Place of Grace: Antimodernism and the Transformation of American Culture, 1880–1920*. New York: Pantheon.

Lee, Felicia R. 1990, "Non Academic Rules Increase in Schools." *New York Times*, 11 March 1990.

Legislative Analyst. 1987–1988, 1988–1989, 1989–1990. *Analysis of the Budget Bill: Report of the Legislative Analyst to the Joint Legislative Budget Committee*. Sacramento: California Legislature.

Levine, Richard. 1990. "Young Immigrant Wave Lifts New York Economy." *New York Times*, 30 July 1990.

Magaziner, Ira C., and Robert B. Reich. 1982. *Minding America's Business: The Decline and Rise of the American Economy*. New York: Harcourt Brace Jovanovich.

Maltz, Michael. 1984. *Recidivism*. Orlando: Academic Press.

March, James G., and Johan P. Olsen. 1989. *Rediscovering Institutions: The Organizational Basis of Politics*. New York: Free Press.

Marx, Gary. 1988. *Undercover: Police Surveillance in America*. Berkeley and Los Angeles: University of California Press.

Massachusetts Parole Board. 1987. *Intensive Parole Supervision, Program Update*. Springfield, Mass.: State of Massachusetts.

Mauer, Marc. 1990. *Young Black Men and the Criminal Justice System*. Washington, D.C.: The Sentencing Project.

McCoy, John L., and Kerry Weems. 1988. "Disabled-Worker Beneficiaries and Disabled SSI Recipients: A Profile of Demographic and Program Characteristics." *Social Security Review Bulletin* 52:16–28.

McGlothlin, W. C. 1979. "Criminal Justice Clients." In *Handbook on Drug Abuse*. Rockville, Md.: National Institute on Drug Abuse.

McGlothlin, W. C., M. D. Anglin, and B. D. Wilson. 1975. "Outcome of the California Civil Addict Commitments: 1961–1972." *Drug and Alcohol Dependence* 1:165.

McKelvey, Blake. 1977. *American Prisons: A History of Good Intentions*. Montclair, N.J.: P. Smith.

McLanahan, Sarah, Irwin Garfinkel, and Dorothy Watson. 1988. "Family Structure, Poverty, and the Underclass." In *Urban Change and Poverty*. Washington, D.C.: National Academy Press, 102–47.

Mead, Lawrence. 1986. *Beyond Entitlement: The Social Obligations of Citizenship*. New York: Free Press.

Meehl, Paul. 1954. *Clinical Versus Statistical Prediction*. Minneapolis: University of Minnesota Press.

Melossi, Dario, and Massimo Pavarini. 1981. *The Prison and the Factory: Origins of the Penitentiary System*. Totowa, N.J.: MacMillan Press.

Messinger, Sheldon. 1969. "Strategies of Control." Ph.D. dissertation, University of California, Los Angeles.

Messinger, Sheldon L., and John E. Berecochea. 1990. "Don't Stay Too Long But Do Come Back Soon: Reflections on the Vicissitudes of California's Prisoner Population." Paper presented at Conference on Growth and Its Influence on Correctional Policy, May 1990, University of California, Berkeley.

Messinger, Sheldon L., John E. Berecochea, Richard A. Berk, and David Rauma. 1988. *Parolees Returned to Prison and the California Prison Population*. Sacramento: Bureau of Criminal Statistics.

Messinger, Sheldon L., John E. Berecochea, David Rauma, and Richard Berk. 1983. "The Foundations of Parole in California." *Law and Society Review* 19:69–106.

Messinger, Sheldon, and Philip E. Johnson. 1980. "Determinate Sentencing: Reform or Regression?" In *The Criminal Justice System: Materials on the Administration of Justice and Reform of the Criminal Law*. Boston: Little, Brown.

Michelman, Frank. 1969. "Forward: On Protecting the Poor through the Fourteenth Amendment." *Harvard Law Review* 83:746.

Mitford, Jessica. 1971. *Kind and Usual Punishment: The Prison Business*. New York: Random House.

Monkkonen, Eric H. 1975. *The Dangerous Class: Crime and Poverty in Columbus, Ohio, 1860–1885*. Cambridge: Harvard University Press.

———. 1988. *America Becomes Urban: The Development of U.S. Cities and Towns, 1780–1980*. Berkeley and Los Angeles: University of California Press.

Morris, Norval, and Michael Tonry. 1990. *Between Prison and Probation: Intermediate Punishments in a Rational Sentencing System*. New York: Oxford University Press.

Morris, William A. 1910. *The Frankpledge System*. New York: Columbia University Press.

Murray, Charles. 1984. *Losing Ground: American Social Policy, 1950–1980*. New York: Basic Books.

Musto, David. 1973. *The American Disease: Origins of Narcotic Control*. New Haven: Yale University Press.

Mydans, Seth. 1992. "Blacks Complaining of Neglect as Los Angeles is Rebuilt." *New York Times*, 30 August 1992.

National Institute of Justice. 1990. *Research in Action—Drug Use Forecasting*. Washington, D.C.: National Institute of Justice.

Newman, Graeme. 1985. *Just and Painful: The Case for Corporal Punishment of Criminals*. New York: Macmillan.

Newman, Oscar. 1972. *Defensible Space*. New York: Macmillan.

New Republic Editors. 1992 "Race Against Time: Our Response to the Conflagration in L.A." *The New Republic*, 25 May 1992.

Nietzsche, Friedrich. 1969. *On the Genealogy of Morals*. New York: Vintage Books.

O'Malley, Pat. 1992. "Risk, Power and Crime Prevention." *Economy and Society* 21: 252–75.

Painter, Nell I. 1987. *Standing At Armageddon: The United States, 1877–1919*. New York: Norton.

Park, Robert E., and Ernest W. Burgess. 1925. *The City*. Chicago: University of Chicago Press, 1967.

Parole and Community Services Division. 1959, 1960, 1987. *Parole Agent Manual*. Sacramento: California Department of Corrections.

———. 1979. *The New Model of Parole*. Sacramento: California Department of Corrections.

———. 1988. *SARD: Substance Abuse Revocation Program, Program Summary*. Sacramento: California Department of Corrections.

———. 1989. *Implementation of Consistent Decision-Making Project*. Sacramento: California Department of Corrections.

Pearson, Frank S. 1987. *Final Report of Research on New Jersey's Intensive Supervision Program*. Washington, D.C.: National Institute of Justice.

Petersilia, Joan. 1987. *Expanding Options for Criminal Sentencing*. Santa Monica: Rand Corporation.

Pindyck, Robert S., and Daniel L. Rubinfeld. 1981. *Econometric Models and Economic Forecasts*. 2d ed. New York: McGraw-Hill.

Pollard, Sidney. 1963. "Factory Discipline in the Industrial Revolution." *Economic History Review* 16:254–71.

President's Commission on Law Enforcement and Administration of Justice. 1967. *The Challenge of Crime in a Free Society*. Washington, D.C.: Government Printing Office.

Rainwater, Lee. 1966. "Work and Identity in the Lower Class." In *Planning for a Nation of Cities*. Cambridge: M.I.T. Press, 105–23.

———. 1967. "Crucible of Identity: The Negro Lower-Class Family." *Daedalus* 95:172.

Rainwater, Lee, and William L. Yancey. 1967. *The Moynihan Report and the Politics of Controversy*. Cambridge: M.I.T. Press.

Reichman, Nancy. 1986. "Managing Crime Risks: Toward an Insurance-Based Model of Social Control." *Research in Law, Deviance, and Social Control* 8:151.

Rhine, Edward E., William R. Smith, and Ronald Jackson. 1991. *Paroling Authorities: Recent History and Current Practices*. Laurel, Md.: American Correctional Association.

Richmond, Mary. 1917. *Social Diagnosis*. New York: Russell Sage.

Robison, James O. 1969. "It's Time to Stop Counting." *Technical Supplement No. 2: Assembly Report on the Costs and Effects of the California Criminal Justice System*. Sacramento: California Assembly.

Robison, James O., et. al. 1971. *By the Standard of His Rehabilitation: Information, Decision, and Outcome in Terminations from Parole*. CDC Research Division, Report No. 39. Sacramento: California Department of Corrections.

Robison, James O., and Paul Takagi. 1968. *Case Decisions in a State Parole System*. Sacramento: California Department of Corrections.

Rossi, Peter. 1989. *Without Shelter, Homelessness in the 1980's*. New York: Priority Press.

Rothman, David J. 1971. *The Discovery of the Asylum: Social Order and Disorder in the New Republic*. Toronto: Little, Brown.

———. 1980. *Conscience and Convenience: The Asylum and Its Alternatives in Progressive America*. Toronto: Little, Brown.

Rule, James B. 1972. *Private Lives and Public Surveillance*. London: Allen Lane.

Rusche, Georg, and Otto Kirchheimer. 1939. *Punishment and Social Structure*. New York: Columbia University Press.

Samaha, Joel B. 1981. "The Recognizance Bond in Elizabethan Law Enforcement." *American Journal of Legal History* 25:189–204.

Schmidt, William. 1992. "Bristol Journal: These Youths are Sparks, Living in a Powder Keg." *New York Times*, 1 August 1992.

Schuwerk, Robert P. 1984. "Illinois Experience with Determinate Sentencing: A Critical Reappraisal, Part I." *DePaul Law Review* 33:631.

Scull, Andrew. 1977. *Decarceration: Community and the Deviant—A Radical View*. Englewood Cliffs, N.J.: Prentice Hall.

Selznick, Philip. 1949. *T.V.A. and the Grass Roots*. Berkeley and Los Angeles: University of California Press.

Shearing, Clifford, and Philip Stenning. 1983. "Private Security: Its Growth and Implications." In *Crime and Justice: An Annual Review of Research*, Vol. 3. Chicago: University of Chicago Press.

———. 1984. "From the Panopticon to Disney World: The Development of Discipline." In *Perspectives in Criminal Law*. Aurora, Ontario: Canada Law Books.

Simon, Jonathan. 1987. "The Emergence of a Risk Society: Insurance, Law, and the State." *Socialist Review* no. 95: 61–89.

———. 1988. "The Ideological Effects of Actuarial Practices." *Law and Society Review* 22:772.

———. 1991. "Doing Time: Post-Modernity and the Crisis of Penal Reform." Unpublished manuscript.

Skolnick, Jerome H. 1989. "The Fire in Our Ghettos Still Burns: In a Little-to-Lose, Crime Replaces the '60s Protest." *Los Angeles Times*, 15 August 1989.

Skolnick, Jerome H., and David H. Bailey. 1986. *The New Blue Line: Police Innovation in Six American Cities*. New York: Free Press.

Spierenburg, Pieter. 1984. *The Spectacle of Suffering: Executions and the Evolution of Repression from a Pre-Industrial Metropolis to the European Experience*. Cambridge: Cambridge University Press.

———. 1991. *The Prison Experience: Disciplinary Institutions and Their Inmates in Early Modern Europe*. New Brunswick, N.J.: Rutgers University Press.

Spitzmiller, Rebecca Jean. 1984. "Note: An Examination of Issues in the Florida Sentencing Guidelines." *Nova Law Journal* 8:687.

Stack, Carol. 1974. *All Our Kin: Strategies for Survival in a Black Community*. New York: Harper and Row.

Star, Deborah. 1974. *Conditions of Parole: 1949–1973*. Sacramento: California Department of Corrections.

Star, Deborah, John E. Berecochea, and David Petrocchi. 1978. *Returns to Prison Ordered: Policy in Practice and Change*. Sacramento: California Department of Corrections.

State Board of Prison Directors. 1918–1942. *Biennial Report of the State Board of Prison Directors*. Sacramento: Superintendent of State Printing.

State of Illinois. 1941. "Work for Parolees." *Journal of Criminal Law and Criminology* 32:561.

Studt, Eliot. 1981. "Parole in California." Unpublished manuscript.

Suttles, Gerald. 1968. *The Social Order of the Slum: Ethnicity and Territory in the Inner City*. Chicago: University of Chicago Press.

Takagi, Paul. 1967. "Evaluation Systems and Adaptations in a Formal Organization: A Case Study of a Parole Agency." Ph.D. dissertation, Stanford University.

Terry, Don. 1992a. "More Familiar, Life in a Cell Seems Less Terrible." *New York Times*, 13 September 1992.

————. 1992b. "Carjacking: New Name for an Old Crime." *New York Times*, 13 September 1992.

Tesh, Sylvia. 1988. *Hidden Arguments: Political Ideology and Disease Prevention Policy*. New Brunswick, N.J.: Rutgers University Press.

Texas Criminal Justice Division. 1990. *Intermediate Sanctions: An Overview of the Texas System*. Austin: Office of the Governor.

Thompson, E. P. 1967. "Time, Work Discipline, and Industrial Capitalism." *Past and Present* 38:56–97.

Tibbits, Clark. 1931. "Success or Failure on Parole Can be Predicted." *Journal of Criminal Law and Criminology* 22:11.

Trachtenburg, Alan. 1982. *The Incorporation of America: Culture and Society in the Gilded Age*. New York: Hill and Wang.

United States Sentencing Commission. 1987. *Sentencing Guidelines and Policy Statements*. Washington, D.C.: Government Printing Office.

Vold, George. 1931. *Prediction Methods and Parole*. Hanover, N.H.: Sociological Press.

Whyte, Edward H. 1916. "The Parole System in California." *Journal of Criminal Law and Criminology* 7:1.

Wickersham Commission. 1931. *National Commission on Law Observance and Enforcement, Penal Institutions, Probation and Parole*. Washington, D.C.: Government Printing Office.

Wiebe, Robert. 1967. *The Search for Order, 1877–1920*. New York: Hill and Wang.

Wilkins, Leslie. 1973. "Crime and Criminal Justice at the Turn of the Century." *Annals of the American Academy of Political and Social Science* 208:13.

Williams, Terry. 1989. *Cocaine Kids: The Inside Story of a Teenage Drug Ring*. Reading, Mass.: Addison-Wesley.

Wilson, J. Q. 1986. *Thinking About Crime*. 2d ed. New York: Basic Books.

Wilson, William J. 1980. *The Declining Significance of Race*. 2d ed. Chicago: University of Chicago Press.

————. 1985. "The Urban Underclass in Advanced Industrial Society." In Paul E. Peterson *The New Urban Reality*. Washington, D.C.: Brookings Institution, 460–82.

————. 1987. *The Truly Disadvantaged: The Inner City, the Underclass, and Public Policy*. Chicago: University of Chicago Press.

————. 1991. "Public Policy Research and the *Truly Disadvantaged*." In *The Urban Underclass*. Washington, D.C.: Brookings Institution.

Wish, Eric. 1982. "Are Heroin Users Really Non-Violent?" Paper presented at the annual meeting of the Academy of Criminal Justice Sciences, Louisville, 1982.

————. 1987. *Drug Use Forecasting*. Washington, D.C.: National Institute of Justice, United States Department of Justice.

Wish, Eric, Mary Toborg, and John Bellassai. 1988. *Identifying Drug Users and Monitoring Them During Conditional Release*. Washington, D.C.: National Institute of Justice.

Yaley, Barbara. 1980. "Habits of Industry: Labor and Penal Policy in California, 1849–1940." Ph.D. dissertation, University of California, Santa Cruz.

Zimring, Franklin E. 1983. "Sentencing Reform in the States: Lessons from the 1970s." In

Reform and Punishment: Essays on Criminal Sentencing. Chicago: University of Chicago Press.

Zimring, Franklin E., and Gordon Hawkins. 1991. *The Scale of Imprisonment*. Chicago: University of Chicago Press.

Zuboff, Shoshana. 1988. *In the Age of the Smart Machine: The Future of Work and Power*. New York: Basic Books.

INDEX

Account system of linking prison production to market, 31, 32

Aid to Families with Dependent Children (AFDC) for parolees, 154

Army, disciplinary parole and, 63

Arrest hold, guidelines for, 234–35

Auburn prison model, 25–27, 29–31

Behavior: of parolees, work and, 156–60; violation, incidence of, in California, 215–16

Bohr, 19

Bonds: good behavior, 21–22; peace, 21, 22; recognizance, in Elizabethan England, 20–22, 23–24

California Civil Addicts program, 93–94

Caseload size: in clinical parole, 81–84; in Narcotic Treatment and Control Program, 87

Casework: in clinical parole, 76; significance of, 190–93

Citizenship, common, poor and, 251–52

Civilizing process, punishment and, 43

Classes, 253–56. *See also* Underclass(es)

Classification, 170; politics of discretion and, 173–74; and prediction in New Model, 174–77; Wisconsin system of, 174–75

Clinical parole: caseload size in, 81–84; casework in, 76; employment and, 95–98; intensive supervision in, 80–84; narcotic addiction and, 71–72, 181–87; parole agent manual for, 71, 74–80; parolee–parole agent relationship in, 76–77, 79; rate of, 102; research program and, 71, 94–95; resistance to, 78; set of ideas for, 70–71; therapeutic community and, 72–74

Cocaine addiction: containment of, 185–86; growing, 180–81; heroin addiction compared to, 182, 185–86

Collateral complaints, disposition of drug use cases and, 223–24

Common citizenship, poor and, 251–52

Community: capacity to absorb released prisoners of, 160–63; private social control in, in intensive supervision programs, 241–43

Community discipline, investing penal resources in, 263–65

Community service work, 263–64

Community supervision: historical perspective on, 17–38; suretyship and, 17–24

Computerized data bases, 170, 177–80

Concentration zones in waste management model, 260–61